SERVANT LEADERSHIP

What Others Say about
Servant Leadership

"There are very few books which can be truly called seminal works. Robert K. Greenleaf's *Servant Leadership* is one of those rare books that will live far beyond the life of its creator. While its impact on leadership is already felt every day in organizations all over the world, I predict its influence will only become greater as more and more leaders and would-be leaders come to understand the power of its message and come to experience the results of its practice. In fact, the final measure of Greenleaf's work may even become more fully manifest among leaders not yet born. Let us hope so!"

James A. Autry, author, *The Servant Leader* and *Love & Profit*

"Robert K. Greenleaf's wisdom has inspired us for over twenty-five years. It is my fervent hope that this most welcomed new edition of *Servant Leadership* will influence a new generation worldwide to transform global capitalism, to serve better the whole of humanity and our planet."

Godric Ernest Scott Bader, Life President, Scott Bader Commonwealth Ltd.

"Servant leadership is now part of the vocabulary of enlightened leadership. Bob Greenleaf, along with other notables such as McGregor, Drucker, and Follett, have created a new thought-world of leadership that contains such virtues as growth, responsibility and love. This book incarnates those values."

Warren Bennis, Distinguished Professor, Marshall School of Business at the University of Southern California; author of *Organizing Genius*

"With this new and expanded edition, *Servant Leadership* fortifies its claim for the high ground of books on corporate management. Yes, it is idealism writ large, but practical idealism that will help to build a better business—better for leaders and servants, and better for clients too. Greenleaf's timeless wisdom provides a beacon that will light the way for creating an enterprise that stands for something: a distinguished serving institution that is at once successful and principled."

John Bogle, Founder and Chairman Emeritus, The Vanguard Group; author, *Bogle on Mutual Funds*

"I am convinced, as a governance theorist and practitioner, that responsible board behavior is impossible in the absence of the servant leadership Robert Greenleaf helped us all to understand. This silver anniversay edition of *Servant Leadership* is both symbol and substance on the shelf of anyone blessed with the opportunity to lead."

John Carver, author, *Boards That Make a Difference*

"If you have tried to put into practice Bob Greenleaf's elegant concepts or if you have seriously pondered his penetrating questions, you are probably taking pleasure in the resulting islands of relational literacy. In the midst of seemingly unrestrained and individualized materialism, Greenleaf's sense of civil community as a preserving principle of the free market system is still our best hope."

Max DePree, author, *Leadership Is an Art*

"With its deeper resonances in our spiritual traditions, Greenleaf reminds us that the essence of leadership is service, and therefore the welfare of people. Anchored in this way, we can distinguish between the tools of influence, persuasion, and power from the orienting values defining leadership to which these tools are applied."

Ronald Heifetz, author, *Leadership Without Easy Answers*

"*Servant Leadership* belongs in every leader's library. It is the indispensable companion on the journey."

Frances Hesselbein, Chairman, The Drucker Foundation

"*Servant Leadership* is a timeless, classic book not only because there was no conflict between the man, Robert Greenleaf, his beliefs, his deeds, and what he wrote about them, but because we know he was right, even when we fail to do it."

Dee Hock, Founder and CEO Emeritus, VISA International; author, *Birth of the Chaordic Age*

"Those of us actively involved in the servant leadership movement around the world are thankful to Robert Greenleaf and the tremendous awareness he raised to the life-changing principles of servant leadership."

James C. Hunter, author, *The Servant*

"Greenleaf's writings grow with you, revealing more depth and opportunities with each reading."

Ann McGee-Cooper, coauthor, *You Don't Have to Go Home from Work Exhausted!*

"Robert Greenleaf's great ideas—written about with care in *Servant Leadership*—are slowly but surely transforming the way leadership is understood and practiced. All who engage in the activity of leadership in the trenches are indebted to Robert Greenleaf for showing us the way we can be effective, productive, *and* humane."

Russ Moxley, Senior Fellow, Center for Creative Leadership; author, *Leadership & Spirit*

"During the past quarter of a century, Robert Greenleaf and his writings have been used to instruct, encourage, and motivate leaders to serve as they lead. We have all benefited from his work and have been reminded that no leader is greater than the people he or she leads, and even the humblest of tasks, as Jesus taught His disciples over two thousand years ago, is worthy for a leader to do."

William Pollard, Chairman, ServiceMaster, author, *The Soul of the Firm*

"Robert Greenleaf conceived the idea of servant leadership during a time of chaos in the United States—the late '60s. But by exploring his idea in the multiple essays gathered in this book, he left a legacy by which people in very different times can continue to be inspired and motivated. The power of his idea and his evolving understanding and expression of its is forever available to us through this book."

Sister Joel Read, President, Alverno College

"*Servant Leadership* is the pacesetting book in the area of transformational leadership. The seminal thoughts of Robert Greenleaf are crucial for the renewal of religious institutions. The Greenleaf Center is to be highly commended for expanding the work of servant leadership and, with Paulist Press, for publishing this silver anniversary edition."

David Young, author, *Servant Leadership for Church Renewal* and *A New Heart and a New Spirit*

Other books by Robert K. Greenleaf
available from other publishers

The Power of Servant Leadership, 1998
On Becoming a Servant Leader, 1996
Seeker and Servant, 1996
Teacher as Servant, 1979

25TH ANNIVERSARY EDITION

SERVANT LEADERSHIP

A JOURNEY INTO THE NATURE OF LEGITIMATE POWER AND GREATNESS

Essays by Robert K. Greenleaf
Edited by Larry C. Spears

Foreword by Stephen R. Covey
Afterword by Peter M. Senge

PAULIST PRESS
New York/Mahwah, N.J.

Book design by Theresa M. Sparacio

Jacket design by Morris Berman Studio

Copyright © 1977 by Robert K. Greenleaf; copyright © 1991, 2002 by the Robert K. Greenleaf Center, Inc.

All rights reserved. No part of this book may be reproduced or transmitted in any form or by any means, electronic or mechanical, including photocopying, recording or by any information storage and retrieval system, without permission in writing from the Publisher.

Library of Congress Cataloging-in-Publication Data

Greenleaf, Robert K.
    Servant leadership : a journey into the nature of legitimate power and greatness / essays by Robert K. Greenleaf ; edited by Larry C. Spears ; foreword by Stephen R. Covey ; afterword by Peter M. Senge. — 25th anniversary ed.
        p.   cm.
    Includes index.
    ISBN 0-8091-0554-3
    1. Leadership. 2. Associations, institutions, etc.—Management. 3. Organizational effectiveness. I. Spears, Larry C., 1955-   II. Title.
HM1241 .G74 2002
303.3′4—dc21

                                                                    2002007618

Published by Paulist Press
997 Macarthur Blvd.
Mahwah, New Jersey 07430

www.paulistpress.com

Printed and bound in the
United States of America

Contents

Foreword by Stephen R. Covey.. 1

Introduction by Robert K. Greenleaf 15

   I. The Servant as Leader.. 21

  II. The Institution as Servant.. 62

 III. Trustees as Servants... 104

 IV. Servant Leadership in Business 147

  V. Servant Leadership in Education 176

 VI. Servant Leadership in Foundations 215

VII. Servant Leadership in Churches 231

VIII. Servant-Leaders 262

 IX. Servant Responsibility in a Bureaucratic Society......... 304

  X. America and World Leadership 320

 XI. An Inward Journey 326

XII. Postscript 341

Afterword by Peter M. Senge.. 343

Index 361

About Robert K. Greenleaf and the Greenleaf Center
for Servant-Leadership 369

ACKNOWLEDGMENTS

C.A.S. Williams, *Encyclopedia of Chinese Symbolism and Art Motives*. New York, The Julian Press, 1960. Used with permission. Aldous Huxley, *Perennial Philosophy*. New York, Harper & Row, 1970. Used with permission. Hermann Hesse, *Journey to the East*. Hilda Rosner, translator. New York, Farrar, Straus & Giroux, 1956. Noonday edition. Used with permission. Helmut Wilhelm, *Change: Eight Lectures on the I Ching*, trans. Cary F. Baynes. Bollingen Series LXII. © 1960 by Bollingen Foundation. Short selections from pp. 17, 18, 19, 20, 22 reprinted by permission of Princeton University Press. London, Routledge and Kegan Paul, Ltd. Used with permission. Elizabeth Gray Vining, *Friend of Life: A Biography of Rufus Jones*. Philadelphia, J. B. Lippincott & Company. Reprinted by permission of Curtis Brown, Ltd. Copyright © 1958 by Elizabeth Gray Vining. Merrimon Cuninggim, *Private Money and Public Service: The Role of the Foundations in American Society*. New York, McGraw-Hill, 1972. Used with permission. Robert K. Greenleaf, "The Art of Knowing" from *Friends Journal—Quaker Thought and Life Today*, October 15, 1974, Philadelphia, Pennsylvania. Used with permission. Excerpt from *A Conversation With Abraham Joshua Heschel*, and "Eternal Light" special production of the Public Affairs Department of NBC News. Used with permission. Abraham Joshua Heschel, *A Passion for Truth*. New York, Farrar, Straus & Giroux, 1973. London, Martin Secker & Warburg Ltd. Used with permission. Nikos Kazantzakis, *Report to Greco*. © 1965 by Simon & Schuster, Inc. Reprinted by permission of the publisher. Oslo, Norway, Max Tau. Used with permission. Albert Camus, "Create Dangerously" from *Resistance, Rebellion and Death*. New York, Alfred A. Knopf, Inc., 1961. Used with permission. Stephen Spender, "The Truly Great" from *Selected Poems*. New York, Random House. London, Faber & Faber, Ltd. Used with permission. *The Poetry of Robert Frost* edited by Edward Connery Lathen. Copyright 1923, 1930, 1939, 1947, © 1969 by Holt, Rinehart and Winston. Copyright 1951, © 1958 by Robert Frost. Copyright © 1967, 1975 by Lesley Frost Ballantine. Reprinted by permission of Holt, Rinehart and Winston, Publishers. London, Jonathan Cape, Ltd. Used with permission. James Thurber, "The Unicorn in the Garden" from *Fables for Our Time*. Copyright 1940 by James Thurber. New York, Harper & Row. Used with permission. London, Hamish Hamilton, Ltd. Used with permission.

To Esther

without whose loving concern,
sustaining spirit, and critical judgment
none of this would have been written

STEPHEN R. COVEY

Foreword

It is a profound honor to have been asked to write a foreword to this Silver Anniversary Edition of *Servant Leadership*—a book that has had enormous influence over the last twenty-five years, both directly and indirectly. Through my work with many organizations over the years, I am a first hand witness of its tremendous impact—and I'm convinced that its greatest influence is yet to come. Why? Because, as Victor Hugo once said, "There's nothing as powerful as an idea whose time has come." Servant leadership's time has come.

The deepest part of human nature is that which urges people—each one of us—to rise above our present circumstances and to transcend our common nature. If you can appeal to it, you tap into a whole new source of human motivation. Perhaps this is why I have found Robert Greenleaf's teaching on servant leadership to be so enormously inspiring, so uplifting, so ennobling.

There is a great movement taking place throughout the world today. Its roots, I believe, are to be found in two powerful forces. One is the dramatic globalization of markets and technology. And in a very pragmatic way, this tidal wave of change is fueling the impact of the second force: the force of timeless, universal principles that have, and always will govern all enduring success, especially those principles that give "air" and "life" and creative power to the human spirit that *produces* value in markets, organizations, families, and most significantly, individual's lives.

Servant Leadership Will Continue to Increase in Relevance

One of these fundamental, timeless principles is the idea of servant leadership, and I am convinced that it will continue to dramatically increase in its relevance. There is a growing awareness and consciousness around it in the world. One of the things that is driving it, as I have mentioned, is the global economy, which absolutely insists on quality at low cost. We've got to produce more for less, and with greater speed than we've ever done before. The only way to do that in a sustained way is through the empowerment of people. And the only way you get empowerment is through high-trust cultures and an empowerment philosophy that turns bosses into servants and coaches, and structures and systems into nurturing institutionalized servant processes.

A low-trust culture that is characterized by high-control management, political posturing, protectionism, cynicism, and internal competition and adversarialism simply cannot compete with the speed, quality, and innovation of those organizations around the world that *do* empower people. It may be possible to buy someone's hand and back, but not their heart, mind, and spirit. And in the competitive reality of today's global marketplace, it will be only those organizations whose people not only willingly volunteer their tremendous creative talent, commitment, and loyalty, but whose organizations align their structures, systems, and management style to support the empowerment of their people that will survive and thrive as market leaders.

Leaders are learning that this kind of empowerment, which is what servant leadership represents, is one of the key principles that, based on practice, not talk, will be the deciding point between an organization's enduring success or its eventual demise.

The "Strange Attractor"

I love this statement made by Stan Davis, "When the infrastructure shifts, everything rumbles." Well, everything is rumbling because the old rules of traditional, hierarchical, high-external-control, top-down management are being dismantled: they simply aren't working any longer. They are being replaced by a new form of "control" that the chaos theory proponents call the "strange attractor"—a sense of vision that people are drawn to, and united in, that enables them to be driven by motivation *inside* them toward achieving a common purpose. This has changed the role of manager from one who drives results and motivation from the outside in, to one who is a servant-leader—one who seeks to draw out, inspire, and develop the best and highest within people from the inside out. The leader does this by engaging the entire team or organization in a process that creates a shared vision, which inspires each person to stretch and reach deeper within himself or herself, and to use everyone's unique talents in whatever way is necessary to independently and interdependently achieve that shared vision.

In order to get the kind of trust in a culture that enables an empowerment approach to thrive, we must not only have individuals who are trustworthy and whose vision is shared with the organization, but we must have a trustworthy organization—one that fosters and supports empowerment. Again, unless systems and structures that foster empowerment are institutionalized, there will be no reinforcement. That was the basic message of W. Edwards Deming—that arguably, over 90 percent of problems are due to bad systems, not bad people. However, Greenleaf correctly points out that people are the programmers. They are the ones who write the systems. Ultimately, however, we must work with people to give them a new concept of their stewardship and to redefine leadership as service and stewardship.

Changeless Principles at the Core

There has to be something at the soul of an organization that does not change but that will enable people to live *with* change. This unchanging core is natural principles. I certainly didn't invent them. Greenleaf didn't invent them. These are natural laws that are self-evident and universal. We all know them. They are common sense. It is as T. S. Eliot so beautifully stated, "We must not cease from exploration. And the end of all our exploring will be to arrive where we began and to know the place for the first time."

Leadership that Endures

I believe that the essential quality that sets servant-leaders apart from others is that they live by their *conscience*—the inward moral sense of what is right and what is wrong. That one quality is the difference between leadership that *works* and leadership—like servant leadership—that *endures.* There is a mass of evidence that shows that this moral sense, this conscience, this inner light, is a universal phenomenon. The spiritual or moral nature of people is also independent of religion or of any particular religious approach, culture, geography, nationality, or race. Yet all of the enduring major religious traditions of the world are unified when it comes to certain basic underlying principles or values.

Immanuel Kant said, "I am constantly amazed by two things: the starry heavens above and the moral law within." *Conscience* is the moral law within. It is the overlapping of moral law and behavior. Many believe, as do I, that it is the voice of God to his children. Others may not share this belief but still recognize that there is an innate sense of fairness and justice, an innate sense of right and wrong, of what is kind and what is unkind, of what contributes and what detracts, of what beautifies and what destroys, of what is true and what is false. Admittedly, culture translates this basic moral sense into different kinds of practices and words, but this translation does not negate the underlying sense of right and wrong.

As I work in nations of different religions and different cultures, I have seen this universal conscience revealed time and again. There really is a set of values, a sense of *fairness, honesty, respect,* and *contribution* that transcends culture—something that is timeless that transcends the ages and that is also self-evident. It is as self-evident as the requirement of trust-worthiness to produce trust.

Natural Authority and Moral Authority

Because people are uniquely endowed with the power and freedom to choose, they have natural authority over all other creation. The rest of creation does not have this power and freedom to choose. It is not a matter of degree; it is a matter of kind. This is why people have a natural authority over animals and the environment.

Because we have a natural authority resulting from our power and freedom to choose, we need to use it in a principled way. Some of us haven't. We have violated our stewardship concerning the earth and the other creations with which we live, so we need laws to protect the environment and endangered species.

Moral authority is different from natural authority. Moral authority comes from the principled use of that natural power and that freedom to choose. When people live by their conscience, responding to the universal principles we discussed earlier, their behavior echoes in everyone's souls. People instinctively feel trust and confidence toward them. This is the beginning of moral authority.

If an entire culture were imbued with this kind of moral authority, it wouldn't need external laws. People would live and be governed by the moral law within. They would all follow a common value system. By exercising their freedom responsibly, they would live in what the turn-of-the-century British parliamentarian Lord Moulton called "the third domain," the law of the unenforceable. Not the first domain, freedom, or the second, law, but the third domain, a unified value system governed by a universal conscience.

Moral authority is another way to define servant leadership because it represents a reciprocal choice between leader and follower. If the leader is principle centered, he or she will develop moral authority. If the follower is principle centered, he or she will follow the leader. In this sense, both leaders and followers are followers. Why? They follow truth. They follow natural law. They follow principles. They follow a common, agreed-upon vision. They share values. They grow to trust one another. Moral authority is mutually developed and shared.

Four Dimensions of Moral Authority (Conscience)

Let us briefly consider the four dimensions of moral authority, the core of servant leadership.

1. *The essence of moral authority or conscience is sacrifice*—the subordinating of one's self or one's ego to a higher purpose, cause, or principle. This sacrifice can take many forms as it manifests itself in the four dimensions of our lives: making physical and economic sacrifices (the body); cultivating an open inquisitive mind and purging ourselves of prejudices (the mind); showing deep respect and love to others (the heart); and subordinating our will to a higher will for the greater good (the spirit).

Conscience is the still, small voice within. It is quiet. It is peaceful. Ego is tyrannical, despotic, and dictatorial.

Ego focuses on one's own survival, pleasure, and enhancement to the exclusion of others; ego is selfishly ambitious. It sees relationships in terms of threat or no threat, like little children who classify all people as "nice" or "mean." Conscience, on the other hand, both democratizes and elevates ego to a larger sense of the group, the whole, the community, the greater good. It sees life in terms of service and contribution, in terms of others' security and fulfillment.

Ego works in the face of genuine crisis but has no discernment in deciding how severe a crisis or threat is. It can't discern *then* from *now* and *when*. Conscience is filled with discernment and senses the degree of threat. It has a large repertoire of responses. It has the patience and wisdom to decide *what* to do *when*. Conscience sees life on a continuum. It is capable of complex adaptation.

Ego can't sleep. It micro-manages. It disempowers. It reduces our capability. It excels in control. Conscience deeply reveres people and sees their potential for self-control. Conscience empowers. It reflects the worth and value of all people and affirms their power and freedom to choose. Then natural self-control emerges, imposed neither from above nor from the outside.

Ego is threatened by negative feedback and punishes the messenger. It interprets all data in terms of self-preservation. It constantly censors information. It denies much of reality. Conscience values feedback and attempts to discern whatever truth it contains. It isn't afraid of information and can accurately interpret what's going on. It has no need to censor information and is open to an awareness of reality from every direction.

Ego is myopic and interprets all of life through its own agenda. Conscience is a social ecologist listening to and sensing the entire system and environment. It fills the body with light, is able to democratize ego to reflect more accurately the entire world.

2. *Conscience inspires us to become part of a cause worthy of our commitment.* While imprisoned in the death camps of Nazi Germany, Doctor Viktor Frankl first asked himself the question, "What is it that I want?" But gradually he submitted himself to his higher nature, his conscience, and changed the question to "What is wanted of me?" This totally changed his world. Instead of attempting to invent answers to his questions, he listened to his conscience, the moral voice within, and detected the answers. He would then do the same thing with other prisoners. He confronted them directly. He would ask a man who was despairing, for example, "Then why don't you take your own life?" The response would be, "Because of the suffering it would cause my wife." And in that answer, the person found meaning behind his own suffering.

When we change our question from asking *what is it we want* to *what is being asked of us,* our conscience is opened up and we allow ourselves to be influenced by it. What a change of mind and heart that is! Feel the passion in George Bernard Shaw's conviction:

> This is the true joy in life, being used for a purpose recognized by yourself as a mighty one. Being a force of nature instead of a feverish, selfish little clod of ailments and grievances complaining that the world will not devote itself to making you happy. I am of the opinion that my life belongs to the whole community, and as long as I live, it is my privilege to do for it whatever I can. I want to be thoroughly used up when I die, for the harder I work, the more I live. I rejoice in life for its own sake. Life is no "brief candle" to me; it is sort of a splendid torch which I've got to hold up for the moment, and I want to make it burn as brightly as possible before handing it on to future generations.

3. *Conscience teaches us that ends and means are inseparable*, that ends actually preexist in the means. Immanuel Kant taught that the means used to accomplish the ends are as important as those ends. Machiavelli taught the opposite, that the ends justify the means.

Gandhi taught that there are seven things that will destroy us. As we study them slowly and carefully, we see in a powerful way how each represents an end being accomplished through an unprincipled or unworthy means:

- Wealth without work.
- Pleasure without conscience.
- Knowledge without character.
- Commerce without morality.
- Science without humanity.
- Worship without sacrifice.
- Politics without principle.

Isn't it interesting how each one of these admirable ends can be falsely attained? But if we reach an admirable end through the wrong means, the ends ultimately turn to dust in our hands.

In our business dealings, we know those who are honest with us and who keep their promises and commitments. We also know exactly those who are duplicitous, deceitful, and dishonest. Even when we reach a contract agreement with them, do we really trust that they will come through and keep their word?

It is conscience that constantly tells us the value of both ends and means and how they are inseparable. But it is ego that tells us that the end justifies the means, unaware that a worthy end can never be accomplished with an unworthy means. It may appear that it can, but there are unintended consequences that are not evident at first that will eventually destroy the end. For instance, we can yell at our kids to clean their rooms, and if our end is to have a clean room, we may accomplish just that. But I guarantee that not only will the means negatively affect the relationships, but the room won't stay clean when we leave town for a few days.

4. *Conscience introduces us into the world of relationships.* It moves us from an independent to an interdependent state. When this happens, everything is altered. We realize that vision and values must be shared before people will be willing to accept the institutionalized discipline of structures and systems that embody those shared values. Such shared vision creates discipline and order without demanding it. Conscience often provides the *why*, vision identifies *what* we are trying to accomplish, discipline represents *how* we are going to accomplish it, and passion represents the strength of *feelings* behind the why, the what, and the how.

Conscience also transforms passion into compassion. It engenders sincere caring for others, a combination of both sympathy and empathy, where pain is shared and received. Compassion is the interdependent expression of passion. JoAnn C. Jones relates an experience in which her university professor teaches her to live and learn guided by her conscience:

> During my second year of nursing school, our professor gave us a quiz. I breezed through the questions until I read the last one: "What is the first name of the

woman who cleans the school?" Surely this was a joke. I had seen the cleaning woman several times but how would I know her name? I handed in my paper, leaving the last question blank. Before the class ended, one student asked if the last question would count toward our grade. "Absolutely," the professor said. "In your careers, you will meet many people—all are significant. They deserve your attention and care. Even if all you do is smile and say hello." I have never forgotten that lesson. I also learned her name was Dorothy.

When people strive to live by their conscience, it produces integrity and peace of mind. William J. H. Boetcker says, "That you may retain your self-respect, it is better to displease the people by doing what you know is right, than to temporarily please them by doing what you know is wrong." This self-respect and integrity, in turn, produces the ability to be both kind and courageous with other people—kind in showing a great respect and reverence for other people, their view, feelings, experiences, and convictions, but also courageous in expressing their own convictions without personal threat. The interplay between differing opinions can produce those third alternatives that are better than what either had initially proposed. This is true synergy in which the whole is greater than the sum of the parts.

People who do not live by their conscience will not experience this internal integrity and peace of mind. They will find their ego attempting to control relationships. Even though they might pretend or feign kindness and empathy from time to time, they will use subtle forms of manipulation and will even go so far as to engage in kind but dictatorial behavior.

The private victory of integrity is the foundation for the public victories of establishing a common vision, discipline, and passion. Leadership becomes an interdependent work rather than an immature interplay between strong, independent, ego-driven rulers and compliant, dependent followers.

Moral Authority and Servant Leadership

I define moral authority as *Our Moral Nature + Principles + Sacrifice*. Many of us know we ought to behave in a certain way, but sacrifice enables us *actually* to behave in those ways that are in alignment with universal principles. Therefore, sacrifice is the essence of moral authority, and *humility* is the foundational attribute of sacrifice.

Moral authority comes through sacrifice in the four basic elements of our nature: physical and economic sacrifice is temperance and giving back; emotional/social sacrifice is surrendering self to the value and difference of another, to apologize, and to forgive; mental sacrifice is placing learning above pleasure and realizing that true freedom comes from discipline; and spiritual sacrifice is living life humbly and courageously, living and serving wisely.

The interesting thing about moral authority is what a paradox it is. The dictionary discusses *authority* in terms of *command, control, power, sway, rule, supremacy, domination, dominion, strength, might*. But its antonyms are *civility, servitude, weakness, follower*. Moral authority is the gaining of influence through following principles. Moral dominion is achieved through servanthood, service, contribution. Power and moral supremacy emerge from humility, where the greatest becomes the servant of all. Moral authority is achieved through sacrifice. Robert Greenleaf put it this way:

> A new moral principle is emerging which holds that the only authority deserving one's allegiance is that which is freely and knowingly granted by the led to the leader in response to, and in proportion to, the clearly evident servant stature of the leader. Those who choose to follow this principle will not casually accept the authority of existing institutions. *Rather, they will freely respond only to individuals who are chosen as leaders because they are proven and trusted as servants.* To the extent that this principle prevails in the future, the

only truly viable institutions will be those that are predominantly servant led.

It has generally been my experience that the very top people of truly great organizations are servant-leaders. They are the most humble, the most reverent, the most open, the most teachable, the most respectful, the most caring, and the most determined. When people with the formal authority or positional power refuse to use that authority and power except as a last resort, their moral authority increases because it is obvious that they have subordinated their ego and positional power and use reasoning, persuasion, kindness, empathy, and, in short, *trustworthiness* instead.

On the other hand, when people use their formal authority early on, their moral authority will be lessened. When we borrow strength, we build weakness in three places: in self, because we are not developing moral authority; in the other, because they become co-dependent with our use of formal authority; and in the quality of the relationship, because authentic openness and trust are never developed.

Islands of Excellence in a Sea of Mediocrity

What if we could get model communities in this country, and model institutions, schools, businesses, and government units that would become islands of excellence in seas of mediocrity? What if they could become models and then transport what they learn and become mentors to others so that this whole spirit of stewardship, of servant leadership, of working at the empowerment process through structures and systems could take root and flourish? I honestly think we could heal our country. I believe that the overwhelming majority of the people in this country, with the right kind of servant leadership at all levels—most important, at the family level—could heal our country. Otherwise, these social problems will worsen and deepen until eventually they will overwhelm the economic machinery—and this will discombobulate everything.

I have hope and confidence that we can. I have the same hope for people in every nation, for the principles of servant leadership are universal. I believe that hope is a moral imperative, and that as we keep our flame of hope burning by our own efforts, we become a big part of the solution.

I congratulate the Greenleaf Center for Servant-Leadership for its invaluable service to society, for carrying the torch of servant leadership over the years, and for initiating this new edition. To the reader, I humbly and most sincerely commend this book and its absolute treasure of insights to you.

© 2001 Franklin Covey Co. Printed with permission of Franklin Covey Co.

Dr. Stephen Covey *is vice-chairman of Franklin Covey Company, the largest management and leadership development organization in the world. He is perhaps most widely known as the author of* The Habits of Highly Effective People, *a book with a compelling message that has kept it on numerous best-seller lists for more than ten years running. Those familiar with his work will not be surprised to learn that Dr. Covey has been recognized as one of* Time *magazine's twenty-five most influential Americans.*

Introduction

Were I to read a book like this I would want to know something of the source of the ideas presented. Assuming that the present reader has a similar interest, a brief summary is given.

As late as the last half of my senior year in college I was without a clear vocational aim. I knew that, on graduation, I would work at something, but I was not much concerned about what it would be. In due course, I assured myself, I would give that important matter some attention. The only certainty was that I wanted no more formal education. I would settle for a bachelor's degree.

In that last term I elected a course entitled "The Sociology of Labor Problems." The professor, an old man—or so he seemed to me—was neither an exciting teacher nor an exceptional scholar. But he had been around, and he was wise in the ways of both people and institutions. Some of his wisdom spoke to me. Early on I made a distinction between wisdom and scholarship; and the former, what works well in practice, has long been my central interest. This is not said to denigrate scholarship. It has its place, and there is a subtle interaction between the two, but they are different things. The wise are not necessarily scholars, and scholars are not necessarily wise. Intelligence (that which intelligence tests measure) has something to do with both.

One day, in the course of a rambling lecture, my old professor made a statement along these lines: "There is a new problem in our country. We are becoming a nation that is dominated by large institutions—churches, businesses, governments, labor unions, universities—and these big institutions are not serving us well. I hope that all of you will be concerned about this. Now you can do as I do, stand outside and criticize, bring pressure if you can, write and argue about it. All of this may do some good. But nothing of substance will happen unless there are people inside these institutions who are able to (and want to) lead them into better performance for the public good. Some of you ought to make careers inside these big institutions and become a force for good—from the inside."

My doors of perception were open a bit wider than usual that day, and his message got through. There was a brief discussion later with the professor, and I decided, without much deliberation, that this was the work for me—in a business. I chose the field of business, not because I had a particular leaning toward business, but because it was possible to enter that field with no further formal education. Also, business seemed to be on the frontier. It was crude but open. And, as it proved to be in time, it was the right choice for one like me, a student of organization—how things get done, and a pursuer of wisdom—what works well in practice. It was rough at times but satisfying in the end.

I quickly learned that American Telephone and Telegraph Company employed more people than any other business in the world, and that one fact settled my choice. That was where I wanted to work. The mid-1920s were a boom period, and it was not difficult to be hired. The local personnel officer of the construction-and-maintenance department in Cleveland took me on, and I was assigned to a line construction crew in Youngstown, Ohio, as a "groundman"—a common laborer digging post holes and carrying tools.

The personnel officer who hired me kept an eye on me, and in a few months I was shifted to the engineering department in Akron. Near the end of my first year I was selected to take a training course at the departmental headquarters in Cleveland in how to lead foremen's conferences. This was the first move of this very large company (now over one million employees) into formal management training. For one year, every other Monday morning, I received a group of twelve foremen, ranging in age from late twenties to sixties (I was twenty-three). We sat informally around a large table, and I guided them through a two-week series of discussions, without a published agenda and with no assigned reading, on the multifaceted job of being a foreman. I learned much from these foremen. This was my graduate education.

For another year I was director of training for this unit of the company and was then moved to the corporate staff in New York where, with the exception of four of the next thirty-five years, I held only positions that did not exist before I had them. My last position, which was held for seven years prior to retirement in 1964, was director of management research, an internal consulting group with a loosely defined commission to be concerned for values, attitudes, organization, and the growth of people, especially executives. In the years since my retirement from A.T.&T. I have worked as a consultant for businesses, foundations, professional societies, church organizations, and universities—not just here, but also in Europe and in the developing nations. I give you this much of a view of my adult life so that you will have some perspective on where the content of this book comes from, because it comes largely out of my own experience, plus watching and talking to able practitioners, and not from scholarship.

The servant-leader concept emerged after a deep involvement with colleges and universities during the period of campus turmoil in the late 1960s and early 1970s. It was a searing experience to watch distinguished institutions show their fragility and crumble, to search for an understanding of what happened to them (and never be satisfied that I knew), and to try to help heal their wounds.

The first chapter of this book, "The Servant as Leader," was written in 1969 out of concern for pervasive student attitudes which then, and now, although the manifestations are different, seemed devoid of hope. Hope, it seems to me, is absolutely essential to both sanity and wholeness of life. In pursuit of a structural basis for hope, two further essays came—"The Institution as Servant" and "Trustees as Servants"—which serve as the second and third chapters of this book.

The remaining chapters were written over twenty years as articles and talks. They express in different ways my wish that leaders will bend their efforts to serve with skill, understanding, and spirit, and that followers will be responsive only to able servants who would lead them—*but that they will respond.* Discriminating and determined *servants as followers* are as important as servant-leaders, and everyone, from time to time, may be in both roles.

But, alas, we live in the age of the anti-leader, and our vast educational structure devotes very little care to nurturing leaders or to understanding followership. If there is any influence, formal education seems to discourage such pursuits. Educators argue, speciously I believe, that such preparation is implicit in general education. If that is true, how can it be that we are in a crisis of leadership in which vast numbers of "educated" people make such gross errors in choosing whose leadership to follow, and in which there is so little incentive for able and dedicated servants to take the risks of asserting leadership? The conclusion I reach is that educators are avoiding the issue when they refuse to give the same care to the development of servant-leaders as they do to doctors, lawyers, ministers, teachers, engineers, scholars. Even schools of administration give scant attention to servant leadership. I have spent a great deal of time and energy trying to persuade educators to accept the obligation, and I am certain that, generally, they recognize neither the obligation nor the opportunity. Thus far in my experience, they appear unpersuadable. An occasional gifted teacher will take some initiative, but the institutions rarely sanction the effort. The outlook for better leadership in our leadership-poor society is not encouraging.

To whom, then, am I speaking in this collection of articles and essays?

Is it the large number of natural servants who might lead, or lead with greater spirit and force?

Could it be students still in their formative years who are groping for a basis for hope?

Large numbers of persons serve as trustees and directors—too often in a nominal way. Could their sights be raised, and could their concept of trust be clarified and enlarged?

The clergy and the churches they serve: do they not have the opportunities to specify in detail a new moral basis for an institution-bound society and give insistent guidance to those who have power to render these institutions more serving? And could some churches thereby venture into the growing edge positions that are crying out to be taken?

Many, many teachers at both secondary and college levels have sufficient latitude in dealing with students that they could, on their own, help nurture the servant-leader potential that, I believe, is latent to some degree in almost every young person. Could not many respected teachers speak those few words that might change the course of a life or give it a new purpose, as Professor Oscar Helming did with me?

Among those now in titular leadership positions in institutions both large and small are some who would find greater joy in their lives if they raised the servant aspect of their leadership and built more serving institutions. Can they be helped to make this change?

We live at a time when holders of power are suspect, and actions that stem from authority are questioned. *Legitimize power* has become an ethical imperative. Can discriminating people be helped to find the means for legitimizing power?

There are legions of persons of good will who could sharpen and clarify their view of the more serving society they would like to live in and help build—if in no other way than by holding a deepened interest and concern about it and speaking to the condition of others. Is not such widespread action necessary if the climate that favors service, and supports servants, is to be maintained?

Behind what is said in the collection presented here is a twofold concern. My first concern is for the individual in society and his or her seeming bent to deal with the massive problems of our times wholly in terms of systems, ideologies, and movements. These have their place, but they are not basic because they do not make themselves. The basics are the incremental thrusts of individuals who have the ability to serve and lead—the prime movers.

My second concern is for the individual as a serving person and the tendency to deny wholeness and creative fulfillment to oneself by failing to lead when there is the opportunity.

Overarching these is a concern for the total process of education and what appears to be indifference to the individual as servant and leader, as a person and in society, on the tacit assumption that intellectual preparation favors optimal growth in these ways where quite the reverse may be true.

Part of the problem is that *serve* and *lead* are overused words with negative connotations. But they are also good words and I can find no others that carry as well the meaning I would like to convey. Not everything that is old and worn, or even corrupt, can be thrown away. Some of it has to be rebuilt and used again. So it is, it seems to me, with the words *serve* and *lead*. Both words are essential for what is undertaken in the following pages.

I

The Servant as Leader

Servant and leader—can these two roles be fused in one real person, in all levels of status or calling? If so, can that person live and be productive in the real world of the present? My sense of the present leads me to say yes to both questions. This chapter is an attempt to explain why and to suggest how.

The idea of the servant as leader came out of reading Hermann Hesse's *Journey to the East*. In this story we see a band of men on a mythical journey, probably also Hesse's own journey. The central figure of the story is Leo, who accompanies the party as the *servant* who does their menial chores, but who also sustains them with his spirit and his song. He is a person of extraordinary presence. All goes well until Leo disappears. Then the group falls into disarray and the journey is abandoned. They cannot make it without the servant Leo. The narrator, one of the party, after some years of wandering, finds Leo and is taken into the Order that had sponsored the journey. There he discovers that Leo, whom he had known first as *servant*, was in fact the titular head of the Order, its guiding spirit, a great and noble *leader*.

One can muse on what Hesse was trying to say when he wrote this story. We know that most of his fiction was autobiographical, that he led a tortured life, and that *Journey to the East* suggests a turn toward the serenity he achieved in his old age. There has been much speculation by critics on Hesse's life and work, some of it centering on this story which they find the most puzzling. But to me, this story clearly says that *the great leader is seen as servant first*, and that simple fact is the key to his greatness. Leo was actually the leader all of the time, but he was servant first because that was what he was, *deep down inside*. Leadership was bestowed upon a person who was by nature a servant. It was something given, or assumed, that could be taken away. His servant nature was the real man, not bestowed, not assumed, and not to be taken away. He was servant first.

I mention Hesse and *Journey to the East* for two reasons. First, I want to acknowledge the source of the idea of the servant as leader. Then I want to use this reference as an introduction to a brief discussion of prophecy.

Fifteen years ago when I first read about Leo, if I had been listening to contemporary prophecy as intently as I do now, the first draft of this piece might have been written then. As it was, the idea lay dormant for eleven years until, four years ago, I concluded that we in this country were in a leadership crisis and that I should do what I could about it. I became painfully aware of how dull my sense of contemporary prophecy had been. And I have reflected much on why we do not hear and heed the prophetic voices in our midst (not a new question in our times, nor more critical than heretofore).

I now embrace the theory of prophecy, which holds that prophetic voices of great clarity, and with a quality of insight equal to that of any age, are speaking cogently all of the time. Men and women of a stature equal to the greatest of the past are with us now addressing the problems of the day and pointing to a better way and to a personeity better able to live fully and serenely in these times.

The variable that marks some periods as barren and some as rich in prophetic vision is in the interest, the level of seeking, the responsiveness of the hearers. The variable is not in the presence or absence or the relative quality and force of the prophetic voices. Prophets grow in stature as people respond to their message. If their early attempts are ignored or spurned, their talent may wither away.

It is *seekers*, then, who make prophets, and the initiative of any one of us in searching for and responding to the voice of contemporary prophets may mark the turning point in their growth and service. But since we are the product of our own history, we see current prophecy within the context of past wisdom. We listen to as wide a range of contemporary thought as we can attend to. Then we *choose* those we elect to heed as prophets—*both old and new*—and meld their advice with our own leadings. This we test in real-life experiences to establish our own position.

Some who have difficulty with this theory assert that their faith rests on one or more of the prophets of old having given the "word" for all time and that the contemporary ones do not speak to their condition as the older ones do. But if one really believes that the "word" has been given for all time, how can one be a seeker? How can one hear the contemporary voice when one has decided not to live in the present and has turned that voice off?

Neither this hypothesis nor its opposite can be proved, but I submit that the one given here is the more hopeful choice, one that offers a significant role in prophecy to every individual. One cannot interact with and build strength in a dead prophet, but one can do it with a living one. "Faith," Dean Inge has said, "is the choice of the nobler hypothesis."

One does not, of course, ignore the great voices of the past. One does not awaken each morning with the compulsion to reinvent the wheel. But if one is *servant*, either leader or follower, one is always searching, listening, expecting that a better wheel for these times is in the making. It may emerge any day. Any one of us may find it out from personal experience. I am hopeful.

I am hopeful for these times, despite the tension and conflict, because more natural servants are trying to see clearly the world as it is and are listening carefully to prophetic voices that are speaking *now*. They are challenging the pervasive injustice with greater force, and they are taking sharper issue with the wide disparity between the quality of society they know is reasonable and possible with available resources, and, on the other hand, the actual performance of the whole range of institutions that exist to serve society.

A fresh critical look is being taken at the issues of power and authority, and people are beginning to learn, however haltingly, to relate to one another in less coercive and more creatively supporting ways. A new moral principle is emerging, which holds that the only authority deserving one's allegiance is that which is freely and knowingly granted by the led to the leader in response to, and in proportion to, the clearly evident servant stature of the leader. Those who choose to follow this principle will not casually accept the authority of existing institutions. *Rather, they will freely respond only to individuals who are chosen as leaders because they are proven and trusted as servants.* To the extent that this principle prevails in the future, the only truly viable institutions will be those that are predominantly servant led.

I am mindful of the long road ahead before these trends, which I see so clearly, become a major society-shaping force. We are not there yet. But I see encouraging movement on the horizon.

What direction will the movement take? Much depends on whether those who stir the ferment will come to grips with the age-old problem of how to live in a human society. I say this because so many, having made their awesome decision for autonomy and independence from tradition, and having taken their firm stand against injustice and hypocrisy, find it hard to convert themselves into *affirmative builders* of a better society. How many of them will seek their personal fulfillment by making the hard choices and by undertaking the rigorous preparation that building a better society requires? It all depends on what kind of leaders emerge and how they—we—respond to them.

My thesis, that more servants should emerge as leaders, or should follow only servant-leaders, is not a popular one. It is much more comfortable to go with a less demanding point of view about what is expected of one now. There are several undemanding, plausibly argued alternatives to choose. One, since society seems corrupt, is to seek to avoid the center of it by retreating to an idyllic existence that minimizes involvement with the "system" (with the "system" that makes such withdrawal possible). Then there is the assumption that since the effort to reform existing institutions has not brought instant perfection, the remedy is to destroy them completely so that fresh new perfect ones can grow. Not much thought seems to be given to the problem of where the new seed will come from or who the gardener to tend them will be. The concept of the servant-leader stands in sharp contrast to this kind of thinking.

Yet it is understandable that the easier alternatives would be chosen, especially by young people. By extending education for so many so far into the adult years, normal participation in society is effectively denied when young people are ready for it. With education that is preponderantly abstract and analytical it is no wonder that there is a preoccupation with criticism and that not much thought is given to "What can I do about it?"

Criticism has its place, but as a total preoccupation it is sterile. In a time of crisis, like the leadership crisis we are now in, if too many potential builders are taken in by a complete absorption with dissecting the wrong and by a zeal for instant perfection, then the movement so many of us want to see will be set back. The danger, perhaps, is to hear the analyst too much and the artist too little.

Albert Camus stands apart from other great artists of his time, in my view, and deserves the title of *prophet* because of his unrelenting demand that each of us confront the exacting terms of our own existence, and, like Sisyphus, *accept our rock and find our happiness in dealing with it.* Camus sums up the relevance of his position to our concern for the servant as leader in the last paragraph of his last published lecture, entitled "Create Dangerously":

> One may long, as I do, for a gentler flame, a respite, a pause for musing. But perhaps there is no other peace for the artist than what he finds in the heat of combat. "Every wall is a door," Emerson correctly said. Let us not look for the door, and the way out, anywhere but in the wall against which we are living. Instead, let us seek the respite where it is—in the very thick of battle. For in my opinion, and this is where I shall close, it *is* there. Great ideas, it has been said, come into the world as gently as doves. Perhaps, then, if we listen attentively, we shall hear, amid the uproar of empires and nations, a faint flutter of wings, the gentle stirring of life and hope. Some will say that this hope lies in a nation, others, in a

man. I believe rather that it is awakened, revived, nourished by millions of solitary individuals whose deeds
and works every day negate frontiers and the crudest
implications of history. As a result, there shines forth
fleetingly the ever-threatened truth that each and every
man, on the foundations of his own sufferings and joys,
builds for them all.

One is asked, then, to accept the human condition, its sufferings and its joys, and to work with its imperfections as the
foundation upon which the individual will build wholeness
through adventurous creative achievement. For the person with
creative potential there is no wholeness except in using it. And, as
Camus explained, the going is rough and the respite is brief. It is
significant that he would title his last university lecture "Create
Dangerously." And, as I ponder the fusing of servant and leader,
it seems a dangerous creation: dangerous for the natural servant
to become a leader, dangerous for the leader to be servant first,
and dangerous for a follower to insist on being led by a servant.
There are safer and easier alternatives available to all three. But
why take them?

As I respond to the challenge of dealing with this question
in the ensuing discourse, I am faced with two problems.

First, I did not get the notion of the servant as leader from
conscious logic. Rather, it came to me as an intuitive insight as I
contemplated Leo. And I do not see what is relevant from my
own searching and experience in terms of a logical progression
from premise to conclusion. Rather, I see it as fragments of data
to be fed into my internal computer from which intuitive insights
come. Serving and leading are still mostly intuition-based concepts in my thinking.

The second problem, related to the first, is that, just as
there may be a real contradiction in the servant as leader, so my
perceptual world is full of contradictions. Some examples: I
believe in order, and I want creation out of chaos. My good society will have strong individualism amid community. It will have
elitism along with populism. I listen to the old and to the young

and find myself baffled and heartened by both. Reason and intuition, each in its own way, both comfort and dismay me. There
are many more. Yet, with all of this, I believe that I live with as
much serenity as do my contemporaries who venture into controversy as freely as I do but whose natural bent is to tie up the
essentials of life in neat bundles of logic and consistency. But I
am deeply grateful to the people who are logical and consistent
because some of them, out of their natures, render invaluable
services for which I am not capable.

My resolution of these two problems is to offer the relevant
gleanings of my experience in the form of a series of unconnected
little essays, some developed more fully than others, with the
suggestion that they be read and pondered separately within the
context of this opening section.

Who Is the Servant-Leader?

The servant-leader *is* servant first—as Leo was portrayed. It
begins with the natural feeling that one wants to serve, to serve
first. Then conscious choice brings one to aspire to lead. That person is sharply different from one who is *leader* first, perhaps
because of the need to assuage an unusual power drive or to
acquire material possessions. For such, it will be a later choice to
serve—after leadership is established. The leader-first and the servant-first are two extreme types. Between them there are shadings
and blends that are part of the infinite variety of human nature.

The difference manifests itself in the care taken by the servant-first to make sure that other people's highest priority needs
are being served. The best test, and difficult to administer, is this:
Do those served grow as persons? Do they, *while being served*,
become healthier, wiser, freer, more autonomous, more likely
themselves to become servants? *And*, what is the effect on the
least privileged in society? Will they benefit or at least not be further deprived?

As one sets out to serve, how can one know that this will be
the result? This is part of the human dilemma; one cannot know

for sure. One must, after some study and experience, hypothe-size—but leave the hypothesis under a shadow of doubt. Then one acts on the hypothesis and examines the result. One contin-ues to study and learn and periodically one reexamines the hypothesis itself.

Finally, one chooses again. Perhaps one chooses the same hypothesis again and again. But it is always a fresh, open choice. And it is always a hypothesis under a shadow of doubt. "Faith is the choice of the nobler hypothesis." Not the *noblest;* one never knows what that is. But the *nobler,* the best one can see when the choice is made. Since the test of results of one's actions is usually long delayed, the faith that sustains the choice of the nobler hypothesis is psychological self-insight. This is the most depend-able part of the true servant.

The natural servant, the person who is *servant-first,* is more likely to persevere and refine a particular hypothesis on what serves another's highest priority needs than is the person who is *leader-first* and who later serves out of promptings of conscience or in conformity with normative expectations.

My hope for the future rests in part on my belief that among the legions of deprived and unsophisticated people are many true servants who will lead and that most of them can learn to discriminate among those who presume to serve them and identify the true servants whom they will follow.

Everything Begins with the Initiative of an Individual

The forces for good and evil in the world are propelled by the thoughts, attitudes, and actions of individual beings. What happens to our values, and therefore to the quality of our civiliza-tion in the future, will be shaped by the conceptions of individu-als that are born of inspiration. Perhaps only a few will receive this inspiration (insight) and the rest will learn from them. The very essence of leadership, going out ahead to show the way, derives from more than usual openness to inspiration. Why would anybody accept the leadership of another except that the other sees more clearly where it is best to go? Perhaps this is the current problem: too many who presume to lead do not see more clearly, and in defense of their inadequacy, they all the more strongly argue that the "system" must be preserved—a fatal error in this day of candor.

But the leader needs more than inspiration. A leader ventures to say, "I will go; come with me!" A leader initiates, provides the ideas and the structure, and takes the risk of failure along with the chance of success. A leader says, "I will go; follow me!" while knowing that the path is uncertain, even dangerous. One then trusts those who go with one's leadership.

Paul Goodman, speaking through a character in *Making Do*, has said, "If there is no community for you, young man, young man, make it yourself."

What Are You Trying to Do?

"What are you trying to do?" is one of the easiest to ask and most difficult to answer of questions.

A mark of leaders, an attribute that puts them in a position to show the way for others, is that they are better than most at pointing the direction. As long as one is leading, one always has a goal. It may be a goal arrived at by group consensus, or the leader, acting on inspiration, may simply have said, "Let's go this way." But the leader always knows what it is and can articulate it for any who are unsure. By clearly stating and restating the goal the leader gives certainty to others who may have difficulty in achieving it for themselves.

The word *goal* is used here in the special sense of the overarching purpose, the big dream, the visionary concept, the ultimate consummation that one approaches but never really achieves. It is something presently out of reach; it is something to strive for, to move toward, to become. It is so stated that it excites the imagination and challenges people to work for something they do not yet know how to do, something they can be proud of as they move toward it.

Every achievement starts with a goal—but not just any goal and not just anybody stating it. The one who states the goal must elicit trust, especially if it is a high risk or visionary goal, because those who follow are asked to accept the risk along with the leader. Leaders do not elicit trust unless one has confidence in their values and competence (including judgment) and unless they have a sustaining spirit *(entheos)* that will support the tenacious pursuit of a goal.

Not much happens without a dream. And for something great to happen, there must be a great dream. Behind every great achievement is a dreamer of great dreams. Much more than a dreamer is required to bring it to reality, but the dream must be there first.

Listening and Understanding

One of our very able leaders recently was made the head of a large, important, and difficult-to-administer public institution. After a short time he realized that he was not happy with the way things were going. His approach to the problem was a bit unusual. For three months he stopped reading newspapers and listening to news broadcasts; and for this period he relied wholly upon those he met in the course of his work to tell him what was going on. In three months his administrative problems were resolved. No miracles were wrought; but out of a sustained intentness of listening that was produced by this unusual decision, this able man learned and received the insights needed to set the right course. And he strengthened his team by so doing.

Why is there so little listening? What makes this example so exceptional? Part of it, I believe, with those who lead, is that the usual leader in the face of a difficulty tends to react by trying to find someone else on whom to pin the problem, rather than by automatically responding: "I have a problem. What is it? What can *I* do about *my* problem?" The sensible person who takes the latter course will probably react by listening, and somebody in the situation is likely to say what the problem is and what should be done about it. Or enough will be heard that there will be an intuitive insight that resolves it.

I have a bias about this which suggests that only a true natural servant automatically responds to any problem by listening *first*. When one is a leader, this disposition causes one to be *seen* as servant first. This suggests that a non-servant who wants to be a servant might become a *natural* servant through a long arduous discipline of learning to listen, a discipline sufficiently sustained that the automatic response to any problem is to listen first. I have seen enough remarkable transformations in people who have been trained to listen to have some confidence in this approach. It is because true listening builds strength in other people.

Most of us at one time or another, some of us a good deal of the time, would really like to communicate, really get through to a significant level of meaning in the hearer's experience. It can be terribly important. The best test of whether we are communicating at this depth is to ask ourselves first: Are we really listening? Are we listening to the one with whom we want to communicate? Is our basic attitude, as we approach the confrontation, one of wanting to understand? Remember that great line from the prayer of Saint Francis, "Lord, grant that I may not seek so much to be understood as to understand."

One must not be afraid of a little silence. Some find silence awkward or oppressive, but a relaxed approach to dialogue will include the welcoming of some silence. It is often a devastating question to ask oneself—but it is sometimes important to ask it— "In saying what I have in mind will I really improve on the silence?"

Language and Imagination

Alfred North Whitehead once said, "No language can be anything but elliptical, requiring a leap of imagination to understand its meaning in its relevance to immediate experience." Nothing is meaningful until it is related to the hearer's own experience. One may hear the words, one may even remember them and repeat them, as a computer does in the retrieval process. But *meaning*, a growth in experience as a result of receiving the communication, requires that the hearer supply the imaginative link from the hearer's fund of experience to the abstract language symbols the speaker has used. As a leader (including teacher, coach, administrator), one must have facility in tempting the hearer into that leap of imagination that connects the verbal concept to the hearer's own experience. The limitation on language, to the communicator, is that the *hearer* must make that leap of imagination. One of the arts of communicating is to say just enough to facilitate that leap. Many attempts to communicate are nullified by saying too much.

The physicist and philosopher Percy Bridgman takes another view of it when he says: "No linguistic structure is capable of reproducing the full complexity of experience...The only feasible way of dealing with this is to push a particular verbal line of attack as far as it can go, and then switch to another verbal level which we might abandon when we have to...Many people...insist on a single self-consistent verbal scheme into which they try to force all experience. In doing this they create a purely verbal world in which they can live a pretty autonomous existence, fortified by the ability of many of their fellows to live in the same verbal world." This, of course, is what makes a cult— a group of people who thus isolate themselves from the evolving mainstream. By staying within their own closed verbal world they forfeit the opportunity to lead others. One of the great tragedies is when a proven, able leader becomes trapped in one of these closed verbal worlds and loses the ability to lead.

A commentator once observed: "If you have something important to communicate, if you can possibly manage it—put your hand over your mouth and point." Someday we will learn what a great handicap language is.

Withdrawal—Finding One's Optimum

People who go for leadership (whether they are servants or non-servants) may be viewed as one of two extreme types. There are those who are so constituted physically and emotionally that they like pressure—seek it out—and they perform best when they are totally intense. And there are those who do not like pressure, do not thrive under it, but who want to lead and are willing to endure the pressure in order to have the opportunity. The former welcome a happy exhaustion and the latter are constantly in defense against that state. For both the art of withdrawal is useful. To the former it is a change of pace; to the latter it is a defense against an unpleasant state. The former may be more the natural leader; the latter needs a tactic to survive. The art of withdrawal serves them both.

The ability to withdraw and reorient oneself, if only for a moment, presumes that one has learned the art of systematic neglect, to sort out the more important from the less important—and the important from the urgent—and attend to the more important, even though there may be penalties and censure for the neglect of something else. One may govern one's life by the law of the optimum (optimum being that pace and set of choices that give one the best performance over a lifespan)—bearing in mind that there are always emergencies and the optimum includes carrying an unused reserve of energy in all periods of normal demand so that one has the resilience to cope with the emergency.

Pacing oneself by appropriate withdrawal is one of the best approaches to making optimal use of one's resources. The servant-leader must constantly ask: How can I use myself to serve best?

Acceptance and Empathy

These are two interesting words, *acceptance* and *empathy*. If we can take one dictionary's definition, *acceptance* is receiving what is offered, with approbation, satisfaction, or acquiescence, and *empathy* is the imaginative projection of one's own consciousness into another being. The opposite of both, the word *reject*, is to refuse to hear or receive—to throw out.

The servant always accepts and empathizes, never rejects. The servant as leader always empathizes, always accepts the person but sometimes refuses to accept some of the person's effort or performance as good enough.

A college president once said, "An educator may be rejected by students and must not object to this. But one may never, under any circumstances, regardless of what they do, reject a single student."

We have known this a long time in the family. For a family to be a family, no one can ever be rejected. Robert Frost in his poem "The Death of the Hired Man" states the problem in a conversation on the farmhouse porch between the farmer and his wife about the shiftless hired man, Silas, who has come back to their place to die. The farmer is irritated about this because Silas was lured away from his farm in the middle of the last haying season. The wife says that theirs is the only home he has. They are then drawn into a discussion of what a home is. The husband gives his view:

"Home is the place where, when you have to go there,
They have to take you in."

The wife sees it differently. What is a home? She says,

"I should have called it
Something you somehow haven't to deserve."

Because of the vagaries of human nature, the halt, the lame, half-made creatures that we all are, the great leader (whether it is the mother in her home or the head of a vast organization) would say what the wife said about home in Robert Frost's poem. The interest in and affection for one's followers that a leader has—and it is a mark of true greatness when it is genuine—is clearly something the followers "haven't to deserve." Great leaders, including "little" people, may have gruff, demanding, uncompromising exteriors. But deep down inside the great ones have empathy and an unqualified acceptance of the persons of those who go with their leadership.

Acceptance of the person, though, requires a tolerance of imperfection. Anybody could lead perfect people—if there were any. But there aren't any perfect people. And the parents who try to raise perfect children are certain to raise neurotics.

It is part of the enigma of human nature that the "typical" person—immature, stumbling, inept, lazy—is capable of great dedication and heroism *if* wisely led. Many otherwise able people are disqualified to lead because they cannot work with and through the half-people who are all there are. The secret of institution building is to be able to weld a team of such people by lifting them up to grow taller than they would otherwise be.

People grow taller when those who lead them empathize and when they are accepted for what they are, even though their performance may be judged critically in terms of what they are capable of doing. Leaders who empathize and who fully accept those who go with them on this basis are more likely to be trusted.

Know the Unknowable—
Beyond Conscious Rationality

The requirements of leadership impose some intellectual demands that are not measured by academic intelligence ratings. They are not mutually exclusive, but they are different things. The leader needs two intellectual abilities that are usually not formally assessed in an academic way: the leader needs to have *a sense for the unknowable* and be able to *foresee the unforeseeable*. Leaders know some things and foresee some things that those they are presuming to lead do not know or foresee as clearly. This is partly what gives leaders their "lead," what puts them out ahead and qualifies them to show the way.

Until quite recently many would attribute these qualities of knowing the unknowable and foreseeing the unforeseeable to mystical or supernatural gifts—and some still do. Now it is possible at least to speculate about them within a framework of natural law. The electrical body-field theory suggests the possibility of an interconnection between fields and could explain telepathy. Some are willing to explore the possibility of memory traces being physical entities, thus providing a basis for explaining clairvoyance. In far-out theorizing, every mind, at the unconscious level, has access to every "bit" of information that is or ever was. Those among us who seem to have unusual access to these "data banks" are called "sensitives." What we now call intuitive insight may be the survivor of an earlier and greater sensitivity. Much of this is highly speculative, but it is inside the bounds of what some scientific minds are willing to ponder within the framework of what is known about natural phenomena. Information recall under hypnosis is suggestive of what is potentially available from the unconscious.

What is the relevance of this somewhat fanciful theory to the issue at hand, the thought process of a leader? One contemporary student of decision-making put it this way: "If, on a practical decision in the world of affairs, you are waiting for *all* of the information for a good decision, it never comes." There always is more information, sometimes a great deal more, that one might have if one waited longer or worked harder to get it—but the delay and the cost are not warranted. On an important decision one rarely has 100 percent of the information needed for a good decision, no matter how much one spends or how long one waits. And if one waits too long, one has a different problem and has to start all over. This is a terrible dilemma of the hesitant decision-maker.

As a practical matter, on most important decisions there is an information gap. There usually is an information gap between the solid information in hand and what is needed. The art of leadership rests, in part, on the ability to bridge that gap by intuition, that is, a judgment from the unconscious process. The person who is better at this than most is likely to emerge the leader because of the ability to contribute something of great value. Others will depend on such persons to go out ahead and show the way because their judgment will be better than most. Leaders, therefore, must be more creative than most; and creativity is largely discovery, a push into the uncharted and the unknown. Every once in a while a leader needs to think like a scientist, an artist, or a poet. And a leader's thought processes may be just as fanciful as theirs—and as fallible.

Intuition is a *feel* for patterns, the ability to generalize based on what has happened previously. Wise leaders know when to bet on these intuitive leads, but they always know that they are betting on percentages. Their hunches are not seen as eternal truths.

Two separate "anxiety" processes may be involved in a leader's intuitive decision, an important aspect of which is timing, the decision to decide. One is the anxiety of holding the decision until as much information as possible is in. The other is the anxiety of making the decision when there really isn't enough information—which, on critical decisions, is usually the case. All of this is complicated by pressures building up from those who "want an answer." Again, trust is at the root of it. Has the leader a really good information base (both hard data and sensitivity to feelings and needs of people) and a reputation for consistently good decisions that people respect? Can the leader defuse the anxiety of other people who want more certainty than exists in the situation?

Intuition in a leader is more valued, and therefore more trusted, at the conceptual level. An intuitive answer to an immediate situation can be a gimmick and conceptually defective. Overarching conceptual insight that gives a sounder framework for decisions (so important, for instance, in foreign policy) is the greater gift.

Foresight—The Central Ethic of Leadership

The common assumption about the word *now* is that it is this instant moment of *clock* time—*now*. In usage, we qualify this a little by saying *right now*, meaning this instant, or *about now*, allowing a little leeway. Sometimes we say, "I'm going to do it now," meaning "I'm going to start soon and do it in the near future," or "I have just now done it," meaning that I did it in the recent past. The dictionary admits all of these variations of usage.

Let us liken *now* to the spread of light from a narrowly focused beam. There is a bright intense center, this moment of clock time, and a diminishing intensity, theoretically out to infinity, on either side. As viewed here, *now* includes *all* of this—all of history and all of the future. As one approaches the central focus, the light intensifies as this moment of clock time is approached. All of it is *now*, but some parts are more *now* than others, and the central focus that marks this instant of clock time moves along as the clock ticks. *This is not the way it is!* It is simply an analogy to suggest a way of looking at now for those who wish better to see the unforeseeable—a mark of a leader.

Prescience, or foresight, is a better than average guess about *what* is going to happen *when* in the future. It begins with a state of mind about *now*, something like that suggested by the light analogy. What we note in the present moment of clock time is merely the intense focus that is connected with what has gone on in the past and what will happen in the future. The prescient person has a sort of "moving average" mentality (to borrow a statistician's term) in which past, present, and future are one, bracketed together and moving along as the clock ticks. The process is continuous.

Machiavelli, writing three hundred years ago about how to be a prince, put it this way. "Thus it happens in matters of state; for knowing afar off (which it is only given a prudent man to do) the evils that are brewing, they are easily cured. But when, for want of such knowledge, they are allowed to grow so that everyone can recognize them, there is no longer any remedy to be found."

The shape of some future events can be calculated from trend data. But, as with a practical decision mentioned earlier, there is usually an information gap that has to be bridged, and one must cultivate the conditions that favor intuition. This is what Machiavelli meant when he said "knowing afar off (which it is only given a prudent man to do)." The prudent person is one who constantly thinks of *now* as the moving concept in which past, present moment, and future are one organic unity. And this requires living by a sort of rhythm that encourages a high level of intuitive insight about the whole gamut of events from the indefinite past, through the present moment, to the indefinite future. One is at once, in every moment of time, historian, contemporary analyst, and prophet—not three separate roles. This is what the practicing leader is, every day of his or her life.

Living this way is partly a matter of *faith*. Stress is a condition of most of modern life, and if one is a servant-leader and carrying the burdens *of* other people—going out ahead to show the way, one takes the rough and tumble (and it really is rough and tumble in some leader roles)—one takes this in the belief that, if one enters a situation prepared with the necessary experience and knowledge at the conscious level, *in the situation* the intuitive insight necessary for one's optimal performance will be forthcoming. Is there any other way, in the turbulent world of affairs (including the typical home), for one to maintain serenity in the face of uncertainty? One follows the steps of the creative process, which requires that one stay with conscious analysis as far as it will carry one, and then withdraw, release the analytical pressure, if only for a moment, in full confidence that a resolving insight will come. The concern with the past and future is gradually attenuated as this span of concern goes forward or backward from the instant moment. The ability to do this is the essential structural dynamic of leadership.

Foresight is seen as a wholly rational process, the product of a constantly running internal computer that deals with intersecting series and random inputs and is vastly more complicated than anything technology has yet produced. Foresight means regarding the events of the instant moment and constantly comparing them with a series of projections made in the past and at the same time projecting future events—with diminishing certainty as projected time runs out into the indefinite future.

The failure (or refusal) of a leader to foresee may be viewed as an *ethical* failure, because a serious ethical compromise today (when the usual judgment on ethical inadequacy is made) is sometimes the result of a failure to make the effort at an earlier date to foresee today's events and take the right actions when there was freedom for initiative to act. The action that society labels "unethical" in the present moment is often really one of no choice. By this standard a lot of guilty people are walking around with an air of innocence that they would not have if society were able always to pin the label "unethical" on the failure to foresee and the consequent failure to act constructively when there was freedom to act.

Foresight is the "lead" that the leader has. Once leaders lose this lead and events start to force their hand, they are leaders in name only. They are not leading but are reacting to immediate events, and they probably will not long be leaders. There are abundant current examples of loss of leadership that stems from a failure to foresee what reasonably could have been foreseen, and from failure to act on that knowledge while the leader had freedom to act.

There is a wealth of experience available on how to achieve this perspective of foresight, but only one aspect is mentioned here. Required is that one live a sort of schizoid life. One is always at two levels of consciousness. One is in the real world—concerned, responsible, effective, value oriented. One is also detached, riding above it, seeing today's events, and seeing oneself deeply involved in today's events, in the perspective of a long sweep of history and projected into the indefinite future. Such a split enables one better to foresee the unforeseeable. Also, from one level of consciousness, each of us acts resolutely from moment to moment on a set of assumptions that then govern our life. Simultaneously, from another level, the adequacy of these assumptions is examined, in action, with the aim of future revision and improvement. Such a view gives one the perspective that makes it possible for one to live and act in the real world with a clearer conscience.

Awareness and Perception

Framing all of this is awareness, opening wide the doors of perception so as to enable one to get more of what is available of sensory experience and other signals from the environment than people usually take in. Awareness has its risks, but it makes life more interesting; certainly it strengthens one's effectiveness as a leader. When one is aware, there is more than the usual alertness, more intense contact with the immediate situation, and more is stored away in the unconscious computer to produce intuitive insights in the future when needed.

William Blake has said, "If the doors of perception were cleansed, everything will appear to man as it is, infinite." Those who have gotten their doors of perception open wide enough often enough know that this statement of Blake's is not mere poetic exaggeration. Most of us move about with very narrow perception—sight, sound, smell, tactile—and we miss most of the grandeur that is in the minutest thing, the smallest experience. We also miss leadership opportunities. There is danger, however. Some people cannot take what they see when the doors of perception are open too wide, and they had better test their tolerance for awareness gradually. A qualification for leadership is that one can tolerate a sustained wide span of awareness so that one better "sees it as it is."

The opening of awareness stocks both the conscious and unconscious minds with a richness of resources for future need. But it does more than that: it is value building and value clarifying, and it armors one to meet the stress of life by helping build serenity in the face of stress and uncertainty. The cultivation of awareness gives one the basis for detachment, the ability to stand aside and see oneself in perspective in the context of one's own experience, amid the ever present dangers, threats, and alarms. Then one sees one's own peculiar assortment of obligations and responsibilities in a way that permits one to sort out the urgent from the important and perhaps deal with the important. Awareness is *not* a giver of solace—it is just the opposite. It is a disturber and an awakener. Able leaders are usually sharply awake and reasonably disturbed. They are not seekers after solace. They have their own inner serenity.

Leaders must have more of an armor of confidence in facing the unknown—more than those who accept their leadership. This is partly anticipation and preparation, but it is also a very

firm belief that in the stress of real life situations one can com-
pose oneself in a way that permits the creative process to operate.

This is told dramatically in one of the great stories of the
human spirit—the story of Jesus when confronted with the
woman taken in adultery. In this story Jesus is seen as a person,
like all of us, with extraordinary prophetic insight of the kind we
all have to some degree. He is a leader; he has a goal—to bring
more compassion into the lives of people.

In this scene the woman is cast down before him by the mob
that is challenging Jesus' leadership. They cry, "The *law* says she
shall be stoned. What do *you* say?" Jesus must make a decision; he
must give the *right* answer, *right* in the situation, and one that
sustains his leadership toward his goal. The situation is deliberately stressed by his challengers. What does he do?

He sits there writing in the sand—a withdrawal device. In
the pressure of the moment, having assessed the situation rationally, he assumes the attitude of withdrawal that will allow creative
insight to function.

He could have taken another course; he could have regaled
the mob with rational arguments about the superiority of compassion over torture. A good logical argument can be made for it.
What would the result have been had he taken that course?

He did not choose to do that. He chose instead to withdraw
and cut the stress—right in the event itself—in order to open his
awareness to creative insight. And a great one came, one that has
kept the story of the incident alive for two thousand years: "Let
him that is without sin among you cast the first stone."

Persuasion—Sometimes One Person at a Time

Leaders work in wondrous ways. Some assume great institutional burdens. Others quietly deal with one person at a time.
Such a leader was John Woolman, an American Quaker who
lived through the middle years of the eighteenth century. He is
known to the world of scholarship for his journal, a literary classic. But in the area of our interest, leadership, he is the man who

almost singlehandedly rid the Religious Society of Friends (Quakers) of slaves.

It is difficult now to imagine the Quakers as slave holders, as indeed it is difficult now to imagine anyone being a slave holder. One wonders how the society of two hundred years hence will view "what man has made of man" in our generation. It is a disturbing thought.

But many of the eighteenth-century American Quakers were affluent, conservative slave holders, and John Woolman, as a young man, set his goal to rid his beloved Society of this terrible practice. Thirty of his adult years (he lived to age fifty-two) were largely devoted to this. By 1770, nearly one hundred years before the Civil War, no Quakers held slaves.

His method was unique. He didn't raise a big storm about it or start a protest movement. His method was one of gentle but clear and persistent persuasion.

Although John Woolman was not a strong man physically, he accomplished his mission by journeys up and down the East Coast by foot or horseback visiting slave holders—over a period of many years. The approach was not to censure the slave holders in a way that drew their animosity. Rather, his approach was to raise questions: What does the owning of slaves do to you as a moral person? What kind of an institution are you binding over to your children? Person by person, inch by inch, by persistently returning and revisiting and pressing his gentle arguments over a period of thirty years, the scourge of slavery was eliminated from this Society, the first religious group in America formally to denounce and forbid slavery among its members. One wonders what would have been the result if there had been fifty John Woolmans, or even five, traveling the length and breadth of the Colonies in the eighteenth century *persuading* people one by one with gentle non-judgmental argument that a wrong should be righted by individual voluntary action. Perhaps we would not have had the war with six hundred thousand casualties and the impoverishment of the South, and with the resultant vexing social problem that is at fever heat one hundred years later with no end in sight. We know now, in the perspective of history, that just a slight alleviation of the tension in the 1850s might have avoided the war. A few John Woolmans, just a *few*, might have made the difference. Leadership by persuasion has the virtue of change by convincement rather than coercion. Its advantages are obvious.

John Woolman exerted his leadership in an age that must have looked as dark to him as ours does to us today. We may easily write off his effort as a suggestion for today on the assumption that the Quakers were ethically conditioned for this approach. All persons are so conditioned, to some extent—enough to gamble on.

One Action at a Time—The Way Some Great Things Get Done

Two things about Thomas Jefferson are of special interest here. First, as a young man he had the good fortune to find a mentor, George Wythe, a Williamsburg lawyer whose original house still stands in the restored village. George Wythe was a substantial man of his times, a signer of the Declaration of Independence and a member of the Constitutional Convention. But his chief claim to fame is as Thomas Jefferson's mentor. It was probably the influence of mentor on understudy, as Jefferson studied law in Wythe's office, that moved Jefferson toward his place in history and somewhat away from his natural disposition to settle down at Monticello as an eccentric Virginia scholar (which he remained, partly, despite Wythe's influence). The point of mentioning George Wythe is that old people may have a part to play in helping potential servant-leaders to emerge at their optimal best.

Perhaps the most significant aspect of Jefferson, more important in history than the Declaration of Independence or his later term as president, was what he did during the war. With the publication of the Declaration of Independence, the war was on and Jefferson was importuned to take important roles in the war. But he turned them all down. *He knew who he was*, and he resolved to be his own man. He chose his own role. He went back to Virginia and didn't leave the state for the duration of the war.

Jefferson believed that the war would be won by the Colonies, that there would be a new nation, and that that nation would need a new system of law to set it on the course that he had dreamed for it in the Declaration of Independence. So he went back to Monticello, got himself elected to the Virginia legislature, and proceeded to write new statutes embodying the new principles of law for the new nation. He set out, against the determined opposition of his conservative colleagues, to get these enacted into Virginia law. It was an uphill fight. He would go to Williamsburg and wrestle with his colleagues until he was slowed to a halt. Then he would get on his horse and ride back to Monticello to rekindle his spirit and write some more statutes. Armed with these he would return to Williamsburg and take another run at it. He wrote one hundred and fifty statutes in that period and got fifty of them enacted into law, the most notable being separation of church and state. For many years Virginia legislators were digging into the remaining one hundred as new urgent problems made their consideration advisable.

When the Constitution was drafted some years later, Jefferson wasn't even around; he was in France as our ambassador. He didn't have to be around. He had done his work and made his contribution in the statutes already operating in Virginia. Such are the wondrous ways in which leaders do their work—when they know who they are and resolve to be their own persons and will accept making their way to their goal by one action at a time, with a lot of frustration along the way.

Conceptualizing—The Prime Leadership Talent

Nikolai Frederik Severin Grundtvig, whose adult life was during the first three-quarters of the nineteenth century, is known as the Father of the Danish Folk High Schools. To understand the significance of the Folk High School one needs to know a little of the unique history of Denmark. Since it is a tiny country, not many outside it know this history, and consequently Grundtvig and his seminal contribution are little known. A great church dedicated to his memory in Copenhagen attests the Danish awareness of what he did for them.

At the beginning of the nineteenth century Denmark was a feudal and absolute monarchy. It was predominantly agricultural, with a large peasant population of serfs who were attached to manors. Early in the century reforms began that gave the land to the peasants as individual holdings. Later the first steps toward representative government were taken.

A chronicler of those times reports:

> The Danish peasantry at the beginning of the nineteenth century was an underclass. In sullen resignation it spent its life in dependence on estate owners and government officials. It was without culture and technical skill, and it was seldom able to rise above the level of bare existence. The agricultural reforms of that time were carried through without the support of the peasants, who did not even understand the meaning of them....All the reforms were made for *the sake of the peasant*, but not by him. In the course of the century this underclass has been changed into a well-to-do middle class which, politically and socially, now takes the lead among the Danish people.

Freedom—to own land and to vote—was not enough to bring about these changes. A new form of education was designed by Grundtvig explicitly to achieve this transformation. Grundtvig was a theologian, poet, and student of history. Although he himself was a scholar, he believed in the active practical life and he conceptualized a school, the Folk High School, as a short, intensive residence course for young adults dealing with the history, mythology, and poetry of the Danish people. He addressed himself to the masses rather than to the cultured. The "cultured" at the time thought him to be a confused visionary and contemptuously turned their backs on him. But the peasants heard him, and their natural leaders responded to his call to start the Folk High Schools—with their own resources.

"The spirit (not knowledge) is power." "The living word in the mother tongue." "Real life is the final test," as contrasted with the German and Danish tendency to theorize. These were some of the maxims that guided the new schools of the people. For fifty years of his long life Grundtvig vigorously and passionately advocated these new schools as the means whereby the peasants could raise themselves into *the* Danish national culture. And, stimulated by the Folk High School experience, the peasant youth began to attend agricultural schools and to build cooperatives on the model borrowed from England.

Two events provided the challenge that matured the new peasant movement and brought it into political and social dominance by the end of the century. There was a disastrous war with Prussia in 1864, which resulted in a substantial loss of territory and a crushing blow to national aspiration. And then, a little later, there was the loss of world markets for corn, their major exportable crop, as a result of the agricultural abundance of the New World.

Peasant initiative, growing out of the spiritual dynamic generated by the Folk High Schools, fueled the recovery of the nation from both of these shocks by transforming its exportable surplus from corn to "butter and bacon," by rebuilding the national spirit, and by nourishing the Danish tradition in the territory lost to Germany during the long years until it was returned after World War 1.

All of this, a truly remarkable social, political, and economic transformation, stemmed from one individual's conceptual leadership. Grundtvig himself did not found or operate a Folk High School, although he lectured widely in them. What he gave was his love for the peasants, his clear vision of what they must do for themselves, his long articulate dedication—some of it through very barren years—and his passionately communicated faith in the worth of these people and their strength to raise themselves—*if only their spirit could be aroused*. It is a great story of the supremacy of the spirit.

And Now!

These three examples from previous centuries illustrate very different types of leadership for the common good. They are not suggested as general models for today, although some useful hints may be found in them. What these examples tell us is that the leadership of trailblazers like Woolman, Jefferson, and Grundtvig is so "situational" that it rarely draws on known models. Rather, it seems to be a fresh creative response to here-and-now opportunities. Too much concern with how others did it may be inhibitive. One wonders, in these kaleidoscopic times, what kind of contemporary leadership effort will be seen as seminal one hundred years from now, as we can now see the three I have described. Let me speculate.

The signs of the times suggest that, to future historians, the next thirty years will be marked as the period when the person of color and the deprived and the alienated of the world effectively asserted their claims to stature, and that they were not led by a privileged elite (like Woolman, Jefferson, and Grundtvig) but by exceptional people from their own kind.

It may be that the best that some of today's privileged can do is to stand aside and serve by helping when asked *and* as instructed. Even the conceptualizing may be done better not by an elite, as Grundtvig did it in his times, but by leaders from among people of color, the alienated, and the disadvantaged of the world. A possible role for those who are now favored by the old rules may be, as Miguel Serrano has said, that of diving under this big wave and taking with them the accumulated wisdom as they see it, in the hope of coming up on the other side prepared to make it available when the turbulence of these times has passed and people of color and the disadvantaged and the alienated have found their way and can freely choose that which they find useful from what the now-privileged have stored away. Not many of today's privileged may elect this course. But those among them who see themselves as *servants first* may want to consider it as a possible best course for them.

I do not have the prescience to know what will come of all of this. And I am not predicting a golden age, not soon. But I do believe that *some* of those of today's privileged who will live into the twenty-first century will find it interesting *if* they can abandon their present notions of how they can best serve their less favored neighbor and wait and listen until the less favored find their own enlightenment, then define their needs in their own way, and finally, state clearly how they want to be served. The now-privileged who are natural servants may in this process get a fresh perspective on the priority of others' needs and thus they may again be able to serve by leading. In the meantime, Paulo Freire has offered the *Pedagogy of the Oppressed* to ponder while they heed John Milton's advice, "They also serve who only stand and wait."

For those of today's privileged who feel more like joining the fray and serving and leading actively as best they can during what promises to be a long period of unusual turbulence, Woolman, Jefferson, and Grundtvig are suggested as models to be studied closely. Study them not to copy the details of their methods but as examples of highly creative individuals, each of whom invented a role that was uniquely appropriate for him as an individual, that drew heavily on his strengths and demanded little that was unnatural for him, and that was very right for the time and place in which he happened to be.

Healing and Serving

Twelve ministers and theologians of all faiths and twelve psychiatrists of all faiths had convened for a two-day, off-the-record seminar on the one-word theme of *healing*. The chairman, a psychiatrist, opened the seminar with this question: "We are all healers, whether *we* are ministers or doctors. Why are we in this business? What is our motivation?" There followed only ten minutes of intense discussion before they were all agreed, doctors and ministers, Catholics, Jews, and Protestants. "For our own healing," they said.

This is an interesting word, *healing*, with its meaning, "to make whole." The example above suggests that one really never makes it. It is always something sought. Perhaps, as with the minister and the doctor, the servant-leader might also acknowledge that his or her own healing is the motivation. There is something subtle communicated to one who is being served and led if, implicit in the compact between servant-leader and led, is the understanding that the search for wholeness is something they share.

Alcoholics Anonymous, according to some who know, recovers more alcoholics from this dreadful illness than all other approaches combined. Legend has it that the founding meeting to incorporate the organization was held in the office of a noted philanthropist, a very wealthy man. In the course of the discussion of the principles that would guide the new organization, the philanthropist made a statement something like this: "From my experience I think I know about the things that can be done with money and the things that cannot be done with money. What you in AA want to do cannot be done with money. You must be poor. You must not use money to do your work."

There was more conversation, but this advice profoundly influenced the course of AA. The principles that have guided the work of AA over the years were born at that meeting: they will be poor; no one but an alcoholic can contribute money to AA's modest budget; AA will own no real property; the essential work of AA, one recovered (or partly recovered) alcoholic helping another toward recovery, will not be done for money,

Here are two quite different perspectives on healing and serving. Whether professional or amateur, the motive for the healing is the same: for one's own healing.

Community—The Lost Knowledge of These Times

Men and women once lived in communities, and in the developing world, many still do. Human society can be much better than it is (or was) in primitive communities. But if community itself is lost in the process of development, will what is put in its place survive? At the moment there seems to be some question. What is our experience?

Within my memory, we once cared for orphaned children in institutions. We have largely abandoned these institutions as not good for children. Children need the love of a real home—in a family, a community.

Now we realize that penal institutions, other than focusing the retributive vengeance of society and restraining antisocial actions for a period, do very little to rehabilitate. In fact they *de*habilitate and return more difficult offenders to society. What should we do with these people? It is now suggested that most of them should be kept in homes, in community.

There is now the beginning of questioning of the extensive building of hospitals. We need some hospitals for extreme cases. But much of the recent expansion has been done for the convenience of doctors and families, not for the good of patients—or even for the good of families. Only community can give the healing love that is essential for health. Besides, the skyrocketing cost of such extensive hospital care is putting an intolerable burden on health-care systems.

The *school,* on which we pinned so much of our hopes for a better society, has become too much a social-upgrading mechanism that destroys community. Now we have the beginnings of questioning of the school as we know it, as a specialized, separate-from-community institution. And much of the alienation and purposelessness of our times is laid at the door, *not of education,* but of the *school.*

We are in the process of moving away from institutional care for the mentally retarded and toward small, community-like homes. Recent experience suggests that, whereas the former provides mostly custodial care, the small community can actually lift them up, help them grow.

Now the care of old people is a special concern, because there are so many more of them and they live so much longer. But the current trend is to put them in retirement homes that segregate the old from normal community. Already there is the suggestion that these are not the happy places that were hoped for. Will retirement homes shortly be abandoned as orphanages were?

As a generalization, I suggest that human service that requires love cannot be satisfactorily dispensed by specialized institutions that exist apart from community, that take the problem out of sight of the community. Both those being cared for and the community suffer.

Love is an undefinable term, and its manifestations are both subtle and infinite. But it begins, I believe, with one absolute condition: unlimited liability! As soon as one's liability for another is qualified *to any degree*, love is diminished by that much.

Institutions, as we know them, are designed to limit liability for those who serve through them. In the British tradition, corporations are not "INC" as we know them, but "LTD"—Limited. Most of the goods and services we now depend on will probably continue to be furnished by such limited liability institutions. But any human service where the one who is served should be loved in the process requires community, a face-to-face group in which the liability of each for the other and all for one is unlimited, or as close to it as it is possible to get. Trust and respect are highest in this circumstance, and an accepted ethic that gives strength to all is reinforced. Where community doesn't exist, trust, respect, and ethical behavior are difficult for the young to learn and for the old to maintain. Living in community as one's basic involvement will generate an exportable surplus of love that we may carry into our many involvements with institutions that are usually not communities: businesses, churches, governments, schools.

Out of the distress of our seeming community-less society, hopeful new forms of community are emerging: young people's communes, Israeli kibbutzim, and therapeutic communities like Synanon. Seen through the bias of conventional morality, these communities are sometimes disturbing to the older generation. But whatever happens with these specific examples, they show a genuine striving for community and represent a significant new social movement that may foretell the future.

The opportunities are tremendous for rediscovering vital lost knowledge about how to live in community while retaining as much as we can of the value in our present urban, institution-bound society.

All that is needed to rebuild community as a viable life form for large numbers of people is for enough servant-leaders to show the way, not by mass movements, but by each servant-leader demonstrating his or her own unlimited liability for a quite specific community-related group.

Institutions

We differ from the primitives in that it is our task to rediscover the elementary knowledge of community while we refine and radically improve much of the vast non-community institutional structure on which we depend and without which we could not survive. A hopeful sign of the times, in the sector of society where it seems least expected—highly competitive business—is that people-building institutions are holding their own while they struggle successfully in the marketplace. It is not a great revolutionary movement, but it is there as a solid fact of these times. And it is a very simple approach. The first order of business is to build a group of people who, under the influence of the institution, grow taller and become healthier, stronger, more autonomous.

Some institutions achieve distinction for a short time by the intelligent *use* of people, but it is not a happy achievement, and eminence, so derived, does not last long. Others aspire to distinction (or the reduction of problems) by embracing gimmicks: profit sharing, work enlargement, information, participation, suggestion plans, paternalism, motivational management. There is nothing wrong with these in a people-building institution. But in a people-using institution they are like aspirin—sometimes stimulating and pain relieving, and they may produce an immediate measurable improvement of sorts. But these are not the means whereby an institution moves from people-using to people-building. In fact, an overdose of these nostrums may seal an institution's fate as a people-user for a very long time.

An institution starts on a course toward people-building with leadership that has a firmly established context of *people first*. With that, the right actions fall naturally into place. And none of the conventional gimmicks may ever be used. (For a fuller discussion of institutions, see the following chapter, "The Institution as Servant.")

Trustees

Institutions need two kinds of leaders: those who are inside and carry the active day-to-day roles, and those who stand outside but are intimately concerned, and who, with the benefit of some detachment, oversee the active leaders, These are the *trustees*.

Trustees are what their title implies, persons in whom ultimate trust is placed. Because institutions inevitably harbor conflict, trustees are the court of last resort if an issue arises that cannot be resolved by the active parties. If tangible assets are involved, trustees legally hold them and are responsible to all interested parties for their good use. They have a prime concern for goals and for progress toward goals. They make their influence felt more by knowing and asking questions than by authority, although they usually have authority and can use it if need be. If, as is usual, there are several trustees, their chairperson has a special obligation to see that the trustees as a group sustain a common purpose and are influential in helping the institution maintain consistent high-level performance toward its goals. The board chair is not simply the presider over meetings but also must serve and lead the trustees as a group and act as their major contact with the active inside leadership. Although trustees usually leave the "making of news" to active persons in the enterprise, theirs is an important leadership opportunity.

So conceived, the role of trustees provides a great opportunity for those who would serve and lead. And no one step will more quickly raise the quality of the total society than a radical reconstruction of trustee bodies so that they are predominantly made up of able, dedicated servant-leaders. Two disturbing questions: Is there now enough discerning toughness strategically placed to see that this change takes place, in the event that able, dedicated servant-leaders become available in sufficient numbers to do it? And are enough able people now preparing themselves for these roles so that this change *can* be made in the event that it is possible to make it? (For a fuller discussion of the trustee role, see the following two chapters, "The Institution as Servant" and "Trustees as Servants.")

Power and Authority—
The Strength and the Weakness

In a complex institution-centered society, which ours is likely to be into the indefinite future, there will be large and small concentrations of power. Sometimes it will be a servant's power of persuasion and example. Sometimes it will be coercive power used to dominate and manipulate people. The difference is that, in the former, power is used to create opportunity and alternatives so that individuals may choose and build autonomy. In the latter, individuals are coerced into a predetermined path. Even if it is "good" for them, if they experience nothing else, ultimately their autonomy will be diminished.

Some coercive power is overt and brutal. Some is covert and subtly manipulative. The former is open and acknowledged; the latter is insidious and hard to detect. Most of us are more coerced than we know. We need to be more alert in order to know, and we also need to acknowledge that, in an imperfect world, authority backed up by power is still necessary because we just don't know a better way. We may one day find one. It is worth searching for. Part of our dilemma is that all leadership is, to some extent, manipulative. Those who follow must be strong!

The trouble with coercive power is that it only strengthens resistance. And, if successful, its controlling effect lasts only as long as the force is strong. It is not organic. Only persuasion and the consequent voluntary acceptance are organic.

Since both kinds of power have been around for a long time, an individual will be better off by at some point being close enough to raw coercion to know what it is. One must be close to both the bitterness and goodness of life to be fully human.

Servants, by definition, are fully human. Servant-leaders are functionally superior because they are closer to the ground—they hear things, see things, know things, and their intuitive insight is exceptional. Because of this they are dependable and trusted. They know the meaning of that line from Shakespeare's sonnet, "They that have power to hurt and will do none...."

How Does One Know the Servant?

For those who follow—and this is everyone, including those who lead—the really critical question is: Who is this moral individual we would see as leader? Who is the servant? How does one tell a truly giving, enriching servant from the neutral person or the one whose net influence is to take away from or diminish other people?

Rabbi Heschel had just concluded a lecture on the Old Testament prophets in which he had spoken of true prophets and false prophets. A questioner asked him how one tells the difference between the true and the false prophets. The rabbi's answer was succinct and to the point. "There is no *way!*" he said. Then he elaborated, "If there were a *way*, if one had a gauge to slip over the head of the prophet and establish without question that this prophet is or isn't a true prophet, there would be no human dilemma and life would have no meaning."

So it is with the servant issue. If there were a dependable way that would tell us "these people enrich by their presence, these are neutral, or these take away," life would be without challenge. Yet it is terribly important that one *know*, both about oneself and about others, whether the net effect of one's influence on others enriches, is neutral, or diminishes and depletes.

Since there is no certain way to know this, one must turn to the artists for illumination. Such an illumination is in Hermann Hesse's idealized portrayal of the servant Leo, whose servant-hood comes through in his leadership. In stark, modern terms it can also be found in the brutal reality of the mental hospital where Ken Kesey (in *One Flew over the Cuckoo's Nest*) gives us Big Nurse—strong, able, dedicated, dominating, authority-ridden, manipulative, exploitative—the net effect of whose influence diminished other people, literally destroyed them. In the story she is pitted in a contest with tough, gutter-bred MacMurphy, a patient, the net effect of whose influence is to build up people and make both patients and the doctor in charge of the ward grow larger as persons, stronger, healthier—an effort that ulti-mately costs MacMurphy his life. If one will study the two char-acters, Leo and MacMurphy, one will get a measure of the range of possibilities in the role of servant as leader.

In Here, Not Out There

A king once asked Confucius's advice on what to do about the large number of thieves. Confucius answered, "If you, sir, were not covetous, although you should reward them to do it, they would not steal." This advice places an enormous burden on those who are favored by the rules, and it establishes how old is the notion that the servant views any problem in the world as *in here*, inside oneself, not *out there*. And if a flaw in the world is to be remedied, to the servant the process of change starts *in here*, in the servant, not *out there*. This is a difficult concept for that busy-body, modern man.

So it is with joy. Joy is inward, it is generated inside. It is not found outside and brought in. It is for those who accept the world as it is, part good, part bad, and who identify with the good by adding a little island of serenity to it.

Hermann Hesse dramatized it in the powerful leadership exerted by Leo, who ostensibly served only in menial ways but who, by the quality of his inner life that was manifest in his presence, lifted others up and made the journey possible. Camus, in his final testament quoted earlier, leaves us with: "Each and every man, on the foundations of his own sufferings and joys, builds for them all."

Who Is the Enemy?

Who is the enemy? Who is holding back more rapid movement to the better society that is reasonable and possible with available resources? Who is responsible for the mediocre performance of so many of our institutions? Who is standing in the way of a larger consensus on the definition of the better society and paths to reaching it?

Not evil people. Not stupid people. Not apathetic people. Not the "system." Not the protesters, the disrupters, the revolutionaries, the reactionaries.

Granting that fewer evil, stupid, or apathetic people or a better "system" might make the job easier, their removal would not change matters, not for long. The better society will come, if it comes, with plenty of evil, stupid, apathetic people around and with an imperfect, ponderous, inertia-charged "system" as the vehicle for change. Liquidate the offending people, radically alter or destroy the system, and in less than a generation they will all be back. It is not in the nature of things that a society can be cleaned up once and for all according to an ideal plan. And even if it were possible, who would want to live in an aseptic world? Evil, stupidity, apathy, the "system" are not the enemy even though society building forces will be contending with them all the time. The healthy society, like the healthy body, is not the one that has taken the most medicine. It is the one in which the internal health-building forces are in the best shape.

The real enemy is fuzzy thinking on the part of good, intelligent, vital people, and their failure to lead, and to follow servants as leaders. Too many settle for being critics and experts. There is too much intellectual wheel spinning, too much retreating into "research," too little preparation for and willingness to undertake the hard and high-risk tasks of building better institutions in an imperfect world, too little disposition to see "the problem" as residing *in here* and not *out there*.

In short, the enemy is strong natural servants who have the potential to lead but do not lead, or who choose to follow a nonservant. They suffer. Society suffers. And so it may be in the future.

Implications

The future society may be just as mediocre as this one. It may be worse. And no amount of restructuring or changing the system or tearing it down in the hope that something better will grow will change this. There may be a better system than the one we now have. It is hard to know. But, whatever it is, if the people to lead it well are not there, a better system will not produce a better society.

Many people finding their wholeness through many and varied contributions make a good society. Here we are concerned with but one facet: *Able servants with potential to lead will lead, and, where appropriate, they will follow only servant-leaders.* Not much else counts if this does not happen.

This brings us to that critical aspect of realism that confronts the servant-leader, that of *order.* There must be some order because we know for certain that the great majority of people will choose some kind of order over chaos even if it is delivered by a brutal non-servant and even if, in the process, they lose much of their freedom. Therefore the servant-leader will beware of pursuing an idealistic path regardless of its impact on order. The big question is: What kind of order? This is the great challenge to the emerging generation of leaders: Can they build better order?

Older people who grew up in a period when values were more settled and the future seemed more secure will be disturbed by much they find today. But one firm note of hope comes through loud and clear; we are at a turn of history in which people are growing up faster and some extraordinarily able, mature, servant-disposed men and women are emerging in their early and middle twenties. The percentage may be small, and again, it may be larger than we think. Moreover, it is not an elite; it is all sorts of exceptional people. Most of them could be ready for some large society-shaping responsibility by the time they are thirty *if* they are encouraged to prepare for leadership as soon as their potential as builders is identified, which is possible for many of them by age eighteen or twenty. Preparation to lead need not be at the complete expense of vocational or scholarly preparation, but it must be the *first priority*. And it may take some difficult bending of resources and some unusual initiatives to accomplish all that should be accomplished in these critical years *and* give leadership preparation first priority. But whatever it takes, it must be done. For a while at least, until a better-led society is assured, some other important goals should take a subordinate place.

All of this rests on the assumption that the only way to change a society (or just make it go) is to produce people, enough people, who will change it (or make it go). The urgent problems of our day—the disposition to venture into immoral and senseless wars, destruction of the environment, poverty, alienation, discrimination, overpopulation—are here because of human failures, individual failures, one person at a time, one action at a time failures.

If we make it out of all of this (and this is written in the belief that we will make it), the "system" will be whatever works best. The builders will find the useful pieces wherever they are and invent new ones when needed, all without reference to ideological coloration. "How do we get the right things done?" will be the watchword of the day, every day. And the context of those who bring it off will be this: all women and men who are touched by the effort grow taller, and become healthier, stronger, more autonomous, *and* more disposed to serve.

Leo the *servant*, and the exemplar of the *servant-leader*, has one further portent for us. If we may assume that Hermann Hesse is the narrator in *Journey to the East* (not a difficult assumption to make), at the end of the story he establishes his identity. His final confrontation at the close of his initiation into the Order is with a small transparent sculpture, two figures joined together. One is Leo, the other is the narrator. The narrator notes that a movement of substance is taking place within the transparent sculpture.

> I perceived that my image was in the process of adding to and flowing into Leo's, nourishing and strengthening it. It seemed that, in time...only one would remain: Leo. He must grow, I must disappear.
>
> As I stood there and looked and tried to understand what I saw, I recalled a short conversation that I had once had with Leo during the festive days at Bremgarten. We had talked about the creations of poetry being more vivid and real than the poets themselves.

What Hesse may be telling us here is that Leo is the symbolic personification of Hesse's aspiration to serve through his literary creations, creations that are greater than Hesse himself; and that his work, for which he was but the channel, will carry on and serve and lead in a way that he, a twisted and tormented man, could not—except as he created.

Does not Hesse dramatize, in extreme form, the dilemma of us all? Except as we venture to create, we cannot project ourselves beyond ourselves to serve and lead.

To which Camus would add: *Create dangerously!*

II

The Institution as Servant

This is my thesis: caring for persons, the more able and the less able serving each other, is the rock upon which a good society is built. Whereas, until recently, caring was largely person to person, now most of it is mediated through institutions— often large, complex, powerful, impersonal, not always competent, sometimes corrupt. If a better society is to be built, one that is more just and more loving, one that provides greater creative opportunity for its people, then the most open course is to *raise both the capacity to serve and the very performance as servant* of existing major institutions by new regenerative forces operating within them.

This chapter is an elaboration of the above thesis. It is addressed particularly to the trustees of three types of large institutions: churches, universities, and businesses. I have chosen these three because they are institutions where I have personal experience. Furthermore, I believe that if *just one* major institution in each of these three types makes a substantial move toward distinction as servant, and if it sustains this performance and is able to communicate its experience, the quality of the total society—all of our institutions—will start to improve.

What I have to say comes from experience—my own and that of others—that bears on institutional reconstruction. It is a personal statement, and it is meant to be neither a scholarly treatise nor a how-to-do-it manual. It is written more to suggest a context and to frame the dimensions of the problem for those who wish to make a determined effort to raise the servant stature of just one large institution.

Why just one? The answer is one of practicality. The nature of the task calls for a level of dedication such that one person, exerting influence as trustee over a period of years, will do well if a contribution is made to the significant advance of *one* large institution.

Why a *large* institution? Again, because of practical reasons. The staff resources required to make the necessary moves can be afforded only by large institutions. Besides, large complex institutions dominate the American scene, and they are better able to communicate their experience. Unless the quality of large institutions can be raised, not much can be done to improve the total society.

Our legal structure recognizes profit and not-for-profit institutions. The common assumption seems to be that "for profit" is tainted with self-serving, whereas "not-for-profit" is presumed selfless. In my experience both assumptions are false. The self-serving motive is an attribute of individuals who are just as prevalent in not-for-profit as in the profit-making institutions. The corporate form should be chosen as the one most appropriate for the mission and with regard to legal constraints and privileges. The opportunities to serve with distinction are the same.

The concept of *trustee* is used here for members of the governing boards of both profit and not-for-profit large institutions. It includes the accepted sense of fiduciary trust, which, in the absence of malfeasance or threatened collapse of the institution, is usually a somewhat passive role. The trustee role advocated here goes far beyond this limited view and implies a dynamic obligation, an insistent motivating force originating with trustees that *obliges* the institution to move toward distinction as servant. By this is meant that an institution makes a contribution, at least proportional to its opportunity, toward building a society that is more just and more loving, one that offers greater creative opportunities to its people.

A new condition of these times is the need for a high level of trust in institutions. Without it they cannot serve and may even lose much of their present autonomy. The urgent need for *trust* requires this enlarged view of the role of the trustee. For those capable of being trustees, as defined here, this may be their best chance to serve and the most rewarding use of their lives. I hope that some who try will share what they learn. All of us need to know more.

My confidence in the thesis just stated, and in the explanation and the arguments for this thesis that follow, rests upon intimate knowledge of three major American institutions that rose from the ordinary to distinction in the first half of this century, and then dropped back to the ordinary. Each, during its period of greatness, gave a powerful lift to the whole society. Each in its own way, and judged by the expectations of the times, was an exceptional servant.

In all three cases there was an able administrator who received well-deserved public recognition for the achievement. But, largely unknown to the public, behind each of those administrators stood a group of men and women, the trustees, who in my judgment made the greater contribution. I see the trustees' contribution as greater because they supplied the standard of quality and determination so that the institution could be exceptional. If the executive who delivered the distinguished performance had not so performed, the trustees would have sought someone who could. In one of the three cases, new trustees took over an institution that was decrepit and might well have been abandoned. In a very few years they moved the institution to an extraordinary level of quality and service.

The lapse of all three of these major institutions from distinguished to merely ordinary performance came, I believe, because the trustees ceased to demand distinction. Their sense of trust declined probably because able, dedicated trustees were replaced by nominal trustees—not poor performers, but just ordinary—and there was no longer trust that could sustain spirit and unity of purpose.

Both the rise and the decline of these three institutions were matters of circumstance. Perceptive persons representing the public good were not asking *who the trustees of these major institutions were*, either when they rose or when they declined.

In a relatively short period our society has moved from a society of individuals to a society dominated by large institutions. Many of the critics of society do not see our problems as caused by this shift and by the failure of trusteeship in these large institutions. As a consequence we have a crisis of institutional quality, not so much from depredations of "evil" people as from sheer neglect by the "good" people.

Crisis of Institutional Quality

One circumstance that brings on a crisis of institutional quality is that, without attending to the structure and *modus operandi*, we have suddenly shifted our standard of what is *good*. Whereas, up to recently, *good* was a rank order performance at or near the top of the field, now *good* has become doing what is reasonable and possible with available resources. Viewed this way the performance of the best is not good enough. All of the comfortable niches at the top are suddenly gone. And every institution is judged mediocre. We are in dire need of pacesetters, at least one big one in each field, that stand so far ahead that even the good ones feel uncomfortable.

Why do the best of our institutions fall short of performing at the level of what is reasonable and possible with available resources? Possibly because these institutions are seen by too many of us, even some of us who are trustees, as impersonal entities to be used and exploited. Most people do not give to institutions the human caring and serving that they give to other persons.

The problem of institutional quality is relatively new. Much of the traditional wisdom we live by was generated before there were institutions as we know them today. The framers of the U.S. Constitution did not anticipate corporations, making it necessary for the courts to treat them as persons. Corporations have had an established place for only one hundred years, and our nearly total dependence on them has been for a much shorter period.

Reinhold Niebuhr's intriguing theme, "Moral Man, Immoral Society," stems from our willingness as individuals to qualify as moral by caring only for persons. If we are to have a more moral *society*, then moral humanity must also care for institutions. We tend to criticize the impersonal system, but it is our attitude and our level of caring, not the "system," that need criticism and improvement.

How much we care depends somewhat on our estimate of the need for our caring. The following paragraphs summarize what I hear thoughtful and discriminating critics say when they judge the quality of our major types of institutions.

Governments rely too much on coercion and too little on persuasion, leadership, and example. Although they render indispensable services, they too often impose upon society a bureaucracy that is oppressive and corrupting. Rarely does conceptual and inspired leadership come from government. Although we wish for it, we have learned not to expect it. The doctrine of countervailing power, pitting one segment of society as an offsetting force against another, is too freely substituted for creative solutions. We are prone to adventurous and illegal wars. Confidence in the integrity of elected officials is at a low point. The total tax structure is a perversion. The treatment of prisoners is barbaric. The cost of it all is staggering.

Business practice, while more enlightened than it once was, still follows too much the way of the huckster-traders of centuries past. They were only a minor force in their day, but the vast modern business structure has taken on their functions and is shaping our culture and setting its values. Economic performance is cyclical, and the penalties are usually borne by the powerless. Too many firms are manipulated as financial pawns for short-term gain with little regard for social consequences or even for the long-term good of the firm. The sense of business responsibility is inadequate for the influence that business wields. Despite phenomenal production of goods and services, the total social impact of businesses is far below what a late twentieth-century "advanced" society should tolerate. To sum it up, one might say, as in the case of government, that our reasonable expectations of the private sector too far exceed its performance,

Health and social services retain too much from the days when magic potions were administered to banish symptoms. As a consequence, the extensive knowledge we now have about how to live in better total health is effectively denied to large numbers of people, and for many the longer life expectancy made possible by curbing disease is too often an empty achievement. The skyrocketing cost of such health care as we have is proof of the inadequacy of our system of health-care delivery.

The contemporary university is the lineal descendant of the medieval one—a design that is now widely admitted to be suitable for a very small percentage of the population. What once was the goal of education, to provide continuity for a culture in which freedom and rationality would prevail, has given way to preparation for narrow professional careers. For many young people what should be a great creative experience is instead a literal incarceration in rigid, stereotyped academic programs for which they have little aptitude and less interest. The result is enormous institutions that are an impossible meld of elitist tradition and mass education, and which cannot withstand the shattering value changes that other forces are bringing in society. Colleges and universities now enroll about 50 percent of our young people. They should be a major civilizing force, but instead they stand among contemporary institutions as the most troubled, the most fragile, and the least certain of their goals as institutions.

The churches, which once gave security and hope by presuming to mediate between God and human beings, continue to function this way even though many persons, including faithful church attenders, now seek their values in their own experience. As a consequence, the alienated and purposeless have multiplied to devastating proportions for want of sufficient value-shaping influence that once was the churches' major role. And the large human (and material) resources of churches seem to be groping for a way to serve.

I give this summary not to condemn all of society. Our present society *is* being judged harshly, sometimes too harshly. But the truth is that, with the present level of education, and the extent of information sources, too many people judge our institutions as not meeting the standard of what is reasonable and possible in their service. The clamor is now loud enough and insistent enough that something substantial must be done, even in the very best of institutions, to meet this critical judgment.

Trustees have the *primary* obligation to meet this critical judgment *and* to produce institutions that exceed the expectations.

Trustees: Prime Movers in Institutional Regeneration

If more serving institutions are to be built, individuals who want to serve must, on their own, become institution builders *where they are*. Much zeal to build a better society is wasted because too many well-intentioned people flail away in all directions and insist on chemical illusions of instant perfection. If utopia cannot be delivered now, they lose interest. The heat this generates may stir the air a bit, but not much will change until the *builders within institutions*, those who have competence and strength, begin to move.

Large universities, businesses, and churches (especially Protestant churches) have in common governing boards with enough autonomy to become originators of new regenerative forces. Occasionally an institution might move to distinction without the influence of its board, but it is not predictable. However, if a strong board sets distinction as its goal, invests the time and energy, organizes itself for the task, and stays with it, distinction is practically assured. The place to start is with an unequivocal trustee obligation to deliver a new, more serving institution.

The most important qualification for trustees should be that they *care* for the institution, which means that they care for *all of the people the institution touches*, and that they are determined to make their caring count.

Selecting trustees to represent constituencies in the institution in order to make the trustee group a balanced political body dilutes trust.

Serving the trustees is their chair, who leads the trustees by serving. By devoting more time than other trustees may afford, the chair helps make their caring count.

The administrators and professionals carry the work of the institution. In the public eye they will be seen as the achievers. But, inside, the trustee action is the primary requirement. The trustees must stand as the symbol of institutional quality. Everybody else is trying to deliver it. The chair is dedicated to making the total process work. But the chair cannot be chief executive officer, as is now true in some cases, especially in business. Chairs should not be officers of administration at all, for their primary task is to make demands on the administration for performance that the trustees understand and that meets the standards they set.

Board chairs stand apart from administration, but they are inside. They must be well informed, and, as servant-leaders of the boards, they must be influential. But they must also stand outside with some objectivity that allows them to watch and evaluate. There is a subtle paradox in their role—they are both inside and outside.

Trustees ask the questions that lead to institutional goals being set and strategic plans being made. In a large institution the governing board may have its own staff and carry, directly, the goal setting and long-range planning. In any case, these are board, not administrative responsibilities. It is the chair's responsibility to see that both trustees and administration understand and accept the goals and plans for the institution. This may call for a new type of leadership in the chair role and a new career pattern by which chairs evolve.

Trustees of a large institution need a staff that serves their needs alone. Ordinarily they may get some basic information from the certified audits and from what the administration tells them. But this usually will not be enough to answer all their questions. Their staff may be employees or part-time consultants, but they should report to the chair, who is acting for the trustees, to supply the information the trustees need on the total operation. For the trustees to fail to build their own dependable information source and to act on what they have learned is a breach of trust. This adds a substantial dimension to the usual view of their role by the trustees.

It is a trustee function to design the top administration and appoint the top executives, not just to approve and confirm the decisions of others. They should not delegate the administration, they should assign it. A continuous study of organization is a major trustee function, and the chair particularly should be deeply immersed in it.

In my view it is fair to say that the active administrators are not good judges of their organization. Administrators are too involved to have objective judgment about top-level organization. Neither are they best qualified to say who should be a part of their number. The selection of the top administrative group—to make sure that they have the intelligence, integrity, stability, skill, adaptability, and spirit that the task requires—is a basic trustee responsibility. This is why trustees, with their relative detachment from administration, are so important. If they are informed and work at it, they can supply the perspective on organization and staff that cannot be expected of the active administrators.

These suggestions for an enlarged trustee role are made in the belief that the questionable performance of major institutions is *not* the result of incompetence or poor motives or lack of industry in the internal administration and leadership but stems rather from an inadequate concept of trust in the governing boards and their failure to accept a more demanding (and a more rewarding) role. Most people who do the work of the world will be happier and act more responsibly if more is asked of them and if recognition and reward for good performances are more discriminating. Trust implies the obligation to ask and insist and discriminate.

Trustee groups that want to respond to this suggestion might look first at their chairs and ask if they are able and committed enough to serve in the many ways that are needed. Do they have the time and energy to invest in caring for the institution? Is their leadership persuasive? Will the group follow that leadership? If the answer to any of these is no, then the trustees will do well to get a new chair for whom all of these questions can be answered affirmatively. In asking these questions about the chair, some trustees may decide to disqualify themselves. If a trustee cannot accept the full obligation, this may be desirable, because trust by the many constituencies of an institution depends in large measure on all the trustees taking such a dynamic view of their role.

One of the facts of life that trustees should note is that *satisfactory* is too often the goal of administrators. If *distinction as servant* is to be achieved, *that* must be the goal of trustees,

Likewise *organization*, to the extent that the structure of the top administrative group is involved, cannot be dealt with by the top group. This too is the concern of trustees.

Organization: The Neglected Element

The following sections on organization and leadership are suggested as an orientation for trustees. These are some of the things that trustees need to know in order to ask, and insist, and discriminate.

The traditional view sees the *modus operandi* of any institution in three parts, with one overarching element:

1. *Goals and strategy*, including long-range thinking that culminates in plans.

2. *Organization*, the concern with people and structure, the reasonably durable arrangements and the staffing for carrying out plans.

3. *Implementation*, the day-to-day execution of plans, including administrative initiative and response to situations. It is the use made of organization to carry out the plans.

Overarching these three is the exercise of *leadership*, which gives the total process coherence and dynamic force by establishing priorities, allocating resources, choosing and guiding staff, articulating goals and philosophy, and exerting a sustained pull for excellence.

In practice these four are so closely meshed that they cannot be examined separately. They are delineated here so that the trustee concern for *organization* can be identified and discussed in the matrix of elements that operate to move an institution toward distinction.

Implementation is largely the concern of administration and staff.

Organization is the curiously neglected element. Thinking about it critically is not only avoided but sometimes it is spurned with some emotional heat. Perhaps this is because of an intuitive sense that trouble lies hidden there and we had best leave it alone and limp along with the tested and tried, even though it may be archaic and inadequate. Also, organization thinking is mostly about tomorrow, and too much trustee thinking, as well as thinking in administration, is crisis oriented. Obviously, in a crisis one makes do with existing organizational notions and structure. Consequently, even when there appears to be concern with organization, it is usually within close conventional limits. Regarding leadership, goals, and implementation there is a great deal of innovative thinking. The same is not true of organization. Most concern with organization is quite superficial.

Let us take the risk and examine some dimensions of the organization problem and see what trouble we confront.

Organization Structure: Formal and Informal

Looking at the structure of any large institution it is useful to identify its two main parts: *formal* and *informal*.

The *formal* structure consists of the more or less definite arrangements and ways of working that are spelled out in statutes and rules or established in practice. These take care of routine operations, specify lines of reporting and authority for certain actions and expenditures, and outline steps to be taken in certain anticipated circumstances.

The *informal* structure responds more to *leadership:* building purpose and challenging with opportunity, judicious use of incentives, astute ordering of priorities and allocating resources where they count the most. Leadership provides the encouragement and the shelter for venturing and risking the unpopular. It gives support for ethical behavior and creative ways for doing things better. The result is team effort and a network of constructive interpersonal relationships that support the total effort.

The informal structure provides the assurance to individuals and small groups who will initiate innovations and respond to situations on their own with creative solutions that are not likely to be masterminded and directed through the formal structure. These informal initiatives are the "glue" that holds the formal structure together and makes it function well. Bureaucracy is a condition in which there is not enough glue. Formalities are substituted for it.

The formal and informal structures combine to give an institution its organizational strength. However, there is a paradox in this relationship. The necessary order and consistency that the formal structure gives (and that provide indispensable conditions for the informal structure to operate in a large institution) also interfere with and inhibit the informal structure. It is important to realize that order and consistency are both necessary and inhibitive. For optimal performance a large institution needs *administration* for order and consistency, and *leadership* to mitigate the effects of administration on initiative and creativity and to build team effort to give these qualities extraordinary encouragement. The result, then, is a tension between order and consistency, on the one hand, and initiative and creativity and team effort, on the other. The problem is to keep this tension at a healthy level that has an optimizing effect. How well this is done depends upon the abilities and the quality of ideas of those who *oversee* (administer and lead); it depends also on how these resources are organized.

Organization: Two Traditions

If the trustees should concede that their institution is doing as poorly as its critics say it is, then they may wish that there were no organizational traditions and that they could begin afresh to deal with these conditions. But there are traditions, at least two major conflicting ones. And the organization problem, it seems to me, is that we have widely adopted one of the two that may well be the cause of most of the trouble. Yet we are so deeply wedded to it that the assumptions we have made about it are seen as self-evident truths, much as the axioms of Euclid stood unchallenged for two thousand years.

The first of these organization traditions, and the most widely accepted, comes down from Moses. It is the hierarchical principle that places one person in charge as the lone chief atop a pyramidal structure. Nearly all institutions we know about— businesses, governments, armies, churches, universities—have been organized this way so long that it is rare for anyone to question the assumptions that underlie the model. We see no other course than to hold one person responsible. And so the natural reaction to a call for stronger leadership is to try to strengthen the control of the one person at the top. This reaction, in most cases, exacerbates rather than alleviates the problem.

The second tradition, of much more limited use, comes down from Roman times. It is the form where the principal leader is *primus inter pares*—first among equals. There is still a "first," a leader, but that leader is not the chief. The difference may appear to be subtle, but it is important that the *primus* constantly test and prove that leadership among a group of able peers. This principle is more difficult to find in practice, but it does exist in important places—with conspicuous success.

The structure with the single chief may be drawn in this way:

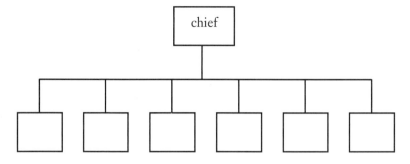

The structure with the *primus* may be diagrammed like this:

Why, the world over, do most trustee bodies choose to delegate administrative responsibility to a chief (in business parlance, chief executive officer or CEO) rather than to a leadership team with a *primus?* The weight of tradition is one reason. But tradition is supported, I believe, because trustees do not want to assume the level of continuing obligation that would be entailed if they were to assign administrative responsibility to a team of equals. They do not want to try to produce and support a chair among them who would have the ability and commitment that this arrangement demands. My experience leads me to argue categorically that in the contemporary world these choices of trustees constitute a breach of trust.

What is proposed here for the top leadership team of large institutions is a shift from the hierarchical principle, with one chief, to a team of equals with a *primus*, preceded by the change in trustee attitude and the role necessary to assure its success. This course may be difficult for the best of boards, and it is not without risk. Trustees will follow it only if they are convinced, first, that the performance of their institution is not what is reasonable and possible with available resources and that it must become so, and, second, that the pyramid with a single chief cannot carry the institution to the distinguished performance that it must attain. Most trustees can know how well or how poorly their institutions perform, but too few are convinced of the limitations of the hierarchical structure.

What is wrong with the idea of one person atop the pyramid? The following section will not argue the merits, only the limitations of the hierarchical principle.

Organization: Some Flaws in the Concept of the Single Chief

To be a lone chief atop a pyramid is *abnormal and corrupting.* None of us is perfect by ourselves, and all of us need the help and correcting influence of close colleagues. When someone is moved atop a pyramid, that person no longer has colleagues, only subordinates. Even the frankest and bravest of subordinates do not talk with their boss in the same way that they talk with colleagues who are equals, and normal communication patterns become warped. Even though a man or woman may have had a long record as an acceptable colleague with equals, on assuming the top spot that person will often become "difficult" (to put it mildly) to subordinates. The pyramidal structure weakens informal links, dries up channels of honest reaction and feedback, and creates limiting chief-subordinate relationships that, at the top, can seriously penalize the whole organization.

A self-protective *image of omniscience* often evolves from these warped and filtered communications. This in time defeats any leader by causing a distortion of judgment, for judgment is often best sharpened through interaction with others who are free to challenge and criticize.

Those persons who are atop the pyramids often suffer from a very real *loneliness.* They cannot be sure enough of the motives of those with whom they must deal, and they are not on the "grapevine." Most of what they know is what other people choose to tell them. They often do not know what everybody else knows, informally.

The idea of one-person-in-control enjoys widespread support because of the decisiveness it affords when decisiveness is needed. Yet a close observation of top persons everywhere reveals the *burden of indecisiveness* to be much greater than the benefit of decisiveness. The difference is that decisiveness is usually conspicuous and sometimes heroic, whereas indecisiveness is often subtle, hard to detect, and sometimes tragic. When one person is chief, the multiple liability to the institution resulting from indecisive moments is much more costly than the asset of the few cases where the chief is conspicuously decisive. I challenge the readers to pause here and think of examples with which they are familiar before dismissing this statement.

Everywhere there is much complaining about *too few leaders.* We have too few because most institutions are structured so that only a few—only one at the time—can emerge. With one person at the top, the full scope of leadership is limited to that one person, no matter how large the institution. As we have become a nation of large institutions (nothing wrong with that, *per se*) we have progressively limited the opportunity for leaders to emerge because our conventional design provides for only one. Such an organizational design aggravates the disadvantages of bigness.

The typical chief who rests uneasily atop the pyramid of any large institution is grossly overburdened. The job destroys too many of them—which is reason enough to abandon the idea. But for the institution there is also damage. For in too many cases the *demands of the office destroy these persons' creativity* long before they leave the office.

When there is but a single chief, there is *a major interruption when that person leaves.* As the chief approaches mandatory retirement, or, as in the university where it is customary to give a year or more of notice so that a successor can be sought, the chief is a "lame duck." In the university the search for a new president is often a ludicrous performance, which is demeaning to the many candidates who must listen to their assets and liabilities being publicly debated while the search continues for "the person who has everything." And there is the inevitable disillusionment. The chosen one turns out to have feet of clay like everybody else.

Being in the top position prevents leadership by persuasion because *the single chief holds too much power.* Chiefs often cannot say persuasively what they would like to say because it will be taken as an order. No one else can effectively speak for the chief because the listeners rightly want to know what the chief thinks.

When more converges on the single chiefs than they can handle, but they must appear to be handling it alone, *they most often resort to concentrated briefing and the support of ghost writing.* As the job is structured, they have no alternative. In the end the chief becomes a performer, not a natural person, and essential creative powers diminish. Thus the concentration of power tends to stunt the growth of the one person in the institution who should be the model of growth in stature, awareness, communication, and human sensitivity. And this growth frustration is inevitably projected downward and imposes its limitation on everybody.

Finally, the prevalence of the lone chief places a burden on the whole society because *it gives control priority over leadership.* It sets before the young the spectacle of an unwholesome struggle to get to the top. It nourishes the notion among able people that one must be boss to be effective. And it sanctions, in a conspicuous way, a pernicious and petty status striving that corrupts everyone.

The above paragraphs have summarized some of the arguments against the concept of the single chief. Against this it can be argued that some people perform brilliantly in the office as it is now structured. This may be because, as in the university, *sheer survival in the job is accounted as brilliant performance.* If the quality of the best of our institutions is as bad as described here, then the heads of these institutions cannot be accorded a high rating merely because they keep the institutions afloat.

In summary, concerning organization, for large institutions the organizational steps are, first, a new role for the trustees and their chair, with a new career pattern for evolving chairs; second, a trustee-designed executive office and assignment of responsibilities and a setup whereby the chair, on behalf of the trustees and with the support of the chair's own staff, closely monitors the performance of an administrative and leadership team that is a group of equals with one of them "first among equals." Beyond these first steps, the details of the organization structure will result from decisions made from day to day in specific situations and with regard to (1) the human and material resources available, (2) the complex of relations and influence among people, (3) the assets and liabilities of the individuals involved, and (4) the central goals of the institution. The aim is distinguished performance as a serving institution.

Leadership: Conceptual and Operational

The prime force for achievement through service in any large institution is a senior administrative group with optimal balance between operators and conceptualizers.

The *operating* talent carries the institution toward its objectives, in the situation, from day to day, and resolves the issues that arise as this movement takes place. This calls for interpersonal skills, sensitivity to the environment, tenacity, experience, judgment, ethical soundness, and related attributes and abilities that the day-to-day movement requires. Operating is more *administering* in contrast to *leading*.

Conceptual talent sees the whole in the perspective of history—past and future. It states and adjusts goals, analyzes and evaluates operating performance, and foresees contingencies a long way ahead. Long-range strategic planning is embraced here, as is setting standards and relating all the parts to the whole. Leadership, in the sense of going out ahead to show the way, is more conceptual than operating. *Conceptual*, as used here, is not synonymous with *intellectual* or *theoretical*. Conceptualizers at their best are intensely practical. They are also effective persuaders and relationship builders.

Highly developed operating and conceptual talents are not completely exclusive. Every able leader-administrator has some of both, even though being exceptional probably in only one of the two.

Both of these talents, in balance and rightly placed, are required for sustained high-level performance in any large institution. By *optimal balance between the two* is meant a relationship in which both conceptualizers and operators understand, respect, and depend on one another, and in which neither dominates the other. In a large institution the council of equals with a *primus inter pares* serves best when it is predominantly conceptual. *Whoever in the council has the greatest team-building ability should be primus*, even though someone else may have a higher-sounding formal title.

A team builder is a strong person who provides the substance that holds the team together in common purpose toward the right objectives. This is accomplished by asking the right questions. If a group is confronted by the right questions long enough, it will see through to the essence and find the right way.

Both the operator and the conceptualizer are result oriented. The operator is concerned primarily with "getting it done." The conceptualizer is primarily concerned with what "ought to be done"—when, how, at what cost, in what priority, *and* how well. They work together as a reinforcing rather than a counteracting team.

The achievement of such optimal balance is hindered by a stubborn fact: *whereas conceptualizers generally recognize the need for operators, the reverse is often not the case.* A conceptualizer in a top spot is quite likely to see that strong operators are placed where needed. But an operator in a top leadership post may not, without some help, see to it that able and influential conceptualizers function as they must. Consequently, if the top post in a hierarchical administration (as opposed to a council of equals) is filled by an operator who is not sharply aware of the need for adequate conceptual influence, the institution does not have a bright long-run future, no matter how able the top person or how brilliant its current performance.

One of the advantages of large decentralized organizations (businesses or multi-campus university systems or church parishes that are under denominational oversight) is that they can accommodate conceptualizers as the major influence in the central staff, while placing operators in the dominant role in the decentralized units. This is good but not sufficient. Also needed is someone who is closely involved with the administration of the decentralized unit and maintains a conceptual link with the central organization. Otherwise, conceptualizers in the central staff may be criers in the wilderness. The urgencies of the times may demand that they be heard—clearly. But if there are only operators in the decentralized units, they may *not* be heard.

Some able people, while they are young, probably can develop exceptional strength in either talent—but usually not in both. Long concentration on one of these talents diminishes the possibility that a switch can be made to the other. A substantial penalty may ensue if a person who has devoted several years, successfully, to one of these talents moves into a key spot that requires an exceptional level of the other; once established as an operator *or* a conceptualizer, one is apt to make any position fit one's habitual way of working. There are exceptions, of course; and if a switch like this is to be made, those overseeing it should be sure they are dealing with an exception.

Highly developed conceptualizers who are effective in top leadership of large institutions seem to be much rarer than able operators. This may be because the number needed is substantially less, or because they do not emerge naturally out of those with long experience in operating work, or because it is harder for an operator to identify a conceptualizer and reward that special talent, or because the need for able conceptualizers is not clearly and explicitly recognized.

American railroads are classic examples of large institutions in which the need for conceptual leadership has been traditionally unrecognized. Nearly everybody in administration was busy running the railroad day to day. Not enough able and well-placed people were thinking about the problems of railroads and the future contingencies.

Some institutions have risen to eminence at one point in their histories because they accidentally evolved at least one able conceptualizer into a key spot. But then they lost eminence when they failed to maintain this talent at a high enough quality and in good balance in their top leadership. *They probably lost their conceptual leadership because they were not guided by an organizational principle that required it. Therefore, not knowing when they accidentally had it, they were not aware when they lost it.*

Able operators are always required for good performance in any institution. An organization may perform well in the short run, as the railroads once did, with an all-operating management. But for long-run good performance, able conceptualizers, rightly placed in top leadership, are absolutely essential. To build and sustain a great institution, one must be able to identify these talented men and women and see that they are always in places where their influence is needed. Providing able operators is an important and larger-scale task, but it is the more obvious and easier to do and therefore less apt to be neglected.

The purely operating motive, unsupported by strong conceptual talent, is likely to settle for doing well within the established pattern. Conceptualizers usually emerge when the institution makes a strong push for distinction—which in our times often means wise, deep-cutting, effective reform and reorganization.

The terms *operator* and *conceptualizer* are not in common use. They are chosen because they more clearly state the central issue of staffing for top performance in any large institution, whether church, university, or business. A critical trustee function is to identify those with exceptional talent as operators and conceptualizers and to select for the top administrative team a balanced group that will give the institution strong leadership and sound administration.

The Trustee as Leader

Part of the problem of moving our institutions along is that persons outside the institution either do not know enough to make a pertinent criticism, or the institution has its guard up and the external critics cannot penetrate it. Those inside who might be critics are sometimes suppressed by an arbitrary discipline or encumbered by loyalty and do not appreciate the importance of criticism to the health of the institution. Sometimes they do not know how to make their criticism effective. It is a major trustee role to build legitimacy by being sensitive to critical thinking from all quarters and helping to interpret the meaning of it to the internal leadership and administration. Thus the trustees should exploit their inside-outside objective position to become instruments of understanding.

Legitimacy begins with trust. No matter what the competence or the intentions, if trust is lacking, nothing happens. One of the positive signs of the times, and one that may have been a major factor in the loss of support that some large institutions are experiencing, is that there has been a substantial decline in two kinds of trust: blind trust (including respect for authority), and trust generated by leadership charisma. It will be a false recovery if all that happens is that these trends are reversed, because now we have the incentive and the opportunity to establish trust on a sounder basis. The only sound basis for trust is for people to have the solid experience of being *served* by their institutions in a way that builds a society that is more just and more loving, and with greater creative opportunities for all of its people. And it is worth the cost of some chaos and disruption if enough people will read the signs and start building institutions that generate a high level of trust through a quality of service that is exceptional by all previous standards.

Trust for these times begins with trustees accepting the obligation to design and oversee a top administration that is capable of making the impossible possible, that is, move the institution toward distinction—and deal with all of the pressures of these times—without asking the single chief executive to do what we have seen is impossible *for any chief.* If anything is clear in organizational experience as I have observed it, once the role of chief executive officer has been passed to a single individual, it is not realistic to expect that that person will redesign the office so as to be no longer the single chief. One may be a great innovative leader, but one will not take *that* step. And the trustees have foreclosed their opportunity for influence on organization until they appoint a successor. The model of the single chief sitting atop the hierarchy is obsolete, and consequently we are at a point of crisis for want of trust in our major institutions.

As a remedy, what is envisioned here for a large institution may be described as *two strong teams,* each led by a *primus inter pares.* The trustees, with the chair as *primus,* are one team, and they have their objective role of being inside the organization but standing apart from operating responsibility. The other team, also with its *primus,* is the top executive group. The cardinal principle is that no single person has unchecked power, but that all of them may be both restrained and encouraged by their peers. The danger in this arrangement is that the trustees might interfere with the executive group. There are two protections against this: a clear definition of the two roles, and the watchfulness of all constituencies who must be fully informed about the arrangement.

This is clearly not the perfect organizational design for all time. With the infinite vagaries of human nature, I doubt that one exists. But I hope that organizational design will become the special competence of able and far-sighted staff people who will be dedicated to the service of trustees. This is the critical question about all of this: If the trustees resolve to take the role advocated here, will they then get the sustained staff support that they must have to be effective in this new role?

The following notes on the institutions of the future—businesses, universities, churches—are an amplification of this line of thought. Some useful perspective on the general argument may come from weighing the similarities and differences among the three.

The Large Business as Servant

Large businesses have been pushed around by social forces in the past forty years more than most other institutions, and the typical large business may be more sensitive to the need to adapt and change than most outsiders are aware. Because they do not have the coercive taxing power of government or the sentimental support given to universities and churches, businesses often feel less secure and find their legitimacy more sharply questioned. Furthermore, businesses are freer from professional hangups than other institutions and therefore they are likely to be more mobile. For reasons like these I believe that we should expect businesses to become conspicuously more serving faster than the others. Three new major pressures may bring this about.

The pressure of consumerism may cause some major businesses to make a determined effort to build a new level of trust in consumer products.

Pollution and the protection of the environment have become major issues and are a costly problem for some businesses. But when sanctions have been taken against polluters, such actions have had a marked effect in raising the level of social responsibility in business.

One great effect of *the revolution of expectation among young people* has been to force companies to try to make their work more significant for their employees. In the end, internal pressure may break down the concept of chief executive officer and force a council of equals. In order to attract and hold enough very able young people to deal with the mounting complexities, the existing chief executive officer may be forced to raise the immediate administrative group to more equal status. And if one is to preside over a successful business, one's major talent will need to evolve from being the *chief* into the *builder of the team.* Furthermore, if the idealism of this generation of young people persists, as I think it will, and as the abler of these young people move into top posts, *they* will insist on more determined efforts to provide significant and meaningful work to more people. This, in the end, will result in a new business ethic. Only one large industry needs to do this with notable success to gain a substantial competitive edge.

These three major forces operating simultaneously may have a profound impact on the servant stature of large businesses. Two quite significant side effects may ensue. The first of these will grow out of the emerging awareness of the limitations inherent in the traditional school that stands aside from the mainstream of society. We built extensive schools partly because of early evils of child labor, partly to keep young people off the labor market, partly just out of momentum. Education was but one of several reasons. But now we are beginning to realize that there is more integrity in useful work than in anything that can be simulated in schools. For those with non-abstracting minds (which may be as many as 85 percent of the population), the sooner they enter a work environment the better. I find the idea appalling that we will try to absorb all the surplus time created by industrial efficiency in ever-expanding leisure pursuits. Many Americans may already have too many *things*, but our capacity to use services rendered to each other is practically limitless. And the great majority will want to be useful as well as rewardingly employed. The combination of the need to merge much of education into the work environment and greatly expand organized services will present a tremendous challenge to business structures to take substantial new initiatives. Perhaps some of the "free enterprise" breast-beating that is narrowly defensive can be brought by new leadership into such socially useful channels.

The second side effect will see more initiative by large businesses to build new relationships with government. It is clear now that the market is not always the best guide for what a business ought to do. Some of what businesses ought to do should be worked out with government agencies that represent the public interest, and this should be done before there is a public crisis. Examples of successful initiatives by business to build these relations with government have not been as numerous as they should be, but there are a few good ones. The signs of the times on this score are auspicious.

The result of these two side effects is that the distinction between *public* and *private* sectors may be progressively blurred in large organizations. With this trend, what will happen to the legal control of ownership is open to question. It is already somewhat of an anachronism in large businesses. However this is resolved, owners of large businesses must make their peace with the idea that these institutions exist by the consent of clients, employees, and society at large—all of whom must be well served, and whose judgment on whether they are being well served is becoming more and more discriminating.

I am sharply aware of the long way to go before large businesses will be judged adequate servants. And I am not envisioning a utopia in which self-serving and manipulation and huckstering and rapaciousness will disappear completely from the business scene. But I do think that some of the forces and trends are right and that there is, among present business leadership, the disposition to respond. Where this will go depends somewhat on the influence wielded by universities and churches—not so much by preaching as by example.

The University as an Institution

How did we get to the decision that a traditional university education was right for 50 percent of the population? And now that we have done it, do we like the result?

I have not been able to find the reasoning in answer to the first question. And I suspect that, when our thoughts get collected, the answer to the second question will be no.

What then will we do with these vast institutions that have been built in the past twenty-five years when we moved from 15 percent of college-age people in the universities to 50 percent? And what alternatives will we offer to the perhaps two-thirds or more of those now in traditional academic environments who want a different kind of education? The lack of answers to these questions defines part of the plight of higher education today.

We have this problem, as I see it, because of the failure of those who hold the public trust for the universities, rather than the administrations or faculties. It is the trustee role to question the assumptions and penetrate the illusions, and too many trustees have failed to do this. Now the universities need to rethink their missions and produce new concepts of what they should do and how they should be governed. They have the internal capability to do this. In fact, the university of the future must be generated inside the university of the present, for that is where the expertise is. The universities must make their own revolution, internally, but they are not likely to do it and carry it to a sound conclusion unless there is an insistent discriminating demand from trustees.

Clearly the trustees cannot take over and manage the universities. They have neither the time nor the competence to do this, and it is not their proper role. What then can they do? These things:

1. Insist that the goals of the university (and its major parts) be stated in clear, unequivocal, behavioral terms. What is supposed to happen? In what measurable ways should students be different after they have met the requirements? The trustees should state the goals, after the internal constituencies—faculty, students, administration—have advised them. If, after a persistent effort to get this done, the trustees are not satisfied that the goals can be defended as adequate and in the public interest, then the trustees should declare a crisis of confidence within the university. It is imperative that at all times the university be pursuing goals that the trustees can defend as adequate and in the public interest. Without this, there is a breach of trust and the trustees are acting, to some extent, as a front for something they either do not understand or do not believe in. A good deal of the difficulties of the universities today may be traced to such a basic flaw of integrity at the trustee level. To the extent that this is material, it must be cleared up before anything can move.

2. Once the goals are stated, the trustees should then ask: "To what extent does the university now reach these goals, at a

reasonable level of excellence, with the students it now has, and with resources it now has—faculty, administration, facilities, money?" If the discrepancy is serious, the trustees should then ask for plans: "How can the gap be closed, and on what kind of timetable—in specific terms that can be measured and evaluated?"

3. If the internal constituencies cannot produce the plans or a reasonable timetable, the trustees may then suggest the engagement of consulting resources to help. If the suggestion is not heeded and plans are not forthcoming, the trustees should shift from suggestion to insistence.

4. If, after a reasonable time, there is still a material gap between goals and performance and concrete plans for better performance, the trustees might ask that the goals be scaled down to what is realistically achievable. If this is done, the trustees should ask that all the students be advised, as clearly and candidly as possible, just what help they can expect from the university. This is an age of great candor, and honesty has risen (commendably) as a student priority. The trustees should insist that this be respected.

5. As an alternative the trustees may have their own study made to try to find ways to set goals and propose innovations that the internal constituencies usually do not originate—such as structural reorganization, joint programs with other institutions, mergers with other institutions, new separately funded and separately governed schools within the university.

6. When the goals are realistically set and plans are fully made, the trustees should then attend to the top leadership of the university. Here the trustees should have, or get from consulting help, the competence to design the top administration—in detail. Anyone who has closely watched the installation of the typical head of a university knows that when that move is made one cannot expect the incumbent to redesign the structure of the office that has just been given. The trustees must design the office (hopefully as a group of equals with a *primus*) and place all members in it with assigned roles. This calls for a level of trustee

knowledge, skill, and dedication that many trustees may not want to assume. If so, reorganization of trustees may need to precede a restructuring of administration. Finally, there should be provision for sustained close oversight by trustees. It is time for trustees to take over for themselves the role of asking the tough questions, rather than leaving them to the soap box, in the idealistic setting of the campus green.

The case made earlier against the single chief needs supplementing when applied to the university. Universities have grown in size and complexity and in the range of requirements to which they must respond, so that large and quite sophisticated administrative staffs are required. Unfortunately, university administration is not viewed by people as offering attractive careers. Administrative work is demeaned by both faculty and students, and career growth channels are not clear enough to keep a spirit of dynamism in the administrative staff. Furthermore, there is sufficient ambiguity in the governance process of the typical university to dull the individual sense of responsibility and make administrative work unrewarding as well as underpaid. As matters now stand the only attractive job in a university outside of the faculty is the president's, and even that has lost its luster. This could be substantially improved by a council of equals leading the university instead of a single chief.

The one-person office of president in a university is misleading. One who did not know the university would think that the president *is* the chief. True, the president is a person who sits in a big office and issues pronouncements, hands out diplomas and, except when dealing with the faculty, acts like a chief. Yet, with regard to the essential work of the university—teaching students—the president is not the chief. With this appearance of office but not the substance, it is no wonder that when tension overtakes the university the president becomes the lone lightning rod who has to absorb all of the shocks without the armor that the structure of the office presumes is there. A council of equals would go far to clear up this ambiguity.

Furthermore, a council of equals would multiply the number of strong people available to lead by persuasion. In fact, the hope for the universities is that they can be restructured so that they can *lead and be led*, as opposed to the more common suggestion that they need tougher management.

The university is a curious institution. It is extraordinarily pliable and innovative when strong initiative emerges from within. But it is practically immovable when criticized or advised from the outside. It is possible to beat it down (as in some recent tragic examples). But the building forces that make a great university are almost entirely produced by strong internal leadership and the widespread initiative that this encourages.

The basic thrusts that build quality in a large university originate in the departments. And any new force that regenerates the university must have the effect of stimulating creative initiatives in the departments. What the typical university so desperately needs is leadership that will, in every nook and cranny, seek out, encourage, discriminately judge, and reward when successful *all* genuine initiatives that will make the university better serving, and penalize, to the point of drying up or radically reorganizing, those departments and schools that fail to maintain themselves by rigorous self-criticism. The structure of schools, departments, programs, centers, and their interrelationships, and whether they are built up, closed down, or modified, is best determined in the process of giving this vigorous and sensitive leadership. And the obligation of the trustees is to design, install, and oversee a leadership team that is capable, *within the existing concept of how a university is governed*, of generating sufficient leadership power to bring the present university quickly to the kind of serving institution it ought to be.

Missing in the university scene, and trustee initiative will be necessary to bring it about, is a strong conceptual staff—part long-term and part one- and two-year full-time faculty deputations— that will help the university bring its own vast resources of intellect and experience to bear on *building* the university into a more serving institution. The usual committee structure of a large university is time consuming and ineffective. These committees try to do through diffuse participation what can only be done by a concentration of effort by the ablest in the university. Only in this way can *trust* be built in leadership so that much of the vast amount of faculty time spent in committees can be turned to teaching and study and work with students. It is a harsh thing to say, but in this regard, American universities resemble the railroads—everybody concerned with the university is busy *operating*. Very, very few are standing aside *thinking* about universities and available to faculty and trustees and administrators for counsel in depth in the critical decisions they make that so vitally affect us all—especially our young people. Conceptual leadership is the most difficult to maintain. The universities think they have this in their faculties—but they don't, because faculty members are too involved. One has to stand aside in some detachment to give conceptual leadership. The universities should set the example. And the initiative of the trustees to do this should be supported by substantial foundation grants.

Perhaps the reason that during these past twenty-five years there have been so few prophetic voices warning us of the perils of unbridled expansion of traditional higher education is that there has been no home for such people *within the university*. The university is too complex an institution and the stakes are too great for the lone philosopher sitting in his study to sound the necessary warnings and point the way to the future. This calls for a critical mass of gifted and dedicated conceptual minds, men and women who have a discernible context, and who, with the help of an able staff leader, will find a rewarding career in making university institution building their goal. As a proportion of the total budget of higher education, the cost of such a staff resource will be insignificant. It is the obligation of university trustees to see that it gets into place—and soon.

The Growing Edge Church

The churches, like all other contemporary institutions, are under pressures and influences that may bring about radical change. The younger half of the population is being exposed to educational and cultural forces that are so different from those that the older half has experienced that it is no wonder that age thirty has come to be the magic dividing line between the generations. The gap is wide.

The central issue that young people are pressing on "established" people is that we are not doing well enough as a society. The churches are judged inadequate, along with all the others. In some ways the churches may be judged more harshly than the others because their role could be so pivotal in the regeneration of what many regard as a sick society.

As a student of organization rather than as a theologian, I view the church as the institutionalization of humankind's religious concern. Conscious religious concern is a part of the gear of civilization—a means to heal humanity's alienation, which our "civilized" state has brought about. The word *religion*, at its root, means "to rebind," to rebind humans to the cosmos. Primitive people may have suffered much from their environment, but they were not alienated. The Lascaux cave paintings attest to that. These ancient people were at home; they belonged. Their total society was bound to the cosmos, and a church, a separate institution specializing in rebinding, was not needed. But we are estranged, particularly our young people, and we have been so for a long time. We need a religion, and a church to steward its service, to heal the pervasive alienation and become a major building force in a new society that is more just and more loving, and that provides greater creative opportunities for its people.

The modern church took its form in a period when, outside the home, the church was the dominant influence in people's lives, and it shaped and sustained the influence of the home. Now both the work environment and the school far outrank the church in influence, and I doubt that churches as they now stand can ever recover their former direct influence. What then will they do?

They will, of course, continue to reach as many individuals directly and in such depth as they can, realizing that influence wielded in this way will not be the religious force in society that it once was or now needs to be. Then some, many I hope, will move out on the growing edge and seek new opportunities for service. One of these will be to become the chief nurturing force, conceptualizer of the opportunity, value shaper, and morale sustainer of leadership everywhere—in business, school, government, health and social service, philanthropy—everywhere. This is not an unrealistic aspiration; the field is wide open. The universities have the immediate task to bring themselves to a model of institutional strength and to extricate themselves from the overexpansion of academic education. The best leadership role that can be expected of most universities is to make of themselves models of institutional excellence and to provide in better ways the technology that leaders use. But the dynamics of leadership—the vision, the values, and the staying power—are essentially religious concerns, and fostering them should become the central mission of the growing edge churches. Where else can it be done? If some of the churches do not accept the opportunity to build leadership strength for other institutions that have greater value-shaping influence on individuals than the churches now have directly, how will churches do their work? What is asked of growing edge churches is that they add to their historic mission of caring for persons, and to their more recent regard for the social order, the mission of caring for institutions—quite specific institutions.

To a student of organization, two events in church history are of special interest. When Martin Luther made his break with the Catholic Church in the sixteenth century, he postulated the priesthood of all believers as his goal. It did not come off because he did not devise a role for the pastor that would permit it. A century later in England George Fox met this challenge by founding the Quakers, who dispensed with the pastor altogether. A small but influential sect survived his effort, but it fell short of his aims because he did not leave it with a way of leading a pastorless flock so that it could grow and adapt.

The first task of the growing edge church is to learn what neither Luther nor Fox knew: how to build a society of equals in which there is strong lay leadership in a trustee board with a chair functioning as *primus inter pares*, and with the pastor functioning as *primus inter pares* for the many who do the work of the church.

Having accomplished this, the second task is to make of the church a powerful force to build leadership strength in those persons who have the opportunity to lead in other institutions and to give them constant support.

If this can be the serious mission of a group of churches, then the central conceptual resource that stands behind these churches will become the architect of the more just, more loving, more serving society. The logical architect in the present structure of things is the seminaries. And I believe that one day the seminaries will become a powerful conceptual resource that stands behind the growing edge churches—those that accept caring for institutions and those who lead them as a major part of their mission. But the reconstruction of the seminaries is not likely to take place until one strong church leads the way.

I know it may be difficult for a single church, on its own, to accept that it will produce and sustain the trustees who will build other serving institutions. I would despair for the future if one strong church will not lead the way, but I am hopeful because I believe one will.

Authority and Strength: The Problem of Power

Much of this chapter deals with two basic changes in the top structure of large institutions. First, trustees will accept a much more exacting level of trust and will assume a firm obligation to bring their institutions to a distinguished level of performance as servant. Second, the trustees will design the administration and leadership of the institution as a group of equals rather than a single chief. Then they will assign the functions including a *primus*, and they will closely monitor the work of the team without interfering in operating decisions.

These changes by themselves will not deliver the distinguished serving institution. But they are advanced as the basic structural changes that will be made before movement toward anything significantly better can begin. I believe that the churches are in the best position to become the prime moving force to produce the trustees who will bring these changes about and to sustain them at a high level of trust.

Part of the failure of our institutions to serve with distinction may be the interaction between two reinforcing elements: low levels of trusteeship and the concept of the single chief executive. Once established, there is a lock-step between trustees, who minimize their obligation by delegating operating responsibility to one person, *and* the chief executive who wants to keep the trustees from interfering. Only to the extent that trustees give support when it is needed does the chief executive want a strong board. Others who have a special interest in the organization—share owners in a business, the various constituencies of a university, members of a church—have expectations that reinforce these relationships. They want a strong board to select and support a strong executive and to make certain checks on the operation, especially financial ones, and they want the board to intervene if the executive—or pastor—fails. But they do not expect the board to lead.

I submit that this is a design for mediocrity. Yet this is what we have, over the whole gamut, when these institutions are judged by what is reasonable and possible with available resources.

How did we get this way, and why have we stayed this way so long? It is deep in our traditional wisdom, at least as old as the story of Moses. The curious thing about this story is that this was the best the ancients knew, but they also knew its faults, which we have forgotten.

Jethro, father-in-law of Moses, came to visit him in the wilderness and found him exhausting himself by dealing personally with all of the problems of his people. He was clearly the leader, but he was "unorganized." Jethro advised him:

You shall represent the people before God, and bring their cases to God; and you shall teach them the statutes and the decisions, and make them know the way in which they must walk and what they must do. Moreover, choose able men from all of the people, such as fear God, men who are trustworthy and who hate a bribe; and place such men over the people as rulers of thousands, of hundreds, of fifties, and of tens. And let them judge the people at all times; every great matter they shall bring to you, but any small matter they shall decide for themselves; so that it will be easier for you and they will bear the burden with you. If you do this, and God so commands you, then you will be able to endure and all of this people also will go their way in peace.

Moses took the advice. Presumably he also accepted the justification: "You will be able to endure and all of this people also will go their way in peace." Nothing was said about the quality of the society that would result, only that Moses will endure and the people will be peaceful (law and order?).

In the end the Lord sacked Moses. Why? Because in that dramatic incident of drawing water from the rock he acted as if he were God.

This confirms the fatal flaw in Jethro's advice. There was no question of Moses' dedication to service, but he accepted bad advice from Jethro on how to structure the leadership of the people so that his own natural power striving would be diminished and his serving enhanced. *Missing was the necessary guardianship of strong trustees and an astute chair.*

In the history of organizational ideas, *primus inter pares* came later, but the notion of a single chief was too firmly entrenched. Too many people were comfortable with it. Unchecked power was still accepted. And the mediocrity of institutions had not yet been challenged the way the revolution of expectations has challenged it today.

It may be that we have stayed with Jethro's advice so long because people have wanted order and they have been willing to pay the price of concentrating power in one person's hands as the only way they knew to get it. Now the costs of this choice are looming too large and it is imperative that we must have what we cannot have if we stay with Jethro's advice.

The abuse of power is curbed if the holder of power is surrounded by equals who are strong, and if there is close oversight by a monitoring group, trustees who are not involved in the daily use of power.

There are several kinds of power. One is coercive power, used principally to destroy. Not much that endures can be built with it. Even presumably autocratic institutions like businesses are learning that the value of coercive power is inverse to its use. Leadership by persuasion and example is the way to build—everywhere.

The Issue of Countervailing Power

An important aspect of power is the fact of countervailing power, which most constituencies of all institutions have to some degree. Faculties of universities, administrators and employees of businesses, and clergy in churches all have contrived some countervailing power—partly as a protection against the arbitrary use of power by those in authority, partly to provide an area of comfort for themselves. Some of this power has been formally granted by trustees—as with university faculties. Partly it is assumed or bestowed by law—as with unions. Partly it is simply organizational inertia resulting from a long tradition of trustee neglect. Whatever the source, in most institutions this countervailing power is real and formidable. While it may be a source of distress to trustees or administrators, and it may be a substantial impediment to improving performance, trustees should recognize that this kind of countervailing power is a necessary condition of all human arrangements. *No one should be powerless!* And it can be taken as axiomatic that if trustee power is not used well, staff power, administrative power, and employee power are also not likely to be used well.

Trustees have too often misused their power by embracing archaic organizational forms that provide for the institution to be governed but not led and by failing to organize themselves so that they give the leadership that only they can give. Consequently, they should not be surprised, when they do attempt to reconstruct their roles, at resistance from administrators and staffs. Any new initiative by trustees will be seen as upsetting an established balance of power.

Therefore, if trustees follow the advice given here, they will proceed first to establish a new basis for trust by making clear to all that they intend henceforth to monitor closely the use of power to assure its much more benign use, that they intend to organize themselves better to serve the institution and all of the people it touches, and that, as individual trustees, they commit themselves to a new level of dedication.

Goals and Purposes

The first step toward trustees becoming optimally effective is to define the institution. They will, of course, have the advice of administrators, staffs, and others who are concerned. But it is a trustee function to state the goals and purposes. What kind of institution is this and what performance is expected of it? By what criteria do trustees wish the performance to be judged by each constituency that is entitled to expect some service from it?

In the course of arriving at the statement of goals and purpose, the trustees may want a canvas made of a sample of each major constituency in order to have a reliable base on which to make their decision concerning what the expected performance will be. In making the decision, trustees should take into account both how each constituency (owner, creditor, student, customer or client, employee, government, vendor, supplier, administrator, parishioner, etc.) states its expectation and what administrators and employees feel is achievable. Astute trustees will set the expected standard just a little above what administrators and employees feel is achievable. Periodic reviews may result in altering this expectancy. "Best possible" performance might be the long-range goal—always a challenge, always something just out of reach, something to strive for. Such a view of the trustee role will require a periodic assessment of performance, a separate judgment on how well each constituency is being served. And this will require that trustees have a kind of staff support that is not now commonly available.

Defining the institution and stating its goals and purposes is probably the most critical task that confronts trustees. Everything else that trustees do rests on this one basic decision.

Trust and Growth: The Value of Understanding

My faith in what is recommended here rests on knowing a few people who are now ready to dedicate themselves to the trustee role as I have described it. And the times are enough out of joint that many will respond if given a little encouragement and assurance that it is a manageable task.

Precisely what trustees need to know, and how they will organize to learn what they need to know, will be worked out in each situation and will be unique to it. And part of the trustees' commitment to leading the institution will be their unrelenting effort to learn what they need to know in order to *oblige* the institution to reach distinction as servant. If trust is to replace the now pervasive cynicism, trustees must clearly stand as having a total understanding of the institution and caring for all of the persons touched by it—caring for those persons in proportion to their involvement in, and their dependence on, the institution.

Suppose every large business, every large church, every large university had a board of trustees that was effectively pushing for distinction as servant in these terms, how many chairs would we need to produce to lead them? Perhaps three thousand? Out of two hundred million people is that unrealistic? I do not think so. But what is involved in doing it?

First, just one in each of the three. That is all it takes to start anything. If one board of trustees in a large church, a large university, and a large business will produce a chair who will grasp the concept of how to move the institution to distinction—and then articulate what is actually happening, not just what is hoped will happen—this will start the movement toward a more serving society, one institution at a time. Will it move fast enough to stem the apparent deterioration? This depends on how many growing edge churches emerge and how hard they work at nurturing and supporting trustees.

How will the church do this? If I had a sure answer to this question it would already have been done. But let me speculate.

Someone in the church must paint the dream. For anything to happen there must be a dream. And for anything great to happen there must be a great dream. The growing edge church will be a painter of great dreams for *all* of its people, something to lift their sights above the ordinary and give them a great goal to strive for—something for each person to strive for.

One of these great dreams is for the good society made up of predominantly serving institutions that shape its character by encouraging serving individuals and providing scope and shelter for large creative acts of service—by individuals and groups.

What is this serving institution like? What does it take to produce it? These questions will have to be answered by those who hold the institution in trust and who are determined to produce it. *This must come first.* Trust is first. Nothing will move until trust is firm.

A serious error of an earlier generation was to put administration first. Administration is important, but it is largely a skill, and skills are secondary. And we can now see that we have put the internal leadership and administration in an untenable spot by expecting them to function without the context of trust that only *trustees*, standing apart from administration, can generate. The stress of these times has exposed this to clear view.

It is the role of the church to *sanction* trustees—to say who is capable of, and prepared for trust. Individuals do not assert this for themselves. (In saying this I am not judging personal ambitious striving in general. It is simply that the trustee may not have it—not in the role of trustee.)

I hope the existing churches will rise to the opportunity to take this role of ultimate sanction on who shall be trustees. But if no existing church, or not enough, will take it on, then whatever group takes this role (and some group must take it) will become a church, perhaps an *ad hoc* church. *But it will be a church* because what is held in trust, the dynamics of leadership—the vision, the values, the staying power—are essentially religious concerns. If it happens this way, then the new thrust will become an *ad hoc* growing edge church and the existing churches may accommodate to it as they have accommodated to another great *ad hoc* church, Alcoholics Anonymous.

If the growing edge church, whether old or new, can build its competence as a nurturer of trustees, and if it will frame its work in a context of values that elicits trust in the church for this vocation, the help of that church will soon be sought by other institutions (including churches not yet so fortunate) that want to strengthen their trustee bodies. Even with today's relatively low level of aspiration for institutions generally, there is a shortage of trustees, and able chairs are really rare.

The challenge of the revolution of expectations can only be met if we can have more people *who will serve as leaders*—everywhere. A top leadership team of equals with a *primus* in our major institutions will grow more leaders faster than any other course available to us. Leaders are not trained. They are competent people to begin with, and they can be given a vision and a context of values. Beyond that they need only opportunity and encouragement to grow. *Our major institutions must give more room for able people to grow.* A top leadership council of equals with a *primus* in place of the lone chief executive is a first big step. They will find ways to expand creative opportunities for large numbers—ways that are appropriate to each situation.

Can it be done? Yes, it can be done by *trustees* who are strong and dedicated, who will limit their trustee service to one major institution and stay with it, and who will organize a capable staff for their own support. Who in these troubled times will be trusted if *trustees* cannot be trusted? And will any less obligation than this merit trust?

There must be someone among the trustees of a university, a business, a church, who wants the joy of achievement and the ease of conscience that substantial movement toward a more serving institution will afford.

More will be welcome, but one is all that is asked for now—just one.

> Now understand me well—It is provided in the essence of things, that from any fruition of success, no matter what, shall come forth something to make a greater struggle necessary.
>
> —WALT WHITMAN

III

Trustees as Servants

George Washington was noted for signing his letters "Your most humble and obedient servant." This chapter is an argument in support of trustees choosing to be servants.

The premise upon which this argument rests is that the best of our voluntary (nongovernmental) institutions, in the service of all of us who depend on them, is too far below what is reasonable and possible with their available resources, human and material. This performance can be raised much closer to the optimal for each institution by governing boards of trustees (including directors of business corporations as trustees) who are determined and who organize themselves to do it.

Trustees and administrators may not readily accept such a categorical statement. However, I sense an uneasiness among many of them, and there is much striving for ways to do better. The trouble is that these efforts are frustrated by outmoded concepts and tangled semantics that are deeply embedded in the way institutions traditionally behave.

There is, to be sure, an abundance of literature on contemporary institutions, but most of it is concerned with "fine tuning" within the limits of conventional language and wisdom. The purpose of this chapter is not to address questions of fine tuning, but rather to question and examine the conventional wisdom and language of contemporary institutional life and to suggest alternative approaches for understanding and dealing with inadequate performance—approaches that will originate with trustees.

Conceptual Flaw

A basic conceptual flaw in the conventional wisdom of institutional structures is the inadequacy—or even absence—of provision for trustees to be a functioning part of the institution's leadership. The role of administrators, as it is commonly established, does not provide for adequate trustee functions. Trustees, for their part, have not seen fit to question the assumptions that administrators make and to assert the affirmative and, in the long run, determining role for themselves that is required both by their legal obligations and by the socio-ethical burden of public trust they carry.

Administrators have been with us for several millennia, ever since the first person undertook to mobilize and direct the energies of other people toward a defined goal. Consequently, administration was seen as a wholly sufficient process long before there were trustees. The original administrators may have been the arm of despotic power, with crude sanctions at their disposal. Later they were circumscribed somewhat by law and custom, whether they were agents of government or of a private employer. Yet much of the notion (established long ago) of absoluteness and self-sufficiency of administrators survives today in the accepted concepts of organization. The pyramidal structure with a single chief at the top (whose adequacy was challenged in the last chapter) is still the conventional model. Today in some large institutions we see encouraging evidence that the assumptions which support the conventional model are no longer accepted as immutable. Yet, in the face of historical precedent and practice, it is small wonder that administrators have not accepted trustees as an important influence, and that trustees have not seen fit to establish their appropriate roles.

The trustee, who first emerged as the individual entrusted with other people's affairs, later became a member of a governing board, usually of a corporation. A society dominated by large corporations with governing boards, both for profit and not for profit, is a historical development that belongs almost entirely to this century. Too much of the public concern for the quality of society is still devoted to caring directly for individuals and not enough attention goes to caring for institutions and the way they are structured. Structural flaws can cause harm to individuals; conversely, conceptually sound and ably administered institutions can build people and enrich society. All too often we seem to disregard this important influence that institutions can have on people.

Unfortunately, government is expected to provide most of the attention that would enlarge the good and reduce the harm in institutional structures. But government has accepted competition in the for-profit realm as the prime regulator and builder when, in fact, it may also be the great destroyer of people and the creator of abuses. Churches, hospitals, universities—even foundations—are also competitive. Trustees, for the most part, do little more than give legal cover to the process. Except in the face of a threatened collapse of the institution, trustees rarely act in the affirmative way that their legal responsibility and the expectations of those served by the institution (and the public interest) suggest that they should. Individual trustees often serve their institutions in useful ways, but for the most part today it is a service that might be rendered as well or better by outside consultants or by volunteers who are not trustees.

Definitions

Much of the tangled semantics that shroud the role of trustees may be cleared up by examining for a moment the meaning of the very word *manage*, which has been appropriated by administrators as the classic label for what they do. I suggest that the etymology of the word comes closer to describing what trustees should do (from the Latin *manus*, "hand," meaning the hand on the reins that guides the horse). In most instances the laws of incorporation clearly establish the claim of trustees to this function by specifying that the institution "shall be managed" by a board of trustees or directors, usually not fewer than three. Typical corporation law does not provide for administrators at all, only for trustees or directors. Throughout this chapter I take the cue from this definition—that the role of trustees is to stand outside the active program of the institution and to *manage*. What they delegate to the inside operating executives is *administration*. With this combination of concept and language (and the two are inextricably related), the title chief executive officer and the single-chief concept it conveys should disappear as an anachronism.

Based on this thinking, then, let us elaborate on the definitions of trusteeship, management, administration, and leadership.

1. *Trusteeship* is the holding of a charter of public trust *for* an institution. As the term is understood here, it represents a function carried out through membership on the governing board of an incorporated institution and is defined by law. Trustees (or directors) are legally and ultimately responsible for the institution and everything that goes on in it. Trustees are not officers of administration—not in the institution where they are trustees. Trustees are members and representatives of the general public, whose trust they hold. They may be professionals and administrators in another—even in a similar—institution, but as trustees they make *trustee judgments*, not administrative or professional judgments.

2. *Management.* The by-laws of the institution usually specify the actions that trustees themselves must take and those they may delegate to administrative officers. Above and beyond these specific actions, the major trustee functions in the management of the institution are:

a. *To set the goals (including long-range plans), to define the obligations and the general premises—or the concept—of the institution, and to approve plans for reaching goals.* All of the parties at interest should be consulted, and administrative and professional staffs should be listened to most carefully. However, the established goals are the trustees' own goals. Ideas may come from any source, but goals are trustee formulated, not just trustee approved or trustee affirmed.

b. *To appoint the top administrative officers, to design the top administrative structure, to design and assign the duties of individuals in that group, and to act so as to motivate administrators and professionals.* Trustees do not "rubber stamp" administrative recommendations on these matters.

c. *To assess, at appropriate times, the performance of the institution,* its major parts, and the work of its top executives in the pursuit of the established goals.

d. *To take appropriate action* based on what is found in the above assessment.

To carry out these functions, the trustees of any institution need leadership by an able and dedicated chair who will invest the time and acquire the skills needed to assure a fully functioning trustee group. This may be a full-time job in a large institution, and some of the other trustees may invest substantial time—much more than attendance at an occasional meeting. Further, some trustee boards will need support from a staff of their own, including full-time or part-time consultants.

The above constitutes a bare model of the *management* of the institution.

3. Administration is a function designed by trustees but carried out by full-time officers (appointed by trustees) who are not trustees. Administration includes all of the overseeing and directing (decision-making) functions not specifically reserved for trustees. (Customarily in business the word *manage* is used in place of *administer*. However, in this chapter I will reserve *manage* for the trustee role, and internal direction of all institutions will be called *administration*.)

The usual administrative functions include the following:

a. *Planning*—both strategic and tactical—to accomplish goals.

b. *Organizing* the total effort (except the executive office, which is designed by the trustees—with the advice, of course, of administrators).

c. *Controlling*—assembling and analyzing data and directing operations.

d. *Supporting* the above by functional staffs (in a business, for instance) in research and development, law, public relations, personnel, finance, marketing, production or program, and so on, depending on the nature of the institution.

Administrators are responsible for all actions necessary to reach the goals set by trustees.

4. *Leadership*—going out ahead to show the way—is available to everyone in the institution who has the competence, values, and temperament for it, from the chair to the least skilled individual. Leadership is a more critical requirement for the chair and for the top executive officers. However, if their leadership should not be adequate, and if the institution is faltering for want of leadership, then it is important that whoever is able to assert leadership should do so. Trustees and administrators are empowered to lead, but if they fail to lead, or if they falter, then the system should be open enough so that they can be challenged (and guided) by anyone who can help to show a better way. The continued threat of challenge to their leadership will strengthen both trustees and administrators.

To recapitulate the model envisioned here, then, *trustees* as a body are legally in charge, and they *manage* the institution. *Administrators operate* the institution under goals and general policies set by trustees and from an executive office designed by trustees. Anyone can lead, and there is no single chief executive officer. There is a problem of getting used to the idea of no single chief, but the passage of time will allay that, especially after the now younger generation takes over.

Trustees lead the administrators. Administrators lead the trustees and the staff. Also, sometimes, leadership comes from unexpected places and from people who theretofore were not suspected of having it.

Trustees lead but they do not administer.

Administrators both administer and lead.

Staffs both administer (because everyone makes some decisions, however small, about what should be done) and sometimes lead (because the structure is open enough for anyone to lead who can effectively assert leadership). Their primary function, however, is to perform the tasks of the institution.

Trustees are accountable to all parties at interest for the best possible performance of the institution in the service of the needs of all constituencies—including society at large. They are the holders of the charter of public trust for the institution.

I
THE TRUSTEE ROLE—
WHY IT IS NOT ADEQUATE NOW
AND WHAT IT NEEDS TO BE

Trustee Initiative—A Historical Precedent

One of the interesting fragments of business history of the period from 1895 to 1915 is how the certified audit of financial statements began. "Chartered" accountants emerged in England in the mid-nineteenth century and first came to this country to check on English investments here. The first law in the United States establishing certified accountancy was enacted in New York State in 1896. Promptly thereafter, as new major companies were launched out of reorganizations and mergers, especially those under the aegis of J. P. Morgan, the elder, they were the first companies to issue financial statements with a certified public accountant's attest (General Electric Company—1898, United States Steel Corporation—1903, American Telephone and Telegraph Company—1913). This procedure is so much a part of all financial reporting today that we have forgotten that it was greeted at its inception with as much apprehension and resistance as is the current suggestion that trustees have their own staffs to supply their needs for information and advice. I do not know that Morgan ordered the C.P.A. audit in his new companies. One can be certain, though, that it was not done without his approval. The C.P.A. audit was but one of the evidences of a new standard of quality, an effort to close the gap that separated mediocrity from excellence, that marked the emergence of these new companies at that time.

In taking these initiatives, Morgan may have been the first trustee in the modern sense. He met four tests that are valid today: (1) he had considerable power over the institution, (2) he was not part of the administration—he had some detachment, (3) he used some of his power to influence moves toward excellence, and (4) he had the good sense to know that the power of neither money nor ideas would change things without exceptional people to lead these new institutions. Furthermore, he was astute in knowing and choosing great institution builders—and he gave them solid support. In my judgment these three companies still bear the mark of that early influence, and they stand in sharp contrast to the get-rich-quick conglomerates of our times that have been put together mostly on the initiative of administrators. The later companies seem not to have the quality of trustee over-sight that was in evidence seventy-five years ago.

Administrators sometimes set high standards of their own and achieve an unusual result with part or all of an institution. But this often is short lived because administrators, by the nature of their predominantly operating responsibilities, cannot have the perspective on the institution that trustees can have. In our times, among discerning people, trustees stand as the public symbol of trust (or lack of it, depending on how they perform) and are completely responsible in the eyes of the law. It is possible that a new ethical imperative concerning institutional performance might find its mark with greater force if addressed to trustees than if it were addressed to administrators, or if, as is usually the case, it were simply addressed to the institution.

Limitations of the Conventional Trustee Role

The principal limitation of the conventional trustee role, as it is practiced today, is the common assumption by trustees that internal officers and staffs, left largely on their own and structured as they usually are, will see to it that the institution performs as it should, that is, close to what is reasonable and possible with its resources. The arguments against this assumption are presented in the last chapter in the section "Organization: Some Flaws in the Concept of the Single Chief," a concept that seems likely to continue in force as long as trustees remain in their conventional nominal roles.

A second limitation grows out of an aspect of human nature. Few of us, regardless of how able, have the ability to perform consistently at a high level of excellence, to set the goals for our own performance, and to judge our own performance objectively. It is not reasonable to expect an internal operating team to do all of these things well, simultaneously.

A third limitation is that nominal trustees customarily accept, somewhat uncritically, data supplied by internal officers and take no steps to equip themselves to be critical. They restrict themselves to affirming goals that are set by administrators and staffs, and, with the exception of the certified audit, trustees largely confine themselves to reviewing performance through administrators' reports on their own work, with little independent data available to them except what they sense intuitively or gather from the "grapevine." When there are adverse conditions, sometimes trustees are the last to know—and they should be among the first. Consequently, they may rest comfortably with the illusion that the administration of the institution is functioning much better than may actually be the case. Since there is no dependable information source responsible directly to them, most trustee bodies have no adequate way of examining performance. Furthermore, if trustees should decide to set goals, rather than simply to affirm or reject those brought to them by internal officers, they usually do not have the staff help they would require to perform that service.

Finally, with trustees in their conventional nominal role, internal constituencies have too much to say about who their leaders will be. When new ones are to be chosen, they want leaders with whom they will be comfortable—and those can be mediocre. They may need leaders who will disturb them, stretch them, goad them if necessary, but their influence is not likely to support the choice of that kind of person. Even great administrative builders of an institution who retire with enough power and prestige to choose their successor too often do not select someone who is as strong. In fact, an adequate successor may not have been groomed at all. Only trustees can have the detachment and the interest necessary for grooming and choosing strong executive leadership. However, in their conventional role they rarely try, and they would not carry much influence if they did try, because they do not know enough.

These are substantial limitations. They are deeply entrenched and are not likely to be set aside until at least the following conditions are met: (1) the inadequacy of the usual trustee is established with sufficient force that trustees as individual persons with their own sense of obligation must heed it; (2) there is a much fuller understanding by trustees of the issues of power and ambiguity in institutional operations; and (3) a new trustee role is clearly delineated, with the probable result that a person with another occupation may not be able to handle more than one or two trusteeships.

The first of these conditions is dealt with in the ensuing section, while the second and third will be handled in subsequent sections.

Trustees Commonly Do Not Function in a Way That Builds Trust

Nominal trustees, as they now commonly function, serve two major purposes: they satisfy the legal requirement, and they provide the cover of legitimacy. If the law did not require them, we would invent them for the second purpose, which is most of the justification that administrators and staffs find for them now. Otherwise, why would so many governing boards have only a token black, a token woman, a token public member?

To be sure, governing boards take those formal actions that their by-laws require. In an emergency they may step in and give direction, and they serve as a useful checking source for internal officers. Some trustees with special talents (such as finance, law, or organization) may give free counsel, especially to nonprofit institutions. These services, however, compromise the objectivity that trustees need. All institutions should pay for the consulting services they require, or if they cannot afford it, they should get it from volunteers who are not trustees.

If one accepts the position that, as trustees now commonly function, they satisfy legal requirements and give the cover of legitimacy but little more, is not this arrangement *neglect* by trustees, administrators, and staffs in which all accept a more limited sense of obligation? Who is being deceived? At whose expense is this carried on? One is inclined to answer, "*All* of those who are served by, or depend on, the institution," which, if it is a major one, can be a large number of people. They could be better served. Perhaps, though, the greater cost is the subtle (and in some cases not so subtle) compromise in the integrity of trustees, administrators, and staffs.

These are harsh words: neglect, compromised integrity. Yet if one speaks of these matters in less pejorative terms, one gets an answer like, "This is a respectable, comfortable, time-honored arrangement. Please do not rock the boat." The matter would rest there were it not for a growing disquiet about the arrangement—a small but nonetheless significant public recognition that trustees and directors of major institutions are largely honorary and ineffective. In other words, they are not seen as trustworthy. The mere presence of trustees, in the absence of the performance that their place and title imply, does not generate trust—enough trust to give our society the stability it needs. In fact, once trustees are clearly and publicly identified as being largely fictitious, their presence may breed more distrust than if there were no trustees at all. And they fuel the cry for more solutions by government.

These assertions may be seen in better perspective within the context of the ensuing discussion of power and ambiguity in institutional life.

II
THE ISSUES OF POWER AND
AMBIGUITY IN INSTITUTIONAL LIFE

Power and Authority—The Central Issue of Trust

Trustees, administrators, staffs, and various outside constituencies all have power. Any one of them may persuade—by articulation or example or both. Having knowledge gives them power. Being persuasive gives them power. Setting a conspicuous example gives them power. They may also overtly compel, if they have authorized sanctions at their disposal, or they may covertly manipulate. All of them also have power because they have unauthorized sanctions available in the form of options to give or to withhold effort, support, or money in ways that give them some coercive power over the others. The power structure of any large institution is a complex network of forces, both seen and unseen. The understanding of its intricacies and close oversight to prevent abuses is a prime trustee obligation.

Trustees have a kind of power that administrators and staffs do not have. They have the legal power to manage everything in the institution; they have all the legal power there is. They may delegate some of it, but they can also take it back. *They cannot give any of it away, irretrievably, and still be trustees.*

Power and its use is one of the central concerns of trustees. The essential definition of the trustee role is that trustees, as a body, hold all of the ultimate (legal) authority. However they do not use power operationally; that is, they do not administer. They use their legal power to secure information and to monitor and to control the operational use of power. This is the central issue of trusteeship: trustees hold ultimate power but they do not use it operationally. Yet they are responsible for its use.

Power and *authority* have many meanings. In this discussion power will mean both "persuasion," where the response is truly voluntary, and "coercion," either overt compulsion or covert manipulation. *Authority* will be taken to mean the sanctions that legitimize the use of power. The history of usage of the words *power* and *authority* from the earliest records in biblical times suggests that the many meanings they represent have long been a preoccupation of thoughtful people. It is an intense preoccupation today.

Trustees are known to have the authority to control the use of power within the institution. However, they are also known to exercise that authority only in the event of gross and flagrant abuse of power. Until recently, there has been little questioning of the resulting nominal or honorary status of trustees and the mediocre institutional performance that results from it. There has not been much concern that the power within the institution be used for socially constructive ends—both within the institution and in its impact on society at large.

Lord Acton's maxim, which I accept, asserts: "Power tends to corrupt and absolute power corrupts absolutely." However, trustees of our major institutions seem not to take this very seriously, or else they would not delegate the use of power as freely and with as little monitoring of its use as is now common. Trustees have the obligation to oversee the use of power in order to check its corrupting influence on those to whom it is entrusted, and to assure that those affected by its use are positively helped and are not harmed. This is a large order. Few trustee bodies are prepared to act on it. The following way of thinking is suggested to guide trustees as they grapple with the obligation.

The role of trustees is to hold what approximates absolute power over the institution, using it operationally only in rare emergencies— ideally never. Trustees delegate the operational use of power to administrators and staffs, but with accountability for its use that is at least as strict as now obtains with the use of property and money. Furthermore, trustees will insist that the outcome be that people in, and affected by, the institution will grow healthier, wiser, freer, more autonomous, and more likely to become servants of society. The only real justification for institutions, beyond a certain efficiency (which, of course, does serve), is that people in them grow to greater stature than if they stood alone. It follows then that people working in institutions will be more productive than they would be as unrelated individuals. The whole is greater than the sum of its parts.

In essence, this view of the use of power holds that no one, *absolutely no one*, is to be entrusted with the operational use of power without the close oversight of fully functioning trustees.

Ambiguity in the Institution—
A Challenge to Trustee Understanding

The trustees' concern for the use of power is complicated by the condition that life within the institution is not wholly rational (no more than anywhere else). If life within a large institution were wholly rational, a computer could probably be designed to administer it better than people. However, it is not wholly rational (fortunately, for us humans who need the ambiguity to test our humanity and our adaptability), and it presents three kinds of challenges that can bring virtual paralysis to the administration if there is none of the effective intervention that trustees are best positioned to make.

First, there is *the operational necessity to be both dogmatic and open to change.* No individual, certainly no institution, can operate for a day without a good deal of dogma. There is too much to decide, too great a variety of situations to be faced, for anyone to consider each situation as if nothing like it had ever appeared before. When people operate under pressure, as is common these days, they can deal with what they confront only by acting within some consistent pattern. One would hope that they will see enough of the nuances of each situation to make suitable adaptations.

Most institutions that survive over a period of time do so because they have a survival pattern, a dogma that gives a general direction of rightness. Those who administer and staff the institution become highly competent in operating within that pattern. Yet unless they are periodically challenged on the adequacy of that pattern, eventually they lose survival ability. Long before that happens, they probably cease to function at their best.

Occasionally an inside administrator will detect, in time, the need for a new pattern and effect a change in course. This, however, is a chance happening; the structure does not favor it. Sometimes even when the key administrators, such as the president of a university, detect the need for a new pattern, they are unable to move the institution. Just keeping it operating on the old pattern presses their leadership to the limit. In such a case the risk of change looms as a greater threat than the risk of failure, even though the old pattern is clearly destined for failure. Administrators, in the nature of things, are preoccupied with the immediate pressing issues of today, when the very real changes in preparation for the future must be made, if they are to be made prudently. The critical signals are those that tell one that action should be taken today in order to forestall impending trouble tomorrow. These are the signals calling for change *now* that the busy administrator may miss.

Trustees have a better chance than the administrator to be open to change. In fact, this is their role—to maintain openness to change, which their relative immunity from day-to-day operational pressures makes possible. Yet administrator and trustee are not sharply differentiated roles. In fact, they are a close mesh, in which the administrator should be mostly dogma and a little bit open to change, and the trustee should be a little bit dogma and mostly open to change. The two roles, closely linked and working in harmony, should take care of both today and tomorrow.

A second ambiguity is *the disability that goes with competence.* Ordinarily we think of competence as a linear "good"—out to infinity. Not so! A critical disability that goes with expanding competence is the inability (or unwillingness) to examine the assumptions by which one operates. In order to achieve great competence, individuals (or institutions) must put their heads down, cut out the peripheral vision that might keep the assumptions always in view, and run! Very few people, as individuals or as parts of the operating mechanism of large institutions, can acquire a high level of specialized competence *and* keep a perspective on what is going on that tells them how good that competence is—in social value or in an ultimate competitive sense.

This disability that goes with competence may seem an abstract concept until one deals with an institution in some crisis, large or small, that requires a shift of goals if it is to continue to prosper and to serve. The task of determining new goals is then clearly seen as an appropriate function of trustees, because only they are sufficiently inside to know and yet far enough outside, free enough from operating involvement, to examine dispassionately the assumptions that now guide those who have high operating competence. Trustees can then help decide which assumptions are still valid and which should be modified or abandoned, and what new ones should be postulated.

Assumptions that guide operating competence are the major stuff of which goals are made, and trustees are best positioned to question, to originate, or to affirm these assumptions. They are not in a very good position to revise old goals or to set new ones unless they have a full understanding of the problem of acting on the present goals.

A third ambiguity is the need for a healthy *tension between belief and criticism* as part of the dynamism that makes a high performing institution. Operating officers and staffs need to be mostly *believing*. Trustees need to be mostly *critical.*

Administrators and staffs need to be mostly believing because the morale of those who do the work of the institution needs to be sustained, and part of the trust of all constituencies rests on a communicated belief in the rightness of what is being done.

Trustees need to be mostly critical because it is the scrutiny of a critical attitude that keeps administrators and staffs on a true course. Part of the basis for trust by all constituencies is an awareness that a critical watch is being kept. It is a sounder arrangement for the critical watch to be kept by those in whom ultimate power is vested, those who control the use of power by requiring a strict accountability for its use.

A critical watch, however, requires more than just a critical frame of mind. It requires that trustees have a level of information and advice sufficient to make their criticism penetrating and meaningful. Few trustees and directors, as their roles are now structured, can be critical in other than a remote consulting sense, and they usually have that only in a narrow field of specialized competence that they bring from another situation. Also, their advice often bears the burden of unexamined assumptions because it is a judgment rooted in specialized competence rather than in the kind of explicitly developed trustee information that is relatively free from the disabilities of competence. Such judgment from competence that a trustee may bring from another situation is useful as a sort of secondary check. However, what is needed as a trustee's critical judgment cannot be built on this source alone, because doing so tends to lock all institutions into a common set of assumptions that may not be adequate for any one of them. This seems inevitable when trustee bodies are selected almost entirely for their competence in some other situation. They cannot be sufficiently critical, and they believe too much in the standard ways of doing things.

Administrators are mostly believing and a little bit critical, while trustees are mostly critical and a little bit believing. There is a subtle overlap between the two roles, yet they are more different than they are alike. The need for trustees to be preponderantly critical requires that they be in a complementary but different role. The next several sections describe such a role.

III
BIGNESS—A NOTE ON THE IMPLICATIONS OF SIZE

The choice of large institutions as the focus of this chapter was made because this has been my predominant experience. By working with a few small institutions I have learned that "small" and "large" are not different-sized copies of the same thing. They are qualitatively different. Those who are familiar with small institutions and who are concerned with the quality of their performance should address this as a separate problem.

Ours is a society that is dominated by large institutions, and some of the criticism of our institutions has been addressed to bigness, as such, as a cause of their failure to serve better and, in some instances, of their positive harm. This may be because a single institution that is big and bad is more of a social problem than if it were small and bad. Bigness concentrates a conspicuous amount of power in a few hands. If that power is not used affirmatively to serve society well, or worse still, if it is negatively used to hurt, there is a tendency to blame bigness as the cause. One the other hand, if the power is dispersed through many small institutions, the service may be as poor and the hurt may be as great or greater, but there is no convenient single institution or a small cluster of them, to blame.

In a complicated, hard-to-manage society such as ours, when power is misused in large institutions to such a degree that government must respond to it, an action like "break up the big ones into small ones and insist on competition" is apt to be the remedy. If trustees and directors of these large institutions maintain their traditional nominal or honorary roles, there may be no feasible alternative to the use of this crude sanction that, in the end, may create more problems than it solves, because it does not have the effect of building quality. It reduces concentrations of power, but it does not assure that many holders of dispersed power will do any better.

The coercive power of government is mostly useful to restrain. The building of voluntary institutions as instruments of quality comes more from the incremental actions of individuals as they serve and lead, and as they gather those complementary talents that give completeness to leadership of an institution. While the antitrust laws are addressed to business institutions, the problem and the opportunity of bigness is as great in the nonprofit field. However, the misuses of power in the latter have not as yet drawn much restraint from government—except in the case of foundations.

Foundations are an interesting illustration of the problem of bigness. They are more vulnerable to restraint by government because they are usually secondary institutions that do not directly serve a need. (They mostly give money to other nonprofit agencies that do serve a need.) Then, some legislators tend to regard foundations as disbursers of government money because, with much of foundation assets, if the money had not been put into a foundation treasury, it would have been paid in taxes. Also, because they do not render a direct service, foundations do not have a constituency—they have few friends. This the foundations discovered when hearings were being held leading to the tax reform act of 1969.

Before the passage of the 1969 law, there had been long-suspected abuses of the foundation instrument—self-dealing and misappropriation by smaller foundations—but it was a few grants by large foundations in the 1960s that members of the Congress judged to be imprudent that brought the new, and very restrictive, foundation law. Judging by the congressional hearings, the law was at least in part an attack on the power of bigness as such. The new law does correct some abuses, but it is a crude and cumbersome law that injects a burdensome bureaucracy into foundation administration that inhibits the creative use of foundation funds—and one of the major criticisms made of foundations is that they tend to be uncreative.

The point of this reference is that there was a long period of warning that some members of Congress were concerned about the misuse of the foundation instrument. These warnings went directly to foundation trustees, through questionnaires addressed to them personally from congressional committees. There was ample opportunity for the trustees of large foundations, which were mostly free of the abuses complained of, to study the problem, to draft a workable law, to take it to the Congress, and to urge its passage. In their own self-interest they would have gotten a law that was easier to live with, and they would have served the country by getting the abuses corrected sooner, and perhaps better, than the law ultimately passed as a result of initiative generated almost wholly within Congress. I was a foundation trustee during some of the pre-1969 years and received these questionnaires. I was not aware that these were my alerting signals to respond creatively as a trustee. Needless to say, there was no suggestion anywhere that this was my role.

This example illustrates one of the recent conspicuous failures of trustees of large institutions, the failure to make an asset out of bigness. *In every field*, if trustees and directors of all large institutions were to accept the full implications of their roles, if they organized themselves to serve their institutions so as to assure performance that is much closer to what is reasonable and possible with their available resources, human and material, and if they had staff support so that they would know what to do—*in every field*, the major voluntary institutions could foresee the need for governmental action, could take the initiative and research the problems, could draft the legislation and the rules, and could urge their adoption by government at all levels. The country would be better governed, and the institutions themselves would be stronger and would serve better.

This is a role for trustees and directors of major institutions. It is not reasonable to expect it from the governing boards of small institutions. Nor should it be expected of administrators of any institution, because they have a preoccupation with current operating details that makes it unlikely that they will take this long view of the part the institution should play in the total social structure. It is one of the opportunities of bigness that is best responded to by trustees. Everything that is big is vulnerable because it is conspicuous and because it is easier to regulate. Yet big institutions have the opportunity to assemble and to use, in a team relationship, exceptional specialized talents that are not as available to small institutions. Important in these talents is the foresight to determine when the regulating power of government should be sought and to become the persuasive promulgator of effective regulations. This, it seems to me, calls for a new trustee role.

IV
A NEW TRUSTEE ROLE—
HOW TO DO IT BETTER

The Problem of Getting It Done

This chapter was not written to help trustees do just a little better with their roles as now defined. The aim here is a substantially new institution, one that serves society much better, far ahead of anything that now exists or that is now dreamed of as possible.

Perhaps some competent, responsible people will say that, human nature being what it is, the recommendations here are too idealistic and therefore impossible. They should be reminded that we got where we are by doing the impossible, and future progress in the quality of our major institutions, which is both inevitable and imperative, will be by the same route!

Three major obstacles stand in the way of taking experimental steps to explore the course recommended here. First, most of the efforts to meet the rising social expectations are *largely coercive*, either through governmental edict, the fostering of countervailing forces, or pressure tactics.

Then, second, we are so wedded to the belief in one-person leadership, even in very large institutions, that many constituencies, including trustees, believe that only with luck in finding a "chief" with miraculous powers will the institution perform better.

A third obstacle grows out of the common assumptions about how things get done in large institutions. Under these assumptions, the administrators and staffs assume the total burden and trustees are kept in a subservient role, partly because it is the custom (and only a rare hard-nosed and determined trustee will challenge the custom), and partly because trustees do not know enough or devote enough time to do differently. As matters now stand, without some carefully taken steps that are guided by a new concept of how a large institution might be better governed, the inside professionals are not likely to welcome a more affirmative trustee role or the intrusion of a new information source that is responsible directly to trustees and that penetrates the closely held data banks inside the institution.

These are substantial obstacles. Obstacles, however, are problems, and problems are things to be solved. The three mentioned are the kind of *ultimate* problems that only trustees have the ultimate power to solve.

The Trustee Role—Initiating Rather Than Reacting

The conventional trustee role may be described as a *reacting* role. In such a reacting role, trustees usually do not initiate or shape the character of the institution, nor do they see it as their role to examine the traditional administrative wisdom. If they are conscientious, and most of them are, they will do the following: try to install competent operating officers, and support and encourage them; maintain some gross controls by requiring trustee approval on certain major actions; check such data as they have for evidences of serious malfeasance; and affirm, deny, or modify policy questions that are submitted to them. This may be labeled fairly a *reacting* role. It is all right as far as it goes, but it no longer goes far enough.

What would be required to put the trustees in an *affirmative* role, so that, if they are capable and dedicated, by their action they can help an institution to function at its optimum?

The answer to this question is that trustees need a new view of people at their best in institutional roles. That view can be simply stated: *No person is complete; no one is to be entrusted with all. Completeness is to be found only in the complementary talents of several who relate as equals.* This flouts one of the time-honored assumptions—almost an axiom—of administrative lore: "You cannot manage by committee! Delegation of authority must be made to an individual." What do we do about that?

We should take the same attitude toward this well-established axiom that modern mathematicians take toward Euclid's assumptions, which stood unchallenged for two thousand years and eventually got in the way of the progress of mathematical thinking.

When they were identified as being in the way, some of Euclid's assumptions were reversed in order to produce mathematical thinking that could do things that were impossible under Euclid's assumptions. We are at a similar point regarding administration. We must reverse the assumption that operating delegations can be made only to individuals. We must reverse it because that assumption is standing in the way of the next big move from mediocre performance toward a much higher level that is reasonable and possible with available resources.

The new assumption is that delegation of authority from trustees to operating executives is best made to a team of several persons whose exceptional talents are complementary and who relate to one another as equals, under the leadership of a *primus inter pares* (as discussed in the last chapter). There is a caution, however. It is also assumed that this is not a workable arrangement unless the trustees fully accept and operate under a definition of their roles as stated earlier in this chapter. If trustees want to remain in their present nominal or honorary roles, then the advice here is to stay with the concept of the single chief and to accept the prevailing mediocre performance that goes with that arrangement. However, if trustees want the institution to break out of its mediocre performance and to sustain a new high level, then the view of people as working best in teams with complementary talents is suggested. If trustees can accept that premise, then they should proceed to design a new role for themselves and be prepared to invest the time required, the principal dimensions of which are as follows:

Set the Goals: What business are we in and what are we trying to accomplish in it? Profit-making business firms have some trouble with this question. Other institutions, such as churches, universities, philanthropies, and social agencies, have a great deal of trouble with it. The first thing an institution needs to do in order to start on a conspicuously higher course is to state clearly where it wants to go, whom it wants to serve, and how it expects those served directly, as well as society at large, to benefit from the service. Unless these are clearly understood, an institution cannot approach its optimum performance. Yet the internal administrators, left to themselves, usually hesitate to state goals so precisely.

Performance Review. Since the administration is involved in the performance of the institution, part of the data the trustees use for their overseeing role should come from a source that is independent of administration. In a later section the trustees' need for their own information source will be discussed in more detail.

Executive Growth and Selection. Every large institution that is to be optimal in its performance should produce leadership out of its own ranks. If it is to be exceptional, it should produce more leadership than it needs and thus export leadership to other institutions. It should import some leaders and other trained persons in order to avoid becoming inbred and to keep the organization stimulated, not because it does not produce enough of its own. Growing people, releasing people for important work elsewhere, and bringing able people from other experiences should be a constant concern for any institution that wants to function at its optimum. However, some otherwise able administrators become so preoccupied with day-to-day performance that they sometimes neglect this vital organization-building work, which needs constant attention. In the long run this neglect can be a fatal flaw, regardless of short-run performance. Therefore, close overseeing of executive growth and selection is suggested as an explicit function for trustees.

Organization of the Top Executive Office. As noted in the last chapter, the organization of the top administrative office and the assignment of functions is not something that the members of that office can do well. They can do it for other parts of the institution, but not for themselves. They cannot be faulted as persons for this. Of course, left to themselves, they work it out somehow, but optimal institutional performance does not result. Because they are not administrators and therefore do not have this problem, trustees are in a position to have the objectivity and the perspective on the institution to work this out.

A New Concept of Trust. Everyone in the institution has a share in building trust. The administrators have the major responsibility for institutional performance that merits trust. However, if there is *not* enough trust (and the premise stated at the beginning of this chapter is that in most institutions today there is not enough trust) and if the level of trust has been low enough long enough, then it must be assumed that internal administrators, as institutions are now structured, will not deliver an adequate amount of it. It is then the obligation of trustees to fulfill what their title implies and become initiating builders of trust. They should see this as their role. They will not supersede administration in doing this. Rather, they will become strengtheners of administrators in *their* trust-building roles.

Trustee acceptance of this view of their role will result in reconstructing trustee bodies substantially, and, if the transformation is successful, it will lead to a whole new era of institutional performance along with the enrichment of the career experience of those who administer and staff our major institutions. As a result, trusteeship will become a much more rewarding experience.

The Trustee Chair

If trustees are to function well within this much broader definition of their role, they need a rather unusual person as their chair. This new chair will be just as different from the present ones as the affirming trustee is from the reacting type that is being replaced.

First and foremost, trustee chairs will *not* be officers of administration. In fact, their best career route may not be through administration at all. In large institutions, chairs will probably be full-time salaried people. They will be the professional leaders of trustees who may be either full-time or part-time. In either case, trustees would be paid adequately for what they do—enough to compensate them for carrying the exacting obligations as defined above.

Chairs, as leaders of the trustees, should be selected by their colleagues for their dedication to optimal performance of the

institution and for their ability to make the trustee role an exciting, creative, and very responsible endeavor, far more rewarding
to the able trustee than the prevailing reactive role. The chair,
thus concerned, will be *primus inter pares*, not chief. In such a
role, chairs will be first among equals and responsible to their
peers, the trustees.

The first step for any trustee of a major institution who feels
the obligation to move the institution much closer to its potential
for service to society is to get a chair who has the ability and the
determination to *lead* it there and who will devote a major portion of the available time, if not full time, to that mission.

We cannot have better institutions unless we have better
leadership in chairs. This chapter is written in full confidence
that an ample supply of able and experienced people exists who
can be trained as both chairs and administrators, as the roles are
defined here. Potentially, there may be many more able people
than seem to be available for these two roles, as they now exist,
because the two proposed roles make a better distribution of the
burdens of leadership and provide for a healthier relationship.

However, it cannot be assumed that everyone who is potentially capable of being an effective chair knows how or will learn
from experience alone. Therefore there needs to be a Chairing
Institute, a place where the art of chairing is researched and taught.
Every new chair should go to the institute for introductory training and should return periodically to keep the skills of chairing in
good order and to learn more as knowledge of the art progresses.

The New Trustee Is Not a Super-Administrator

The roles of trustees (who manage) and of operating executives (who administer) were defined at the beginning of this
chapter as separate and distinct. Definitions, however, do not settle doubts, and one of the doubts about the new trustee role is
expressed in the question: How can the trustee perform this
function without encroaching on what administrators have to do
to lead the institution to the expected achievement?

The best answer to this question is that the trustee chair is professionally trained as a chair, just as the administrator is trained as an administrator. Chairs are not simply former administrators who have been moved to the position of chair without examination of their qualifications for it and without specific training in how the role is best performed. The requirements made of both trustees and administrators will be more exacting, as one would expect, if the performance of the institution is to rise.

Some basic principles will need to be explicitly accepted, such as that *no one, absolutely no one, is to be entrusted with the operational use of power without the close oversight of fully functioning trustees.* If old-style administrators do not accept this, then clearly they will feel encroached upon. There will be a transition period. Some able administrators who cannot make such an adjustment but who are too valuable to lose may continue to operate in the old style. General Eisenhower faced this problem when he had to deal with General Patton after the latter had slapped and cursed a battle-fatigued soldier in a field hospital. It is implied in the report of the handling of this incident that General Eisenhower did not think that someone who did what General Patton had done should be commanding troops, but he just did not have another general who could cope as well with the major actions that lay immediately ahead. Therefore he left Patton in command.

In closing this reference we should note that there are some able people who ought not to be trustees or administrators of major institutions either under the existing arrangement or under the one proposed here. One of the important advantages of the proposed new structure of relations is that it will more quickly and sharply expose those who should not be in institutional leadership at all—either as trustees or as administrators.

V
INFORMATION: THE KEY TO RESTRUCTURING
THE TRUSTEE ROLE

As modern institutions have evolved (and they are very recent), one of the possible reasons that trustees have failed to emerge in their appropriate roles is that they have not been properly informed. Because they are not (and should not be) insiders, as administrators and staffs are, and because their role is different and they may invest only limited time, they cannot be informed as insiders are. They cannot receive all of the formal communications that administrators use, they do not participate in operating decisions, and they are not a part of the informal communication network. *And this is as it should be*, because objectivity and noninvolvement are parts of the strength of the trustee role.

Some of the information that trustees need to know is the same as what inside administrators value. For example, both should have the same basic, summarized financial information and the findings of the independent audit. But most of their information needs are different because their roles are different. Administrators are usually adequately informed for their roles; trustees usually are not.

What do trustees need to know? They need to know what is required to carry the four major functions of trustees as defined earlier: (1) set the goals and define the obligations, (2) appoint the top executive officers and design the top administrative structure, (3) assess the total performance of the institution, and (4) take appropriate action based upon what has been found in that assessment. In addition to these, there usually are certain areas specified in the by-laws for trustee action.

How is the content of this trustee knowledge to be determined? Who will secure it? And how is it best presented and utilized?

The content will be what trustees need to know in order to act, in the first instance, on matters with which they should be concerned. The recommendations of administrators and staffs usually will be a part of the information trustees will want to have. But trustees will need information in addition to what administrators and staffs give them so that they can make their own independent judgment, contrary to administrative advice if that is their considered judgment. The trustees may examine their information in meetings of the whole or in subcommittees. Trustees will decide the extent and nature of the information they require in each area where they will make the decision. It is important, however, that all information to trustees, whether directly from informed people from inside or outside the institution, or through presentations of studies and reports, be designed for the special needs of trustees; it should not be merely selections or abstracts from information prepared for the use of administrators and staffs.

Who will secure the information for trustees? One of the functions of the chair (who is *not* an administrator and, in a large institution, is either full-time or part-time) is to see that trustees are properly informed. Chairs, or staff persons responsible to them, will oversee the informing of trustees, including the design and gathering of the data. Some of this may come from inside the institution, from the efforts of internal staff, and some may be from independent research firms or consultants who will be engaged by trustees and report directly to them. The direction of all of this will be by the chair or the trustee staff.

How shall trustee information be presented and utilized? By a minimum of written material and a maximum of audiovisual presentation to trustees as a group. The reason for this choice is that trustees are a deliberative body and information should be designed to give them what they need for the decisions they must make, to conserve their time, and to facilitate a group decision out of discussion.

In summary, what is wanted is a fresh analysis of trustee information needs and a design of presentations that are carefully tailored to facilitate the specific judgments and decisions that trustees will make.

Carefully and imaginatively designed trustee information will serve three ancillary purposes: (1) It will provide a constant influence to focus attention on clearly designated trustee functions and help prevent involvement with administrative matters. (2) It will provide a structure of knowledge about the function of trustees that will make possible explicit training for the trustee role. (3) It will help make service as a trustee a rewarding involvement for the kind of people who should be trustees, and it will justify a greater time investment than trustees normally make. Furthermore, it will facilitate recruiting the right people as trustees.

Providing information to trustees on the basis suggested here is both difficult and expensive, and it clearly signals a new *initiating* role for trustees as contrasted with the usual *reacting* role in which trustees are *nominal*. If the transition is to be made in a constructive way, with a minimum of loss of vital force and a maximum gain in institutional strength, all constituencies, particularly internal officers and staffs, will need to *want* trustees to perform so that *trustee judgments* will stand on a par with all other judgments by or about the institution. The following section deals with this question.

VI
TRUSTEE JUDGMENT

Although trustees may not have professional or administrative expertise in the particular institution, theirs is not a *lay* judgment. It is a unique thing, a *trustee judgment*, and it stands on a par in importance with any other judgment within the institution.

This is a difficult concept for inside administrators and professionals to accept. The medical staff of a hospital may ask: How can trustee judgment be equated with a medical staff judgment *in a hospital?* The answer is that both hospitals and the medical profession are in deep trouble because doctors have not admitted the parity of trustee judgment with their own (the crisis in malpractice insurance is a case in point). Until quite recently doctors were individual practitioners working alone in their offices and in the homes of their patients. When medical practice evolved to the point where it was deeply enmeshed in *institutions* (hospitals, clinics, research centers, insurance companies), the parity of trustee judgments should have been acknowledged—but it wasn't; hence the problem.

Universities and colleges where faculties have been equally reluctant to accept the parity of trustee judgment are rapidly heading for a different kind of crisis. Mark Hopkins on the end of his log probably did not need trustees. But institutionalized education *does* need them, and their judgments need to be respected.

How, the troubled professional may ask, could we be expected to accept a parity of trustee judgment *with the kind of trustees we have?* That would be folly! Granted. But, I would answer, you were unrealistic in assuming that your professional work could be institutionalized *without* a parity of trustee judgment. You should have insisted on effective trustees, and you ought to insist upon them now—for the good of your work and for your own self-protection. An institution, especially a large one, is not a safe arrangement for any service or for any involved person unless it has effective trustees who can contribute a quality of judgment that no administrative or professional group can generate wholly with its own resources.

What is trustee judgment? It is a meld of the following unique aspects of the role of trustee: (1) trustees have the perspective of detachment that no insider can have; (2) they have their own information source that equips them for their special functions; (3) trustees are free from the pressures and minutia of day-to-day operations so that they can take an overview as well as project the future; (4) trustees do not have a career stake in the institution— their motivation can be less self-centered; (5) effective trustees stand as symbols of trust; therefore they can provide a shelter of legitimacy in a way that deeply committed insiders cannot; (6) because trustees are not colleagues who may have contending interests, they can function creatively as a group on issues that internal constituencies may not be able to resolve; (7) trustees are better able to have a sense of history, past-present-future, and therefore are better able to hold the institution's vision and keep it steady, and they may better see the path to survival and long service; (8) trustees can keep the concept of ultimate purpose in sharp focus and hold it up as a guide at times when the insiders are hard pressed to stay afloat from day to day.

If trustees are well selected and well led by their chair, and if they devote enough time to exploit all of these unique aspects of their role, their judgments merit respect on a par with the best that the rest of the institution can produce.

Consider the following example of what I believe is a major trustee failure of our times.

When the historians of some future age try to sort out the artifacts of our present times, one of the questions they may ask is this: How could we have supported the vast aggregate of society-building institutions—churches, schools, foundations—and allowed them so studiously to avoid the one service that would have assured a great and long durable future for our particular civilization, that is, *preparing those of the young who are capable of it for responsible roles as servants?* I have been around enough among churches, schools, and foundations to be convinced that there is a lack of willingness to rise to the opportunity. Preparing the young for responsible roles as servants is neither expensive nor difficult to do, but it is not now the focus of much explicit effort. It is assumed to be one of those things that is implicit; it is just supposed to happen. And we have charmed ourselves into believing that it is being done. *It is not being done!*

We might make it easy for those future historians and write down a possible answer to their anticipated question and leave it where they will find it. The reason for this gross failure, I believe, is that this is one of those crucial issues on which a respected trustee judgment is absolutely required—and it has not been forthcoming.

Administrators and professionals, left almost wholly on their own without effective trustees (as most of them now are), may fail to take that one step on which sheer survival of the institution depends. They get hung up on a fantasy that it is taken care of. And only the vigilance of strong, effective trustees has

the chance to catch this fault when it happens and demand that
action be taken.

Trustee judgment is the last line of defense within the institution against what are sometimes colossal errors in judgment
and failure to set adequate goals, by the best professionals and
administrators. The failure explicitly to prepare future bearers of
responsible roles *as servants* is such an error by administrators
and staffs of churches, schools, and foundations in our times.
Trustees seem not to have noted this failure.

The trustee who has good trustee judgment, and who wants
to gain ground in building a better institution, will know that
three decisions need to be made about any action that, in the test
of time, turns out well: (1) there is a good idea; (2) good people
are committed to carrying it out; and (3) resources are placed at
their disposal.

A good trustee judgment, one that stands on a par with all
other judgments and is respected by all other constituents, is a
blend of good judgments on all three of these elements. An error
on any one of them will doom the action to failure. Only trustees
are in a position to make a good judgment and to set the policies
to guide others in making such judgments on *any one* of these elements. Trustees do not have all of the answers, but they can best
utilize what data there is in making some crucial judgments and
in establishing policies to guide the judgments of others.

VII
A PEDAGOGY OF TRUSTEESHIP

What trustees should be and do is not yet obvious in the
culture. Therefore trusteeship is a social role that needs to be
explicitly conceptualized by each trustee group. Further, conscientious trustees will accept (1) that it is not sufficient just to
understand their role, (2) that how they should carry that role
will not necessarily evolve out of experience, and (3) that the
trustee role needs to be consciously learned by each board. Also,

some means for assuring sustained high performance is important for trustees, just as it is for everybody else.

Trust begins with good motives. But competence, and a way of sustaining competence, needs to be added to good motives.

If trustees posit a role for themselves that will enable them to be influential in raising the performance of the total institution to the optimal (and I have tried to describe such a role in this chapter), they confront a difficult problem: how to carry that role *as a group*. It is one thing to carry a trustee role as an individual. It is quite another to function effectively as a part of a group process.

If very much of what is advocated in this chapter is accepted, then a trustee board will do well to search for a *coach* who will help them learn an appropriate process so that they will become an effective collegial group whose judgment deserves to be respected as superior wisdom in matters that trustees should consider and decide. Since no group will ever achieve this fully, the coaching process will be continuous.

Engaging a coach to help trustees to operate by a process that favors their optimal performance serves to acknowledge that a conscious learning process is accepted, that trustee performance will always fall short of perfection, but that the full obligation of trust calls for a constant striving for perfection.

Where does one find such coaches, and how do they do their work?

If the trustees acknowledge that they need and want a coach, they can find one. The Yellow Pages do not list such coaches, and they probably never will. Each trustee body has the opportunity to evolve its own coach. This is part of the creative challenge of being a trustee. And part of the excitement of being a trustee is interacting with a coach.

Trustees in search of a coach are advised not to seek among those who profess credentials in group process. This is not said to denigrate the expertise of such persons. It is simply that if the search begins among the "group process" people, the risk is too great that an uncongenial ideology will be imposed. Rather, I suggest that the search be made among those able people known to the trustees who would be accepted among them as a peer, but whose best contribution would be as a coach rather than as a trustee. Such a person's contribution might be greater, in the end, than that of any single trustee.

Trustees will accept strategic and tactical leadership from their chairman. They will accept conceptual leadership from their coach. They will expect from the coach a close monitoring of the *process* of their deliberations but abstention from the value weighing that precedes consensus.

The coach might best be selected, as I have said, from among those who are not established as specialists in group process. But when the role is understood, the coach might then learn what is useful to the new role from specialists in group process.

The primary aim of the coach is to facilitate consensus—achieving one mind. The effective trustee group is not merely one that hears all of the arguments and then votes. Rather, it reaches a consensus—a group judgment that will be accepted as superior wisdom. Without the acceptance of all constituencies that trustee judgment is superior wisdom, there is little leadership possible for trustees. Part of the acceptance of trustee judgment as superior wisdom rests upon a consistent group process that is carefully monitored by a coach.

There is very little sustained performance at the level of excellence—of any kind, anywhere—without continuous coaching. Since trustees have the obligation to monitor the performance of the institution, and since trustees are the court of last resort, trustees who want to do the best they can will provide for the monitoring of their own work. *And this is how they will learn.*

VIII

THE "TRUSTEED" SOCIETY—A POSSIBILITY

I do not see the possibility in the foreseeable future of a golden age in which the nobler motives of humans will emerge as universal. Nor am I sure that I would want to live in such a society if it happened. But I do foresee, and hope for, the possibility that large numbers of trustees will emerge who live up to the possibility for trust that is inherent in their positions, a standard that is now generally missed by a wide margin.

Trustees can become the persons who are trusted partly because they are seen as being unusually sensitive to the corrupting influences of power and partly as an effective bulwark against the abuses of power that are so common today. They would be the people, among all others, who would insist that power be used to serve and not to hurt.

Trustees, then, quite apart from their governing role in the specific institutions they oversee, would, as individual citizens, become a conspicuous leaven in a society that is much too disposed to violence and in which a crippling low level of trust prevails. Where trust is required, they would be the first ones turned to because they are the ones most likely to be trusted—trusted to serve and not to hurt.

As matters now stand, when an issue of importance needs the help of a commission, either *ad hoc* or long term, the usual resource is to turn to status people: administrators, active or retired, lawyers, office holders. And these, too often, are not seen as having credibility as persons to be trusted. They are not necessarily untrustworthy, and they may be wise, judicious, experienced, and dependable. But they are not conspicuously identified in the public mind with *trust*, because they have not carried a role that would justify that view. They are more likely to be seen as persons who are skilled in the operational use of power—able, but not to be trusted except as they function under the close oversight of trustees who are established as servants. Yet they are all we have because *the trustee as servant* has not evolved as a distinctly recognizable role in sufficient numbers to constitute the leaven of which such persons are capable.

As a nation (perhaps as a world society) we stand in dire need of some new visions of our future course. The nuclear sword of Damocles hangs over our head, crime is rampant, too many of the young are alienated, the economy is not functioning well and seems not able to right itself, the environment is in danger—the list is long and ominous. But perhaps the greatest threat is that we lack the *mechanism of consensus*, a way of making up our collective minds. And, with an unprecedented social structure that has rather quickly become overpoweringly vast and complicated, there is no way for the body politic to arrive at the necessary decisions on a representative basis. The necessary consensus is likely to emerge *only* if some persons who know enough are *trusted* to find some ways to go. Most of us will then follow their lead—because they are trusted. I know of no other way that we might get together for our mutual good.

For ours to become a *"trusteed"* society in the sense I have outlined it, as contrasted to a manipulated one, which is mostly what we now have, the large number of trustee positions in all of our voluntary institutions should be consciously used, not only to build serving institutions, which is their primary function, but to constitute a leaven of trust in society at large, a unique resource in the public decision process.

It is no small order. But what is there to lose by trying?

And what is to be gained by trying? What is to be gained is that the trustees can add the precious element of caring—a collegial group that is within the institution but that stands apart from the operation and *cares*.

IX
Having Power; Having an Idea; Having the People—and Caring

Earlier I noted that J. P. Morgan (the elder, who died in 1913) may have been the first trustee, in a major way and in the modern sense. He had power, great power; nobody like him is around today in the nongovernmental sector. He had an idea, a concept of what an institution might become, way ahead of his time, and the times have not yet caught up with his thinking. He knew that strong people were required to build the institutions he wanted—and he knew who they were among his contemporaries.

And he cared. Great institutions were important to him. Evidently he cherished them deeply.

If he were among us today, and if he were just as he was in his prime, he would not be judged acceptable—because of his style of living, his ruthlessness, his disdain for government, and his failure to foresee the ultimate consequences of his kind of one-man power. But in the context of his times, he was a great trustee.

In saying this I am not speaking abstractly. I spent thirty-eight years in one of the businesses that was a result of his genius for caring. I entered it straight from college thirteen years after Morgan had died and six years after the death of the great institution builder he had installed as its head early in the twentieth century. But most of the organization that had built the modern business was still intact, and I had a chance to know some of the builders and talk with them about how the remarkable transformation of this business had come about.

I was a naive youngster from a small town and a small college, and I came to this experience with nothing but a few words of advice from an old professor of sociology to the effect that there is a growing "people" problem in all American institutions and some of us should get inside and work on it. From the outside I could criticize as he did, but I could *do* something about it only from the inside. Nearly fifty years elapsed before I came to the understanding of that advice that I now have. For more than forty years I attributed the remarkable institution I worked for to the effort of the great builder whom Morgan had installed as its head. It was only recently that I acquired the perspective to see that, crucial as the influence of this builder was, he was the secondary cause. The primary source was Morgan, who met the four tests outlined above. If the person who built it had not been available, Morgan would have found somebody who could—and would. And this view came into the business almost as a motto. As people were assigned to tackle large new goals to deal with the colossal problems that beset this business when Morgan took it over, with the assignments went the judgment—sometimes expressed, sometimes implied, but always understood—"If you can't do it, I will find somebody who will!"

I can hear the protesting contemporary trustee, "If I had J. P. Morgan's kind of power, I could build a great institution too." To which I would reply, "Ah, but would you? Plenty who have had Morgan's kind of power did not do it, and you do not use the power you now have to that end. What makes you think you would do more if you had more power?" J. P. Morgan's power was important to his achievement, but what made the result exceptional was that he cared—*he cared for the quality of the institution.*

And a second protest might be, "But I really don't have a great idea for the institution of which I am trustee. And I don't know where the great builders are even if I had the idea." And to that I would reply, "If you cared enough, you would find the idea and the people." Some power is essential. And to do what only a trustee can do you have to get to be a trustee. But most important of all is *caring.* Most trustees I know just don't care enough. If trustees really cared, ideas and people would blossom all over the place. I *know.* I have worked inside institutions, several of them, where trustees did not care. I entered the business that J. P. Morgan built after its trustees had ceased to care; but the momentum of his influence, plus that of the great builder he installed, was still strong. To be sure, I and others like me could do something, but nothing in comparison to what we could have done if the trustees had really cared.

Also, I know because I have been a trustee in several situations where *I* did not care—not enough. And I am keenly aware of what unrewarding experiences those were—for *me* as an ineffective trustee.

What does it mean, *now,* to care for an institution—whether business, church, school, philanthropy? What quality of caring is required in this era?

Having power (and every trustee has some power) one *initiates* the means whereby power is used to serve and not to hurt. *Serve* is used in the sense that all who are touched by the institution or its work become, because of that influence, healthier, wiser, freer, more autonomous, more likely themselves to become servants. Any institution that does not strive with all of its resources, human and material, to achieve the reasonable and the possible in these dimensions is not being adequately cared for by its trustees. That, I believe, is what the times we live in require.

What shall one do, as a trustee who is aware of this necessity, upon finding that one cannot persuade fellow trustees to accept such an obligation, and if one does not foresee the possibility of doing so in a reasonable period?

My advice is to resign. One may do so with a public statement (as Arthur Goldberg did when he resigned from the board of Trans World Airlines a few years ago). This action had a salutary effect and raised the public consciousness about trusteeship. Or one may share one's reasoning with fellow trustees but make no public statement. Or one may simply go away quietly, as I have done when I really had not thought through why I was leaving; I only knew I should not be there.

This advice is arguable. What if all conscientious trustees withdrew and left the control of our institutions in the hands of the casual and the indifferent? There are two answers to that: (1) most boards are so nominal that it wouldn't make much difference; (2) the situation would be more honest, and therefore better. But beyond that, the shock treatment of a major exodus of conscientious trustees may be needed to bring any significant change. I believe that I see the start of this now, and I encourage it. It is part of the basis of my hope for the future.

X

INTRINSIC MOTIVATION OF TRUSTEES

Where are the people to do this—chairs, trustees, and their staffs? This is the most insistent question asked by people who accept the assumptions made in this chapter about the state of society and its major voluntary institutions. Are there such men and women who are prepared to venture as *the new trustees* if they can see a reasonable course to follow?

They are rarer than they should be because of the failure of our society-nurturing institutions—churches, schools, foundations—to prepare them explicitly for this as an immediate prospect. We can only hope that enough people are willing to venture without adequate preparation so that a regenerative movement can begin. If all that happens is that trustees of churches, schools, and foundations begin to use their influence to start some action to prepare such people for the future, there is a chance that, within a generation, the insistent question "Where are the people to do this?" might not need to be asked.

If we grant the failure of our society-nurturing institutions to prepare people for these more exacting trustee roles, then we have only the hope that there are enough people who are, or who might have the chance to be, trustees who have intrinsic motivation to do better and are restless with their present inadequacies.

My hope for the future (and I do have hope despite the critical nature of this chapter) lies in my belief that there are many actual or potential trustees with such motivation who might be roused into action by a realization of the great institution-building opportunity that is before them. I believe further that the meager light on the path ahead that is being shed by the few who are trying to generate it is sufficient for the venturesome to start to move—and the venturesome are all that can be counted on at this stage. Most may wait until the path is clearly marked and well lighted. But the venturesome may start to move *now*. Some would move if just a few of those who profess a concern for the present state of our institutions would focus some of their energy on *trusteeship* and help create a climate of opinion that would encourage trustees to accept a greater sense of obligation and to rise to a much larger opportunity.

Then, where are the administrators and staffs who will operate the optimal institutions under the leadership of able trustees who function as advocated here? They seem just as rare as the serving trustees if one judges by their responses to these suggestions. "If my trustees want to operate that way, they can find themselves a new chief executive" is a commonly heard comment. Realization of these attitudes is enough to discourage even the venturesome trustees who wish to be servants.

Despite such discouragements, I am hopeful that some trustees will venture. My hope rests on attitudes common among the younger generation of executives who are aware of the serious limitations in the conventional wisdom of administration (as discussed in the last chapter). Some of these younger executives are more sensitive to the corrupting influence of power than are their elders. While they realize that some power must be used, they prefer to work in a close collegial relationship, with a team of equals led by a *primus inter pares*, rather than to hold so much power in their own hands. They are more disposed to share the burden, and they will welcome the close monitoring of the use of power by able and fully functioning trustees.

We live amid a revolution of values, some good, some bad (when viewed from the perspective of one of the older generation). And one of the good consequences, in my judgment, is a greater disposition of able people, especially among the young, to work in teams rather than to strive to be prima donnas—not so much for idealistic reasons as because the word is getting around that it makes a more serene and fulfilled life. We may be witnessing the end of individualism as a predominant cultural value (although there may still be some power-hungry people around to add spice to the brew). For the trustee who is disposed to be venturesome as servant, one of the possibilities to be counted on in many of the able older executives is the desire, when their time comes, to lay down their spears with colors flying rather than to leave with the mark "obsolete" indelibly stamped on their backs. And any who wish to avoid that opprobrious state are well advised, while they still stand erect, to learn from those of their younger colleagues who may hold the keys to the future. I know a few of my generation who have had the humility (and the good sense) to learn from those of the young who are with the future. Theirs is an enviable old age.

Trustees as servants face one of the most exciting challenges of our times: to lead our moribund institutions, and some of the seemingly moribund people in them, into a future of greatness.

> The greatest sin of man is to forget that he is a prince—that he has royal power. All worlds are in need of exaltation, and everyone is charged to lift what is low, to unite what lies apart, to advance what is left behind. It is as if all worlds...are full of expectancy, of sacred goals to be reached, so that consummation can come to pass. And man is called upon to bring about the climax slowly but decisively.

> —ABRAHAM JOSHUA HESCHEL

IV

Servant Leadership in Business

Perhaps I reflect the influence of my own vocational choice when I say that in the next few years more will be learned in business than in any other field about how to bring servant leadership into being as a major social force. In my view, businesses not only do as well with their obligations now, under the conditions imposed on them, as other kinds of institutions do with theirs, but businesses are more questioning of their own adequacy, they are more open to innovation, and they are disposed to take greater risks to find a better way.

The three statements that comprise this chapter, one given to a general audience and two addressed to specific businesses—one large and one small—give a fair sample of what contemporary business people are willing to think about. What these three quite different pieces have in common, and they were written between 1958 and 1974, is a call to a new business ethic—a striving for excellence. Businesses are asked not only to produce better goods and services, but to become greater social assets as institutions.

It is important for the nonbusiness reader to note that government attitudes, reflecting, no doubt, the prevailing popular view toward privately owned businesses, are different from those taken toward other types of institutions. By law, with criminal sanctions, profit-making businesses are required to compete as the principal means for compelling them to serve. This is a crude and cumbersome and ambiguous approach. By implication, public policy is saying that if profit is an aim, the institution will not serve unless it is compelled to. The practical consequence of this decision has been to impose, and surround with an aura of sanctity, the law of the jungle. Necessarily, I believe, business schools teach more about how to survive and prosper in the jungle than how, through excellence, to help build a better society. This is a questionable mission for a university.

It is not the purpose here to argue the merits of this approach, or to suggest that there is not a problem of some businesses not serving well. But, in my view, the problem of not serving well is no greater in business than with schools, churches, hospitals, philanthropies, and government itself.

In addressing businesses, therefore, with the intent of encouraging a greater *voluntary* striving for excellence as servant, I am mindful of the special conditions under which businesses operate, as distinguished from other institutions. A principle is suggested: *When any action is regulated by law, the incentive for individual conscience to govern is diminished—unless the law coincides with almost universally held moral standards.* We should have learned this out of our experience with alcohol prohibition. The U.S. Constitution was amended, after World War I, in order to suppress the acknowledged (by the majority) evil of alcohol. In 1933 the amendment was repealed, not because of a change in view about the evil, but because so many disregarded the law that the nation would be destroyed in trying to enforce it. We are repeating this error now with marijuana (although we have recently begun a retreat from it), and logic that says marijuana is evil seems less persuasive than with alcohol.

I cite the examples of prohibitions on alcohol and marijuana because they suggest that before we pass a law we should weigh the possible consequences of diminishing voluntary ethical striving toward the same end, unless, as I have said, the ethical norm is already almost universally accepted. Before the prohibition on alcohol was enacted into law, substantial progress was being made (in the United States) toward containing the evil of alcohol with a voluntary ethic. We seem to have lost much of that ethic by the passage of the law. *We cannot have it both ways.*

In making this point I am not arguing for anarchy, for no law. My point is that we in the United States are more naive than most about what can be done with law, especially with the labyrinth of laws with which business is surrounded. It comes out better if one persuades rather than compels.

Let me suggest to the reader that the assumptions be examined—both about the making of profit and about undertaking to compel service by law. Is all that we want from profit-making business the lowest price we can exact? In my own efforts to help business to become more serving I feel that I am contending with a popular view that *price is all*. Personally, I would prefer to pay a considerably higher price if thereby the institution could become substantially more serving to all who are touched by its actions.

Having said all of this, I recognize the problem of so much of business not serving well. But the core of the problem, as I see it, is not in business institutions; rather, it is in the attitudes, concepts, and expectations regarding business held by the rest of society. People in churches, universities, government, and social agencies *do not love* business institutions. As a consequence, many inside business do not love them either. Businesses, despite their crassness, occasional corruption, and unloveliness, *must be loved* if they are to serve us better. They are much too large a presence in the lives of all of us to have them in our midst and *not* serve us better.

But how, one may ask, can one love this abstraction called the corporation? One doesn't! One loves *only the people* who are gathered to render the service for which the corporation is enfranchised. *The people are the institution!*

ETHICS AND MANIPULATION

(A paper presented at the Conference on "The Manipulation of Man," The Gottlieb Dutweiler Institute, Zurich, Switzerland, February 26, 1970)

Part of the problem of dealing with our subject, "Ethics and Manipulation," is that the words *manipulation* and *management* have a common root in *manus*, "hand," and both words imply shaping other people's destinies. Whereas *manipulation of* people has long been taken as bad because it implies moving them without their knowing fully what is going on, until recently *management* has been accepted as legitimate. Now, as I read the signs, we are in a period of radical transition regarding power, authority, and decision everywhere, and a cloud has settled over all leadership and management in any form. All institutions are affected by these trends, and institutional leadership is now quite different from what it was a few years ago. I expect these trends to continue.

There has emerged from this ferment the expectation, held by many, that a manipulation-free society is a possibility—a "leaderless" society that is governed by a continuing consensus with full participation and with every motive behind every action fully exposed. I respect the motives of those who advocate this ideal state and admit to occasional utopian dreams of life in an influence-free society. But, realistically, I do not see such a society in prospect, and I will deal here with the institution of American business as I know it in my own experience—a state of affairs in which strong, able people must lead, and therefore manipulate, if the goods and services expected are to emerge. Some of us would do better with fewer goods, though we need more services—health care, for instance. But whatever the level of goods and services, institutions will be required to deliver them. These institutions, if they are to rise above mediocrity, will have their ablest people as leaders, and those leaders will manipulate.

The issue then, as I see it, is not whether all manipulation can be banished as evil, but rather, can some manipulation be made legitimate? By what standards, and how? What ethic should govern for these times? Before I conclude, I will speculate on what one new business ethic might be.

I cannot visualize a world without leaders, without those who better see the path ahead taking the risks to lead and show the way. What reason is there for accepting the constraints of a society except that therein the more able serve the less able? One way that some people serve is to lead. And anyone who does this *manipulates* others because one literally helps shape their destinies without fully revealing either one's motives or the direction in which one is leading them. Leaders may be completely honest about their *conscious* intent. But the essential artistry in their leadership, that which makes them more dependable and trustworthy than most, is their intuitive insight, which cannot be fully explained. We have it from the great French jurist Saleilles that a judge makes decisions intuitively and then devises the fine legal reasoning to justify them—after the fact. So it is with the scientist on the growing edge of discovery. And so it is with the leader—whether business person, administrator, politician, clergy, or teacher. I cannot conceive of a duller, less creative world than one in which everything can be fully and rationally explained.

My search, therefore, day by day, is for a path through the maze along which people are accepted as they are and which leads to a world that is more benign. As I look out through my particular window on the world I realize that I do not see all. Rather, I see only what the filter of my biases and attitudes of the moment permits me to see. Therefore if, in the course of this discussion, I make a declaration without appending "it seems to me," please assume such a qualification on everything I say.

Traveling this path, I see the field of American business as almost without professional standards. It is not much supported by sentiment, there is no aura of professional sanctity to mask its shortcomings, and, because it is one of the least restrained—by a professional ethic—of all fields of practice, at the low end of the scale there is much that is corrupt and very bad, while at the high end there is much at a level of excellence that is truly distinguished. The spread between the two extremes is wide.

Performance in any field or calling should be judged in reference to the obligations assumed for society, which differ from field to field. I know something of what goes on in the fields of education, government, religion, philanthropy, and health services. In my judgment, businessmen do as well by their obligations as do the others. None does very well.

The world of practice in all fields, as I see it through my particular window, is, on the average, mediocre. No field does very well when judged by what is reasonable and possible with available resources. This is what makes the subject of manipulation, or almost any other dimension of modern Western society, so interesting. How can we do better? We have the resources to do so much better, far better than the mediocre level that now prevails because so much leadership is poor.

The problem of doing better in the modern world, as I see it, is this: How can people perform better in, and be better served by, *institutions*—especially large ones?

In my country, at least, where business practice is shaped more by the influence of large institutions and where there is a wide range of choice as to what a business may be like, as a sub-culture, there is much to be found that is relevant to our theme, "The Manipulation of Man," by exploring briefly how our big businesses came to be what they are—and how they may be different in the future.

Let me use the three largest American businesses in their fields as examples. Each of them is what it is today because each, at a critical period in its history, was headed by a building genius (not the founding owner) who gave the institution the stamp of his personal values. Each of these building geniuses was an adequate leader and manager for his day, but each brought unusual conceptual powers—in defining the institution and establishing his values as its values.

In General Motors, our largest manufacturing concern, the genius was Alfred Sloan, whose unique gift was remarkable organizational insight and the growing of managers; in Sears Roebuck, our largest merchandising company, the genius was Julius Rosenwald, who brought unusual humanness and trust; in American Telephone and Telegraph Company, our largest public utility (and my old company), the genius was Theodore N. Vail, who gave it dedication to service supported by relentless technical innovation. Although Vail has been gone fifty years (he was the earliest of the three), A.T.&T. is still his business—his personal values still dominate it. There has been an erosion, of course, but fifty years is a long time for one person's recognizable influence to last in something as transient as a business or in an institution as large as this one. It is the same with Sloan and Rosenwald, who came later. General Motors and Sears are still "their" companies. These three companies rose above the level of mediocrity because three great leader-builders brought them there.

I do not cite these companies as paragons or models for the future. They have the same faults and frailties common to all human institutions at this stage of their development. But each of these, at a critical period in its growth, made a lunge forward and contributed something to the art of institution building. Whether it can be done again depends on the quality of the people who emerge, inside, to serve and lead.

The test of leadership has not changed: What does the scorekeeper (or the several scorekeepers) say? The scorekeeper's rules have changed a bit, and they will change even more. There are more "publics" demanding satisfaction, and the intensity of their scrutiny has increased. Business institutions have grown larger and much more complex and the pace of innovation is sometimes breathtaking. Dealing with these conditions, large-business leadership has become a sophisticated calling, and the leaders are much more concerned with building strength and bringing sharpness of focus to many people and building a dependable staff rather than with deciding everything themselves. Contemporary business leaders are just as much determined institution builders as their predecessors, but they work differently and their role is more difficult to understand—from the outside.

The role of top leadership in large American business is shifting away from that of the dominant decision-maker to that of manager of the information system. Leadership depends more on the pull of the overarching goals plus building the competence and sustaining the autonomy of many decision-makers. This, in turn, is supported by wide access to reliable and comprehensive information. The sanctions pressing on individuals for good performance are, first, their own pride and conscience framed within adequate information that guides them and tells them how they are doing; second, the social pressure of peers whose own performance is interlinked with theirs and who have access to the common pool of information so that *they* know how their colleagues are doing; and finally, the last-resort authority of the superior officer, which, in a good institution, is rarely used. The value of coercive power is inverse to its use.

This is a hopeful and encouraging trend. It is made possible by a wide scope of freedom for quite autonomous institutions under the shelter of political democracy. But, in my country, the model for it has not been set by the government, nor is it the product of democratization within the firm. Rather, it is the result of the growth of knowledge, relentless market pressures, and the emergence of some unusual business builders. Political democracy is a necessary condition, but it does not guarantee anything. The only assurance of a good result is the encouragement of the culture for incremental thrusts by large numbers of strong, free, able people as they serve and lead. Individual people doing the right things give a society its moral stature. This does not make a perfect society, but this is how such goodness as it has is built.

Earlier I said that I believed that the decisive creative response to the challenge of the contemporary ferment, the response that is more likely to turn things around than any other I know about, will come from the business firm. I see the tentative first steps already being made.

How then will businesses respond to the new conditions? How can they perform their expected functions in a way that the charge of manipulation recedes as a serious issue?

I have confidence that, after a bit of confusion, a new business ethic will emerge. And the best I can do at this point is to speculate on what that ethic might be. I will confine my speculation to only one facet of the total problem of business ethics— those who work within business. There are many parts of the total business ethic that need attention, but the one I will deal with seems the most basic.

What might the new ethic be? (Not a new idea but new as a firmly held business ethic.)

Looking at the two major elements, the work and the person, the new ethic, simply but quite completely stated, will be: *The work exists for the person as much as the person exists for the work.*

Put another way, the business exists as much to provide meaningful work to the person as it exists to provide a product or service to the customer.

The business then becomes a serving institution—serving those who produce and those who use. At first, the new ethic may put these two on a par. But as the economy becomes even more productive and people get more sensible and settle for fewer "things," in the new ethic service to those who produce may rise in priority above service to those who use, and the significance of work will be more the joy of the doing rather than the goods and services produced. There must, of course, be goods and services at some level, but in an era of abundance they need not be the top priority. This view of it not only will make a better society, but in the future, this may be the only way the consumer can be well served—by accepting that serving is more important than being served, and that the mere possession of money does not give one an unqualified right to command the service of another. (We are partly there already.) Furthermore, users will be better served if they find a way to communicate this belief to those who serve. A new consumer ethic will need to evolve alongside the new business ethic. I am close enough to this restless generation of young people in my country to believe that the more able and discerning among them will not settle for less than this as the prevailing ethic for the future. And they will enforce their view simply by too many of the abler ones refusing to work on any other terms.

I have said that the idea is not new but that its adoption as a firmly held business ethic will be new in our time. In fact, as an idea, it is very old—at least twenty-five hundred years. Its first formulation, to my knowledge, is in the Buddhist ethic, as one step in the noble eightfold path—right vocation, or right livelihood—as given in the famous sermon at Benares.

Speaking to those in business who presume to manage, it is important that this principle be embraced as an ethic and not simply as a "device" to achieve harmony or increase productivity or reduce turnover. Some popular procedures, such as participation or work enlargement or profit sharing, may be manipulative devices if they do not flow naturally out of a comprehensive ethic. "Participative democracy" in industry as it is now advocated in Europe may, in practice, be another such device, especially in a large industry. I do not think it will flourish in my country. Our unions are too astute to permit it, and involvement with it will divert attention from more basic matters.

Manipulative devices, and manipulation as a concept, are attacked because they are visible targets. However, just removing the evidences of manipulation (assuming it can be done) will not produce meaning and significance in individual lives. In an overcrowded industrial society this can only be done by the institutions we now have, where most people spend their working lives, adopting an ethic in which meaning and significance are the goal—at least on a parity with other goals. And to bring it to parity, it must, for a while at least, be the primary goal. This means that business institutions must adopt this goal, and its accomplishment rests on the ability of builders, leaders, to move these institutions (while keeping them intact and functioning), from where they are, with the heavy emphasis on production, to where they need to be, with the heavy emphasis on growing people. And they will do this while meeting all of the other performance criteria that society imposes for institutional survival.

When George Fox gave the seventeenth-century English Quaker businessmen a new business ethic (truthfulness, dependability, fixed prices—no haggling), he did it because his view of right conduct demanded it, not because it would be more profitable. It did, in fact, become more profitable because those early Quaker businessmen quickly emerged out of the seamy morass of that day as people who could be trusted. But the new ethic was a radical demand on those people, and they must have had apprehensions about it when it was urged upon them.

The ethic suggested here is a radical one too, and those in business will probably be apprehensive about it. Those who are moved to act on it are not likely to move so much in response to the moral imperative, simply because the moral leader with sufficient stature to persuade them (as George Fox did with his followers) doesn't seem to be around. The new ethic will come, if it comes, as an acknowledgment (or in anticipation) of the relentless pressure of the revolution in values.

Very soon, across the whole gamut of our institutions, we may know how many determined builders there are who can move creatively with these times in which powerful new forces for integrity are operating. I wager that in American business we have a few leaders who will rise to the challenge. But they will not choose to announce, with great fanfare, a new ethic to deal with the new conditions. If they are wise they will not announce *anything.* There is an ancient moral injunction that tells us to "practice what we preach." A few businesspeople have learned the hard way to follow the modern version of that advice, which says: "Don't practice what you preach; just practice!" Consequently the wise businessperson will simply start the slow process of converting the large numbers of people within the institution who must share this view if it is to be viable. It will be noticed only in practice, and that gradually.

It will take some courage for a large business to make this ethical shift, but only one of them need make the shift initially. When Henry Ford set up his assembly line to manufacture automobiles, ultimately everybody in that kind of business had to convert. So it may be with the new business ethic.

The process has already started in some businesses with the effort to accommodate the very able young people who have a clear, individualistic style that they are determined to preserve and who need the excitement of a dynamic purpose. Such very able individuals are quickly given a track of their own to run on so that they can have the satisfaction of personal achievement. This is easier to do in a small business, but larger firms are learning to decentralize in a way that creates a variety of environments in which different styles of able people will flourish and be themselves. The corporate leader and his or her staff provide a context for all of this so that individuals can have a clear focus of purpose, so that they can be supported when they need it and feel a part of a larger purpose without losing their individuality, and so that all the parts can contribute to the total strength of the enterprise. (If some people want to make their career with a large business and keep their individuality, then they should choose a strong business.) This is the first step—to accommodate the wide differences and needs of the very able. A few strong businesses are well along with this step. The test? They have many able young people and it is difficult to "raid" them and lure them away.

The second step, and the more difficult, is to exert a strong pull for growth on *all* in the enterprise who have unrealized potential and who want to grow. More people will want to grow when the climate is encouraging. Most large businesses have the staff resources to redesign the work so as to capitalize on individual strengths. Sometimes it means taking on a product or service that is not particularly profitable just because someone needs it. The specific imperative that brings this about will probably be the pressure from the *able* young people within the firm who are recruited under arrangements mentioned in the preceding paragraph.

Motivation then becomes what people generate for themselves when they experience growth. Whereas the usual assumption about the firm is that it is in business to make a profit and serve its customers and that it does things for and to employees to get them to be productive, the new ethic requires that *growth* of those who do the work is the primary aim, and the workers then see to it that the customer is served and that the ink on the bottom line is black. It is *their* game. The art, of course, is how to do this in a firm that employs many thousands.

It won't be easy. But neither will it be any harder than other difficult things that large businesses have to do. And this one, ultimately, they will accept that they *have* to do. With that acceptance will come the belief that it is right, which makes it an ethic.

If done well, the change will come slowly, and those who demand instant perfection will probably say that nothing at all is happening. To stay alive and meet all of the other criteria that must be met, a business will probably continue to operate the old way while moving toward the new. There will be inevitable confusion. But this is what makes business leadership interesting.

In my country we are well on the way to accepting that the world owes every person a living. The next step may be to acknowledge that every person is entitled to work that is meaningful in individual terms, and that it is the obligation of employers, *in toto*, to provide it. Whereas "a living" can be dispensed via money through a relief agency, "meaningful work" is likely to be delivered only within an employing institution that is living by a new ethic. And the practice of this ethic is a positive move toward a holistic society.

Except for a few esoteric scholars, the case for the university as a place set apart from the world of work rests on tenuous grounds. Perhaps, experimentally at least, we should move toward a new institution that embraces both work and learning—learning in a deep and formal sense and all of the school influence most people need. This requires a new type of leader, one who can conceptualize such an institution, generate enthusiasm so that many good and able people want to be a part of it, and provide the strong focus of purpose that builds dynamic strength in many. Great things happen when able leaders create these conditions. There are some able leaders in American business who can rise to the challenge to create these conditions. All that is needed is enough incentive to make them want to do it. Our young people are busy building that incentive.

To those who do not know intimately the inner workings of large American businesses it may be difficult to appreciate what a profound effect on the business culture a new ethic like this will have. When the business manager who is fully committed to this ethic is asked, "What are you in business for?" the answer may be: "*I am in the business of growing people*—people who are stronger, healthier, more autonomous, more self-reliant, more competent. Incidentally, we also make and sell at a profit things that people want to buy so we can pay for all this. We play that game hard and well and we are successful by the usual standards, but that is really incidental. I recall a time when there was a complaint about manipulation. We don't hear it anymore. We manage the business about the same way we always did. We simply changed our aim. Strong, healthy, autonomous, self-reliant, and competent people don't mind being manipulated. In fact, they take it as a game and do a little of it themselves. Consequently, as an institution, we are terribly strong. In fact, we are distinguished. How do I know we are distinguished? Because the best young people want to work for us. We select the best of the best and, once inside, they never want to leave. Any business that can do that is a winner."

Utopian?

No, I don't think so. Most of our large American businesses have the capability and the resources to embrace a new ethic like this and act resolutely on its implications. And I believe that among them there are several that have sufficient foresight and creative drive to prefer to run ahead of the changing ethic rather than be run over by it. Such is the way that new ethics are made.

In the long perspective of history, this period of the 1970s may be seen as one in which, in the course of coming to grips with the moral issues of power, authority, *and* manipulation, a new view of how people are best served by institutions may emerge. Institutions are not necessarily more benign when they protest their idealistic motives, nor are they necessarily less benign when they admit to crass commercialism. One should not be surprised that a Ralph Waldo Emerson, who could see "the good of evil born," would observe, when he was weighing his words carefully, that "the greatest meliorator of the world is selfish, huckstering trade."

I predict that under the pressures of the times the typical American business, because it is more flexible, more adaptive, more human, more openly responsive to market forces, and because, in business, integrity of service (or lack of it) is more vividly and concretely demonstrated than in other types of institutions, will more quickly resolve the issues of manipulation—in all of their manifestations. And it will accomplish this not by banishing manipulation but by sublimating it, and, out of the alchemy, it may contribute something significantly new to the evolving knowledge of how people can better live and work together in societies.

If this proves in practice to be generally recognized, then there may be a radical realignment of expectations from institutions, and what society has traditionally expected from businesses, churches, schools, governments, and philanthropic foundations may be considerably scrambled. If this happens, I wager that, out of this scrambling, the business type of institution will emerge with a considerably larger role than heretofore. Witness the agitation in my country to take the Post Office out of the Civil Service and into a public corporation, and the vigorous entry of a few of our aggressive private business firms into the "learning" field. This is happening not because of any inherent virtue in business, but simply because, the way institutions have evolved, businesses are more adaptive and more responsive to opportunity.

Despite the ideological tensions in the world today, when any society really wants to accomplish something, it tends to draw on whatever works best. The builders find the useful pieces wherever they are, and they invent new ones when needed, all without regard to ideological coloration. "How do you get the right things done?" comes to be the watchword of the day—every day.

I admit a bias. If I were young again, I would again cast my lot with a large American business. I would do it because my country is a business-dominated society (not in a formal power sense but simply by the sheer mass of the business presence) and any social advance will move, in part, from forces generated inside business. From my own experience there is enough integrity in the typical business that I would be more useful and my personal growth would be better nourished by working *inside* rather than by trying to influence it from the outside. I would choose to join a large business firm because there would be more satisfaction in being where the action is (the *action*, not just the excitement)—at the point where some of the critical issues of society must be resolved if the work of the world is to be done. And I would do it because I believe that if I accept the challenge to cope with the inevitable manipulation within an institution that is responding sensibly and creatively to issues and situations that require new ethics, I will emerge at the end of my career with a better personal value system than I would have if I had chosen a work where I was more on my own and, therefore, freer from being manipulated.

This is the ultimate test: What values govern one's life—at the end of it?

Manipulation, as I see it, is one of the imperfections of an imperfect world. It is a social problem, but it is not first priority, and the reformer's zeal will blunt its point by attacking it as primary. *Mediocrity* (including self-serving) in positions of influence *is* primary, and it cannot be dealt with by eliminating influence, as in the "leaderless society." Mediocrity will still be there.

Reducing mediocrity is a slow, difficult, person-by-person process in which the less able learn to identify and trust the more able who will diligently and honestly serve them. *It is also a process in which able and honest, serving people prepare themselves to lead and accept the opportunity to lead when offered.*

Reducing mediocrity in positions of influence by replacing the less qualified with more able and honest serving people is a manageable task with our available resources. It can be done. And I am confident that it will be done on a substantial scale when the people and institutions that have the good of society at heart bring a clearer focus to their efforts and concentrate on the one thing that will turn us about the quickest: excellence in place of mediocrity.

MEMO ON GROWING FROM SMALL TO LARGE

(The following memorandum was written for the chief executive and principal owner of a small company that has achieved the reputation for unusual quality of product and service. It has grown rapidly to its present size and has the potential for becoming a distinguished large institution if it can maintain its present quality as it continues to grow. That could be done, it seemed to me, if the

head of it, to whom this memo was addressed, could (1) change roles from sole manager of a small enterprise to leader of a collective of many able people who would administer a large enterprise, and (2) see to it that each work group in the company becomes a positive social force.)

The line that separates a large business from a small one might be drawn at that point where the business can no longer function well under the direct oversight of one individual. If the business has been built largely on one person's drive, imagination, taste, and judgment, as yours seems to have been, it may be difficult to recognize when that point has been reached. The signals that would tell you may not be unmistakably clear. The most immediate risk in your present way of operating may be that you could not be replaced, if there should be a need of that. Another risk is that the day-to-day demands on your leadership may become more taxing at a time when you may wish that they become less so. But the greatest risk may be that the company cannot grow and keep its present quality. I assume that you would like to minimize all of these risks.

I would guess, from our conversation, that your business is on the verge of becoming large in the sense that these risks loom as real possibilities, and it may be timely to consider an alternative that would permit the company to continue to grow while reducing these risks. The alternative I suggest is that you begin to shift your personal effort toward *building an institution* in which you become more the *manager of a process* that gets the job done and less the *administrator of day-to-day operations*. This might be the first step toward the ultimate optimal long-term performance as a large business that is *managed* by a board of directors who act as trustees and is *administered* by a team of equals who are led by a *primus inter pares*. The result would be an institution that would have the best chance of attracting and holding in its service the large number of able people who will be required to give it strength, quality, and continuity. This would require a shift in goals for you, a move from a preoccupation with building and operating the business day to day, to one of building an institution that has an autonomy of its own, that will do as well on a large scale what you have been able to do so well on a smaller scale, and that will have a life span, as a large and exceptional business, that is far beyond what it is likely to have if you continue in your present role.

I do not underestimate the difficulty of doing this. As I told you, I have watched another who has built a unique business as you have, and who accepted, intellectually, the need to transform it into an institution, but who faltered when faced with the practical steps this required. It is not realistic to expect people like you to hand over the control of a business you have built to others who are not as experienced, perhaps not basically as able, as yourself. Yet, if you stay as you are, that is precisely what you will be forced to do—sometime.

If you accept the goal named above as desirable, what then do you do? It seems to me that you take one initial step now, within your present way of operating, that will be the first of a series of steps that move you gradually toward the role of institution builder. Each step should give you a base for a prudent next step so that you can move steadily toward a new role without ever contemplating a move that presents an unwarranted risk to what you have already built.

A possible first step, as I see it, emerged in our conversation. You have a problem that you put to me as a consultant who presumably has ideas on such things. You want to know what you should do to keep at least 80 percent of the able, high potential young people you have hired recently. I responded that I did not think any consultant could give you an answer to that question. The search for an answer is something you should assign to one of your best people as a staff problem.

As I have reflected on our discussion of this idea, I concluded that this may be as good an issue as any on which to make your first move toward building an institution. As long as you see your role in terms of the person who wants a consultant to give you an answer to a question like that, you are standing in your old role of the one-person builder and operator of the business, whereas, if you move on this as a problem for one of your best people to solve as an explicit, and perhaps as an exclusive staff assignment, then you have taken a big step toward building an institution out of a successful small business. Instead of being the seeker of solutions, directly from a consultant to you (which is all that the manager of a small business can do), you will be moving toward being the *manager of the process* by which the best solution can be found. And by continuing to take such steps you will be shifting your role from one-person manager of a small business to builder of a large institution in which (as I think is evolving) directors (under a strong board chair) *manage* and the operating executives *administer.* Let me supply some reasoning that may help to qualify this suggestion as a sound first step:

● Such an assignment to one of your most able people will enable you to get the right question in focus. Maybe you should not keep 80 percent of the people you have hired recently who are presumed to have high potential. Maybe you should *lose* 80 percent of them. I am not suggesting that this is the case, but I have a suspicion that the necessary staff work has not been done to establish that these are the people you should have hired. And there are too many of them for you to know them well enough personally to make that judgment. So you need to get the question framed in a way that I suspect has not yet been done. The right person assigned to this, after a little work, can tell you whether you are asking the right question.

● When you get the question settled, then you may want to provide some consulting help to the person you assign to get the answer. There may be many useful inputs from consulting sources, but probably none that will provide the complete answer—one that is best for your company at this time. Your own staff person will have to work that out.

● Probably the main reason you should assign this problem to one of your best people rather than seek an answer from a consultant is that, in an area like this, getting the right answer into practice in your company is likely to be much more difficult than finding the right answer in the first place. It is possible, on some legal, technical, or financial questions, to get dependable expert advice that may be readily put to use. But anything that cuts deep into the culture, like a new procedure for the future staffing of your executive group, is much more difficult to install than it is to discover. The outside consultant, even if lucky enough to recommend the right answer, would not be able to get it installed.

● The safest way I know for changing the character of any institution is through building a staff of very able people who will get their greatest creative fulfillment in finding and installing good solutions to critical problems. They may be happier doing that than they would be if they were administering part of the business, and they may be more valuable to the business in these roles. Such a group of effective staff people would probably become the core of the administration of the business—its most valuable asset. You can always find capable operating administrators for a business, *provided* that you have a strong staff that can find and install good solutions for its problems. Furthermore, the building and directing of such a staff may be one of the best preparations for a person to move from the one-person management of a small business to board chair of a large business.

● By taking such issues one at a time you can gradually shift your role from that of the finder and installer of answers to that of the administrator of the process by which this takes place. When you have accomplished this, you can then be replaced by a competent professional administrator and move into the board chair position, keeping (as you say you want to keep) the research function under your wing. I suspect, though, that if you take this route you may find institution building (including vitalizing the trustee function) to be such an interesting creative challenge that you may choose to leave research, as you now conceive it, as a part of the operating administration of the business.

In chapters 2 and 3, "The Institution as Servant" and "Trustees as Servants," I have summarized my best thinking about the structure of both the operating administration and the board of trustees of large institutions. But I know of no single model where all that I have suggested above is to be seen in operation. If there were such, there would be no need for me to write this memo; it would be available in manual form. But everything noted here has its roots somewhere in my experience, and I urge with confidence that if all of it is put into practice, it will make a superior model.

However, what I have suggested above deals only with the top structure of the business. If you want to make your present distinguished small business into a distinguished large one, you will need also to attend to the bottom structure of the business, the work group, and make of it something that is as congenial to the times in which it will be judged as I believe the top structure I have recommended will prove to be. And on this, the nature of the optimal work group of the future, I can only speculate.

I am reasonably familiar with current experiments with work and the work group in this country and in Europe, and I do not believe that an adequate philosophy of work has yet been stated, one that you can accept as a guide for the design of the optimal work group for the years ahead. Therefore, I suggest that all those in a spot like yours, people who are actively building the model for the viable future business, will need to state the philosophy, based upon their own experience in following their own reliable intuitive judgment. The intuition of the institution builder will originate the experiment; the philosophy will emerge as the experiment is studied. What follows, then, is not a recommendation. Rather, it is food to nourish your own intuitive process as you plot your course into virgin territory—with confidence.

Twenty-five years ago the late Professor Fritz Roethlisberger of Harvard Business School wrote a provocative article entitled "The Foreman, Master and Victim of Double Talk." This article describes the impossible situation of the typical foreman: impossible as a vocation for a person and impossible for the company because of the unrealistic expectations of what the person in that role should do. The foreman is the one at the end of the chain of command, the one who has to get the work done—somehow—according to someone else's design. The foreman must deal with the union steward, who is sometimes a member of the work group and is viewed as a hostile adversary. The foreman is often responsible for only part of an integrated process and must deal firsthand, with the growing disenchantment with the demands of work. Professor Roethlisberger's article evoked wide comment in industrial circles but not much was done about the problem that was identified at that time. Now, I believe, if one is to build the distinguished business of the future, especially a large business, one will need to do something about work and the work group and the leadership of that group. Let me suggest something.

First there will be, and should be, a labor union. Several large American industries still manage to operate without a union, and they tend to consider it as a notable achievement. Others who have unions sometimes dream of the ideal situation in which they do not have one. In sharp contrast with this attitude, the builder of the distinguished business of the future will accept the union as indispensable to the optimal work group, and, as the leader of a big company, will learn to deal with a big union so as to make of the work group a constructive force for the individual worker, for the company, and for society at large.

In saying this I am not approving of unions as they now stand, any more than I approve of corporations as they now stand. Both have much to do to become the servants of society that their roles make possible, and that influential critics will demand with greater insistence. I simply say that if you want to lead your present distinguished small business to become a distinguished large one, then you should do this in a way that helps a union to evolve as a responsible part of the enterprise.

I believe that you need to assume that work, all work, exists as much for the enrichment of the life of the worker as it does for the service of the one who pays for it. This does not mean that work will not be hard, demanding, and sometimes frustrating. It is just that the workers' life goals (quite apart from the money they earn) will be served by doing the work, and that is at least half the reason the work is there to be done. The implications of this assumption, if you choose to make it, are enormous, and I will not try to trace all of them.

Movement guided by this assumption will begin, I believe, by taking the foreman out of management and arranging the work so that, as far as possible, it will be done by cohesive work groups or teams that are small enough that the group members become a community. The design of the work groups might be done jointly between the administration of the company and the union, with the exception that neither the work leader (who replaces the foreman) nor the union steward will be regarded as an agent of the parent group in contentions that may arise between the union and the company. This is essential if they are not to be regarded as adversaries within the work group. If there is contention between the union and the company (as there is likely to be at times), neither the work leader nor the union steward will be involved.

The essential concept is that the task belongs to the group. Both the work leader and the union steward are designated as persons who are acceptable to the group and who further its growth as a human community. If the product (goods or services) or the arrangements that affect people are not satisfactory, the problem becomes a matter for joint concern of the administration and the union. The administration assumes the primary concern to see that those who pay for the product or service are well served. The union assumes the primary obligation to see that those who do the work are adequately rewarded, psychically and materially. But each has a minor share of the other's primary obligation. If these two parties cannot resolve an issue, then it may be given to an arbitrator to decide, as is sometimes done now, or the ultimate sanction of a strike or a lockout may be resorted to. But whatever happens, the work group remains a cohesive community that includes the work leader and the union steward as full participating members, and all are insulated from the larger controversy.

This kind of thinking conceives of administration as the agent of the owners—whether shareholders, government, or trustees—and of beneficiaries of the effort, that is, clients, patrons, or customers. The union is then seen as guardian of the workers' personal stake in the enterprise, psychic and material, and their channel into the political process. Both are made legitimate by the integrity of the work group. Work groups are the foundation stones of the whole structure of institutions.

The above thoughts on work groups, as I stated earlier, are not given as a plan of action. Rather, they are offered to suggest that you set aside conventional wisdom and begin to think of a wholly new design for a business. If you can build a new structure of administrative leadership, as outlined earlier in this memo, and if you can arrange the work so that strong communities evolve to do it, you may find that you do not need much of the elaborate intermediate structure that has become so burdensome (and sometimes obstructive) in large institutions.

In summary, I am suggesting that a person like you who has been so successful in building a distinguished small business might, at your age, find an even more exciting challenge in transforming this one-person business into an institution that has autonomy and creative drive as a collective of many able people and that has the capacity for expansion into a large business without losing, and perhaps even enhancing, the claim to distinction it has achieved as a small one.

BUSINESS DIRECTORS
INITIATE SOCIAL POLICY

For years I made the strongest pleas I could for our major institutions to become affirmative (as opposed to passive or reactive) servants of society. Surely there was a trustee of a university, business, or church who was ready to move in this direction.

In 1974, the first unequivocal response came to me, saying: "We would like to know how to be that kind of institution."

This response did not come from where the casual observer might guess—a church, a university, a hospital, a social agency. It came from where I expected it: from a business, a large multinational business. I expected this not because I impute any special virtue to business as such, but because, as I know institutions, businesses are least lulled to complacency by idealistic pretensions and the support of sentiment, and they have fewer professional hang-ups than the others. When the heads of eleemosynary institutions are confronted with evidence of a deficiency they cannot deny, they sometimes seem to put on sackcloth and ashes and go in for self-flagellation, but they do not do anything about it. Businesses, when similarly confronted, sometimes stoutly assert their innocence and proclaim their virtue, but then they quietly take some remedial action.

The directors of this company had read my pamphlet version of the earlier chapter on "The Institution as Servant" and decided that they wanted to explore how they could move toward being a more socially responsible company. The chair got in touch with me and arranged for me to have separate conversations with each of the directors. At the conclusion of these conversations, I wrote the following proposal for the directors. With minor changes, it was given to the operating administrators of the company.

Note to Directors

The attached memorandum is suggested as a first communication from the directors concerning the establishment of a new social policy for the company, with accountability, in detail, to the directors.

As a first such policy statement, it contains a minimum of prescriptive direction. Most of it deals with the start of a new information flow to the directors concerning the social performance of the company. This will provide the directors with the data to guide later and more explicit statements of social policy.

The customary outline of items for a social audit are omitted at this time. This can better be constructed for the several divisions of the company after the directors have had the opportunity to study the opinions and attitudes of the major constituencies who normally judge the behavior of the company. The directors will then have a sound basis for establishing reasonable social performance standards for the company.

The aim is that within one year sufficient data will be assembled and analyzed so that agreement can be reached among directors on what social performance it is reasonable to expect from the company in the foreseeable future.

Social Policy for the Company

As a general policy, the company is to be economically successful (both long term and short term) and it is to be regarded as socially responsible by all interested parties: employees (including administrators), vendors, owners, customers, suppliers, church, university, and appropriate agencies of government. Social performance is to be separately judged in each country where the company operates.

The criteria for economic success are well established and the economic performance of the company as a whole is currently good. This is to be maintained.

The criteria for judging social performance, heretofore, have not been made explicit. This first policy statement is a step toward making these criteria more explicit in the company and its subsidiaries, together with procedures for assessing performance.

1. The company will be concerned to develop a leading role in social matters, and hence will take care not only to follow the spirit of existing legal requirements but even to keep ahead of them by elaborating and applying original measures ahead of legal requirements.

In this respect, each major division of the company will present to the directors, for the first time in July 1975, an annual report for the past twelve months giving: (1) a description of all new laws or regulations governing social performance that became effective in that period; and (2) the position of the company as far as these new laws or regulations are concerned, indicating also the new measures taken voluntarily in this field by the company.

2. The central office of the company will devise a general system for assessing the attitudes toward, and opinions about, the

social performance of the company by all eight of the constituencies named above. These will be adapted as appropriate in each of the countries where the company has a substantial operation, but the central office of the company will maintain a sufficient knowledge of variations so that a company-wide assessment can be made. After a review of these findings by the top administrators of the company, they will be reported to the directors not later than July 1, 1975. The directors, with the aid of professional consultants responsible to them, will analyze these reports and will determine whether the data from these surveys give a sufficient basis for the design of a procedure for a social audit. Further detailed policy determinations will emerge from these deliberations.

3. Coincident with the above, each major division of the company will establish a task force study team of five workers and five administrators who will be relieved of their regular duties for three months to conduct a study of opportunities for greater participation of workers in decisions that affect them. The purpose of these studies will be to provide the data that will give the basis for prudent arrangements for effective worker participation that will be appropriate for each location. After reviewing their findings with the top administrators of the company, all study teams will report in person to the directors not later than January 1, 1976. The directors, with the aid of professional consultants responsible to them, will analyze these reports and will formulate explicit policies, appropriate to each subsidiary company, for worker participation.

4. A study team of ten key administrators from as many divisions of the company will be established. These administrators will be relieved of their regular duties for three months to study the structure of power and authority at all levels of the company. Particularly, the team will study the practical functioning of the top executive groups in the company and its subsidiaries with reference to the proposals set forth in the essay on "The Institution as Servant," and it will reach conclusions about the feasibility of top administrative groups composed of governing councils of

equals that are led by a *primus inter pares*. After having reviewed its findings with the top administrators of the company, this study team will report its findings in person to the directors not later than January 1, 1976. The directors, with the aid of professional consultants responsible to them, will analyze the reports and will formulate explicit policies regarding the structure of power and authority in the company.

5. The central office of the company will provide staff help to the study teams described in the previous two paragraphs to assist both in the organization of the studies and in the writing of their reports and recommendations. But such support will not be used to influence the substance of the reports and recommendations, which will be reviewed by the top administrators of the company, but which will be reported in person to the directors for their use in formulating policy. The directors will, of course, take into account the views of top administrators in making their policy decisions.

6. Each major division of the company is expected (1) to be aware of trends and developments in other businesses and other institutions in matters covered by the foregoing paragraphs, (2) to participate in associations and consultations concerning these matters in the countries where they have substantial operations, and (3) to report to the directors on each July 1 on such involvements during the previous year, plus any conclusions reached regarding the application of what is learned to the company.

Concluding Note to Directors

These recommendations are made, as I said at the outset, primarily to start a new and regular flow of information to the directors. The procedures suggested here will establish that the interpretation of these data which the directors need for their policy decisions is different from what administrators need for their operating decisions. Therefore, the directors should begin to build their own independent source of advice to help them interpret the new data. Taking these steps (asking for the data and securing independent advice) will probably be disturbing to administrators, initially. But once the practice is established, and with regular discussions between directors and administrators about it, the administrators will realize that they can operate with greater assurance if the directors establish policy—clearly, firmly, and prudently.

If directors want a more socially responsible company (and this is written with the understanding that you, as directors, do want this) they should start the process by becoming more responsible directors. This will require some adjustment from administrators who are accustomed to nominal (and, therefore, less responsible) directors. Directors should accept that when they move to their proper role they create a problem, and that they should deal with it as a problem. The heightened quality of the company that will result will be to everybody's benefit, including the administrators who will be disturbed by the adjustment they must make.

V

Servant Leadership in Education

A story is told about Frank Lloyd Wright, the pioneering architect, when he was based at his studio near Madison, Wisconsin. He was invited by a women's club in Madison to talk to them on the subject "What Is Art?"

In his prime years Wright was a large, impressive man with a good stage presence and a fine voice. He acknowledged the introduction, produced from his pocket a small book, and, without comment, proceeded to read Hans Christian Andersen's fairy tale about the little mermaid. It took only a few minutes and he read it beautifully. When he finished, he closed the book, looked intently at his audience and said, "That, my friends, is art"—and sat down.

This story poses what I see as a central problem of education as it has developed in our country: how to serve perhaps 85 percent of the population who learn best from experience and have trouble with abstract concepts, which dominate school curricula.

Ivan Illich's book *Deschooling Society* has shaken things a bit, but so much has been committed to the vast educational establishment that a comprehensive revolutionary approach such as he advocates does not seem likely. Yet there is a growing disquiet about the gap between what we need and what we now have in education. And there is a question whether any influential agency has the objectivity and the skills to examine the whole range of assumptions about what is done in education and to chart a new course that pushes the outer limits of the reasonable and the possible.

Within the scope of my concern here, "servant leadership," I fault the whole educational enterprise on three major points.

First, I fault it for the refusal (and I believe it is that) to offer explicit preparation for leadership to those who have the potential for it. Not only do educators seem passive about it, but I suspect that some influential educators not only denigrate leadership but administer what has been called an anti-leadership vaccine. The resistance to encouraging the growth of leadership is so formidable that there seems no other way to account for it.

My second concern for the process of education is the general attitude of educators toward social mobility. Elsewhere I quote the president of my old college as defining democracy as "a state of affairs in which it is possible for the more able who emerge in the lower classes to get into the upper classes." He saw the college he presided over as, in part, a facilitator of this process. Further, the common practice of relating ascending levels of income to levels of education adds emphasis to this point of view.

I would like to see the opportunity offered, at both secondary and college levels, for the poor to be prepared to return to their roots and become leaders among the disadvantaged. This suggestion rests upon the belief that the situation of the poor, particularly the neglect of their children, is a national disgrace in our affluent country, and that, if this condition is to be made right, *the natural leaders who arise among the disadvantaged will find the way and organize the effort themselves.* The best service that a school can render to these people may *not* be to homogenize them into the upper classes but to help those who have a value orientation that favors it to develop their ability to lead their people to secure a better life for many. All people should have a choice about how they want to use their lives, and it is the right of the disadvantaged young people to upgrade themselves in whatever way they wish. But I would argue for educational options that will help those who would be challenged by the opportunity to learn to lead their own people.

The third concern I have for education is the state of confusion I sense regarding the teaching of values. Coincident with the retreat from the posture of schools as the upholders of moral norms there has been a substantial growth, due to student demand, for courses about religion. Along with this, religious services, where religion is practiced, seem to have declined on campuses. This leaves the question: Is it only appropriate to teach *about* values and make no judgments about what they ought to be? Is this really an adequate role for schools and colleges? Should not schools be importantly concerned with *value clarification* so that students are given as firm a basis as possible for making the choices they have always made—even when the schools presumed to know what their values ought to be?

Educators carry two major liabilities that, I believe, stand in the way of rigorous training in value clarification. First they have assumed the role of credentialing. It is interesting to note that Thomas Jefferson would not allow the University of Virginia to give degrees as long as he was rector. He believed that degrees were pretentious and he wanted only students for whom learning was a sufficient motivation. The second liability is that collegiate education, which is optional for the student, has become expanded to the point where a buyer's market governs. The combination of these puts the typical college in an uncomfortable bind and makes innovation difficult, even though innovation is essential to their long-term survival. Trustees have compounded the problem by giving faculties virtual control over academic policy.

The following four papers do not purport to cover the whole field, but they do take into account the existence of these problems, among others. They come out of my effort to encourage greater preparation for servant leadership in schools.

FRIENDS SCHOOLS AND THE ISSUE OF "POWER AND AUTHORITY"

(Notes on a talk given to A Seminar for Trustees—Friends Council on Education, Westtown School, January 19–21, 1973)

The whole process of education seems to be heading for a radical shakeup in the next few years. We seem to be at the end of a period of euphoria about education. We have gone through a phase of fantastic increase of resources devoted to education at all levels in the apparent belief that this was the soundest investment we could make, and there has been little disposition for careful detached examination of the assumptions. Two kinds of disaffection have suddenly appeared: first, the Coleman report and the ensuing controversy among the experts that raise some searching questions about what investment in education, *per se*, will accomplish; and, second, the general view of a deteriorating society at a time when, if education were the panacea we innocently thought it was, the social fabric should appear stronger rather than weaker. With this disaffection there is a gnawing frustration: we have no alternatives. When we feel this way about other goods and services we usually have some options. Even if we decide to abandon something, we may be able to get along without it. But if our present style of education is viewed as counterproductive, as some critics are beginning to assert, we have no place to go because we have built a society on the assumption that it is best to keep people in school until age eighteen to twenty-two—and more—and, at this point, we have no other way for them to fit in. This is one of the consequences of building a social structure based on a labyrinth of limited-liability institutions rather than on community. We have the kind of structure that needs the careful oversight of some agency whose sole function is to judge the worth of what we are doing, as a society, and advise us—*and be heard.* But we do not have that and we are left at the mercy of the crude sanctions that a huge and powerful society, even if frustrated and leaderless, may impose. Our fragile educational institutions may have to bear the brunt of much of this in the next few years. I hold with the preacher in Ecclesiastes that "for everything there is a season and a time for every matter under heaven." My sense of the present tells me that now is the time to *build anew*. Only by building anew will some of our independent schools be likely to survive. And building anew will be carried on amid the value confusion of our times, in which power and authority are being subjected to a searching examination.

Power and Authority

Both of these words have a long and varied history of usage. *Power* takes two and one-half pages in the Oxford Dictionary of the English Language and even more in the Concordance to the Revised Standard Version of the Bible—and *might*, which is related, takes still more. There has been a preoccupation with these words, and the concepts they represent, from the earliest records—and it is at fever heat today.

Power has many meanings, but in this discussion let us take it to be coercive force—either overtly to compel or covertly to manipulate. And let us take authority to mean a sanction bestowed to legitimate the use of power.

The ringing phrase from Zechariah, "Not by might, nor by power, but by my Spirit, says the Lord," suggests that in the ancient wisdom there was at least the hope that *might* and *power* might someday be superseded by *spirit*. My worm's-eye view of things suggests that we have made some progress in checking the overt use of power (although modern mechanisms of destruction make the consequences of its use vastly greater), but, as people have grown more sophisticated, covert manipulation seems greater than ever.

As I have pondered these past weeks on the question of power and authority and their relationship to secondary education, I have centered on what I regard as two fundamental issues that should be faced before many minor issues are dealt with. The exploration of these two issues will, I believe, do much to provide a perspective that may be helpful in dealing with the many uses of and responses to power which those engaged in education at all levels confront every day.

Issue #1: The assumption that some individuals know what another ought to learn, and are justified in imposing their judgment— backed up by sanctions.

I can hear the protest: How would any kind of education ever be organized for the young unless some of the more experienced who are willing to teach them make that assumption? I don't know the answer to that question. But I do believe that when people are of secondary school age they are old enough to understand that an assumption has been made, and that it might be wrong—and, for some individuals, that it might not be good for them. Such understanding might speed their maturation and enhance their respect for institutionalized education if the potential for error (perhaps even for evil) in making the assumption were freely acknowledged.

Because of an assignment I now have, I am immersed in the current problems of philanthropic foundations, and I have just read a most interesting book, *Private Money and Public Service*, by Merrimon Cuninggim, who recently stepped down as president of the Danforth Foundation. Dr. Cuninggim was a theologian before taking the foundation presidency some years ago. As I read his book I kept wondering how a man of his background could deal with that subject without examining the obvious theological aspects. And, near the end, he did. Let me read a few cogent sentences:

> [There is] a recognition that a foundation needs to make about itself, a belief having ethical significance that is basic to its self-understanding. This is the recognition of frailty, the belief in sin. As it applies to a foundation it is the realization—the consciously accepted value, if you will—that giving is potentially an immoral act. Jesus is supposed to have said that it is more blessed to give than to receive, though it was Paul, who wasn't there, who attributed it to him. When Jesus summed up his own list of blesseds, benevolence was absent, yet he believed in it—viz., the story of the Good Samaritan. But on more than one occasion he took pains to point out that giving was ethically dangerous.

What Dr. Cuninggim says about giving is also applicable to teaching or to any helping role for that matter—doctor, nurse, social worker—where the helper presumes to know more of what is in the best interest of the recipients than the recipients know for themselves. I am not saying that the helper does not often, or even usually, know what is best. But if the situation is coercive, either overtly or covertly, then the potentiality for evil is there, just as Dr. Cuninggim says it is with giving. I have done enough foundation staff work to be certain in my own experience that the role of almoner is a corrupting one—for the almoner as well as for the recipient. The recently published Hospital Bill of Rights is an acknowledgment that hospital administrators are sharply aware of the potential evil in the caring role.

Part of the problem of all eleemosynary institutions is the presumption of virtue in the nonprofit posture. There may be moral risk in any idealistic pretensions. An old sociologist friend of mine once, in an off-the-record comment about the relative quality of interpersonal staff relations in large institutions, made this generalization: "The relative quality of staff interpersonal relations is inverse to the idealistic pretensions of the institutions."

I have had a good deal of experience with large institutions—businesses, philanthropies, universities, churches—and my experience confirms the assertion that there is a moral risk in idealistic pretensions. Perhaps because of the more blatant use of raw coercion in some of the businesses, there is less ambiguity about power and authority than in the others. The real test, as I see it, is where compassion is called for. In a discussion of these issues, this question was once put to me: "If you were really down—demoralized, humiliated, disgraced—and nothing but pure compassion, readiness to go the second mile in an effort to restore you as a person would help, in what kind of institution would you have the best chance of being restored?" My instant reply was, "In a business, in a big business—any big business."

If Lord Acton was right when he said "All power tends to corrupt, and absolute power corrupts absolutely" (and I think he was), and if some use of power is unavoidable—in a school or anywhere else (and I think it is unavoidable)—then what do those with tender consciences do? It seems to me they do at least two things: first, they acknowledge the potentiality for evil in the act of doing whatever they do (as Dr. Cuninggim suggests). They acknowledge it to themselves and to all who may be touched by the use of power. In a school, this will be students, parents, teachers, administrators, nonprofessional employees—everybody in sight. Second, they make sure that the balance of power in the institution is optimal. If the teachers have power (as they must), the student, the parent, the administrator, and the nonprofessional employee must have some power. A generalization is offered: The institution is strongest when all the parties have adequate power for their role; it is weakest where one or more of the elements has too little power, because then somebody has too much and the corrupting influence of power is moving toward the absolute.

I will remind you that in offering these observations I am not presuming to tell you how you should think. Rather, I am offering what I think in the hope that you will say what you think and that, out of the dialogue, all of us will be wiser.

Issue #2: The fact that our whole system of education rests on coercion: first the legal requirement for attending school until age 16–18; then the built-in compulsion to continue academic education by the credentialing that begins with the secondary school diploma and continues through the Ph.D. degree—and beyond.

Did you ever reflect on what teaching would be like if all compulsory schooling were abolished and all credentialing in the educational process were prohibited by law—as Ivan Illich recommends? It might have a spectacular effect in the rewards to teachers by giving them greater opportunity to teach people who want to learn. What might it do for students?

As a young man I was asked to help a group of men ranging in age from 35 to 55 whose jobs were threatened by the introduction of a new technology that required them to make elementary algebraic computations—which they could not do. We worked at this in evening sessions twice a week. In our first meeting I discovered that they were very rusty in arithmetic, so a few sessions were devoted to that. Then I worked out a way of introducing them to algebra—without the use of a textbook—which took them in very few sessions as far as most high schools go in a year.

In my youthful enthusiasm I thought I had made a major pedagogical discovery. Then, about that time, I met the principal of a large high school and told him of my discovery, and I asked whether he didn't think my way superior to the dull approach that was common then in high schools. His response was, "There is a factor here that you are not aware of. You were teaching a group of people who wanted to learn algebra. Our problem is that we have to teach algebra to people who don't want to learn it. Your method wouldn't work with them." What a sad commentary! And yet, under compulsory education—either by law or by credentialing—what else can we expect? How much of the total educational effort is devoted to teaching people who do not have a motivation, other than responding to compulsion, to learn what we are trying to teach them? Is there any way out of this dilemma (if you concede that it is a dilemma) other than Ivan Illich's revolutionary approach? Is there an alternative?

Hope for the Future?

I have raised two questions of power: the moral risk in the assumption of virtue, and the extent of coercion in the whole educational process. The least we can do is to acknowledge both the moral risk and the coercion to the students and help them to understand it as a part of the reality of life with which they should learn to deal. Can we go farther than this? Is there a ray of light at the end of the tunnel that may be dark and long? I suspect that the tunnel will be dark and long—but there is a ray of light there for those who believe in *Light*. Let me call your attention to the story of the Danish Folk High Schools (see chapter 1). It tells how an oppressed, dispirited, impoverished people raised themselves by their own effort to assume responsible citizenship.

One might say offhand that there is little in common between mid-nineteenth century Denmark and the United States in the 1970s. However, there is one large common element: the need for rekindling the spirit of young people. The conditions of both societies have a great similarity: oppressiveness. The cause of the oppressiveness and the precise circumstances are different, but the pervasive oppressiveness is very similar. And the remedy, I believe, is the same: raise the spirit of young people, help them build their confidence that they can successfully contend with the condition, work with them to find the direction they need to go and the competencies they need to acquire, and send them on their way. This is the task that is right for secondary education—and the time is right.

How do we do this when our schools are overburdened with their present obligations and are struggling to survive? Your conditions are not as tough as those Grundtvig faced. You have *something* to begin with, and he had *nothing*—nothing but his own vision, and his spirit.

My suggestion is that at the outset you do nothing that seriously interferes with your present obligations or that jeopardizes your survival chances. But add something that is *voluntary*, something that *raises the human spirit*. Try it and see if you are not rewarded. *See if the urge to venture further does not overtake you.*

In Elizabeth Vining's biography of Rufus Jones, *Friend of Life*, there are a few very special lines from a talk he made in London in 1929. "I am not interested anymore in just clinging to the Society of Friends and preserving it. We stand at a crisis and we can be bearers of the torch or we can carefully husband a little flame and keep it from going out a little longer." I wonder what Rufus, the great soul, would say to us here today—forty-four years later—in the face of the kinds of questions that our schools face.

I am sure that Rufus would say something to us about *change*. *And* this would not be a new thought; all of us here are aware of the pressure for change. In our schools we have already changed—sometimes radically—and some of it may have been painful. We know we must change some more, and some of us may be wondering whether we will survive it, and whether, even if we survive, in good conscience we can live with the consequences of the adaptations we make. I know it is a serious problem, and we need to give some thought to the preoccupation with change.

One of the oldest books in the world is of Chinese origin; it antedates Confucius, and is called *I Ching, The Book of Changes*. The counter-culture has embraced it, and you will find it in many college bookstores. *I Ching* is primarily concerned with the philosophy of change, with living with change as an organic part of one's nature rather than thinking of the good as static and change as threatening, as so many of my contemporaries seem to view it.

Back during World War II, when Peking was occupied by the Japanese, there was a little colony of Germans there. One of them was a Chinese scholar, Hellmut Wilhelm, who had done much to acquaint the world with *I Ching*. In an effort to keep their intellectual lights burning during those dark days, they asked Wilhelm to talk to them about *I Ching*. This resulted in a series of eight lectures, which are now available in translation. Let me quote a few lines from Wilhelm's comment on ancient Chinese thought about change:

> Reflection on the simple fundamental facts of our experience brings immediate recognition of constant change. To the unsophisticated mind, the characteristic thing about phenomena is their dynamism. It is only abstract thinking that takes them out of their dynamic continuity and isolates them as static units...[But] it is in constant change and growth alone that life can be grasped at all. If it is interrupted, the result is not death, which is really only an aspect of life, but life's reversal, its perversion...The opposite of change in Chinese thought is growth of what ought to decrease, the downfall of what ought to rule...Change is natural movement, development that can only reverse itself by going against nature...The concept of change is not an external, normative principle that imprints itself on phenomena; it is an inner tendency according to which development takes place naturally and spontaneously...To stand in the stream of this development is a datum of nature; to recognize it and follow it is responsibility and free choice...Safety is the

clear knowledge of the right stand to be taken, security in the assurance that events are rolling in the right direction…In this point of view, which accords the responsible person an influence on the course of things, change ceases to be an insidious, intangible snare and becomes an organic order corresponding to man's nature. No small role is thus assigned to man.

This may suggest our place today, to see ourselves as responsible people at the center of an organic process of change that at this time, may be strenuous and confused. But what is done will be more than a saving action. It will begin with the struggle to survive. However, if survival alone is the aim, it is not likely to succeed. It will include a conserving role; there is much that is good in what we now have and it should be saved. More important, it will build anew, build something that may not yet be dreamed of. *It will be voluntary, and it will raise the spirit.*

A few weeks ago, as we drove to a Meeting on a cold, bright New Hampshire morning, we noticed cars with several dogs inside and a dog sled tied on top and we knew that nearby there was a dog-sled race. My memory jumped back fifty years, and at the Meeting told the children the following story.

The setting was a cold January morning in a little town in Wisconsin, where I then was, on the southern shore of Lake Superior. It happened to be a Saturday when they had their annual dog-sled derby on the ice. A one-mile course had been staked out by sticking little fir trees in the ice. The whole course was easily visible because of the steep slope of the shore.

It was a youngsters' meet and the contenders ranged all the way from large boys with several dogs and big sleds to one little fellow who didn't seem over five with a little sled and one small dog. They took off at the signal and the little fellow with his one dog was quickly outdistanced—he was hardly in the race. All went well with the rest until, about halfway around, the team that was second started to pass the team then in the lead. They came too close and the dogs got in a fight. And as each team came up the dogs joined the fight. None seemed to be able to steer clear of it. Soon, from our position about a half mile away, there was just one big black seething mass of kids and sleds and dogs—all but the little fellow with his one little dog who gave this imbroglio a wide berth, the only one that managed it, *and* the only one to finish the race.

As I reflect on the many vexing problems and the stresses of our times that complicate their solutions, this simple scene from long ago comes vividly to mind. And I draw the obvious moral: No matter how difficult the challenge or how impossible or hopeless the task may seem, *if you are reasonably sure of your course, just keep on going!*

TRUSTEES CONSIDER A HYPOTHETICAL CASE

In the course of helping to lead a conference on the role of trustees that was attended by twenty-five trustees from several universities, I presented a hypothetical case for discussion. This case assumes that the assembled persons are the trustees of Cheswick University and that I am meeting with them as the representative of potential donors who are offering a gift of ten million dollars under rather strict and unusual conditions. Two hours were taken for the discussion. Some excerpts from the record of the conference that represent the tenor of the discussion are given following the statement of the case. In this summary, "T" refers to a comment by a trustee and "D" represents remarks by the donors' representative.

Case Problem for Trustees

You are the trustees of Cheswick University, which is currently operating at a high level of excellence within the conventional wisdom of what a good university should be. Your financial condition and your fund-raising potential are such that you can continue for some time as you are and handle the level of innovation that most universities like you customarily undertake.

You have just received the offer of a ten million dollar gift with these specific conditions:

1. You may not add any of this to your endowment—now or in the future.

2. You may not put any of this into the budget of your present program—now or in the future—or into innovations of your present program.

3. Two million dollars may be spent in analyzing the problem of how best to prepare young people *to serve and be served by the present society and to grow with their opportunities* and in designing a wholly new program to accomplish this end that is feasible at Cheswick University. (By "serve and be served" by the donors mean that the students' education has prepared them to make a constructive contribution to the present society in a way that meets the students' legitimate needs, psychic and material.)

4. If, on the completion of this plan, the donors judge it to be wholly new and feasible, the remaining eight million dollars (plus any remaining portion of the two million dollars) will be available to help finance the introduction of the new program.

5. The advice of your present administration, faculty, and students may be sought, but no part of this fund may be used to compensate for this advice. In other words, until there is a new design that the donors have approved as feasible, and until the trustees have made a firm commitment to proceed to install it, no part of this fund may be spent within Cheswick University.

6. All decisions with respect to the use of this fund must be made by the trustees alone.

7. If you accept this fund under the above conditions, there is no commitment implied to take any action. However, any funds not expended within the above conditions at the end of five years will revert to the donors.

I represent the donors who are offering this fund. I am here to discuss it with you if you want to consider it.

Discussion

T. If the donors assume that Cheswick University is doing reasonably well in a conventional sense, and if they assume that the trustees are persons of integrity, would they not also assume that we already think we are operating this university to produce students who would serve the present society and would grow with their opportunities or we would have no business being trustees? I would think the donors would be looking for some institution that was concerned and uncertain about what it is doing. Why is this proposition being brought to us?

D. The donors are concerned that the best of universities are not adequately preparing young people to serve and be served by the present society and to grow with their opportunities. They are singling you out because you are strong, and they are simply asking you whether it would interest you to find a better way for a university to help its students in this way. Then, if they are satisfied that you have found a better way, they are willing to help you install it, if you want to.

T. But what we may come up with may cost a whole lot more than eight million dollars to install. In that event, how would we finance it?

D. The donors are offering this to you because you are already strong and are able adequately to finance yourselves. They assume that, using the initial two million to find a better way, you will *want* to install it. They are saying, "If you find the better way (and if we accept it), and if you want to install it, we are prepared to put in another eight million." Obviously this is not going to solve your funding needs for all time. The donors assume that your fund-raising operation, which is quite good now, will continue to function.

T. We would have a lot of things to do if we made a radical change—our admissions policy, for instance; move from a homogeneous to a heterogeneous student body, for instance, in terms of age, economic background, academic proficiency, etc. To do what these donors would want, probably, we couldn't use this money to make a better run at the top 10 percent of the scholars.

Then there might be radical curriculum innovations. But you say we can't pay, out of this fund, our own faculty, administrators, or students for working on this. I assume we could pay our trustees. Is that right?

D. Yes, you could pay your trustees out of the two million, if you accept it. You may pay anyone to work on this other than your own students, faculty, or administrators.

T. That is a curious restriction. What are the donors trying to accomplish with that?

D. The donors want the trustees to accept this as their problem. You are not obligated to take any action. You are simply offered two million to find a better way to prepare students to serve and be served by this society and to grow with the opportunity. If you do not want to (or cannot) install it at Cheswick, and if the donors think it is a good idea, they may find another college that wants to try it, and give that college the eight million.

T. I would take the two million.

T. I'm not sure what to talk to you about. I'm not sure whether in the back of the donors' mind is the idea that we can be bought off for ten million. Are they trying to get us to create the kind of university they want?

D. The donors have only two things: (1) a sense of a need for more effort in universities to prepare students to serve and be served by this society and to grow with their opportunities, and (2) money. They don't know how to do this. But they think some strong institution ought to find out. Then, if *that institution* wants to do it (and if the donors are satisfied with what it wants to do), they will give them eight million.

T. This smacks of distrust. I don't like that part of it.

D. The donors do not trust the *governance structure* of the typical university in which trustees are in a nominal and reactive role. They believe that if the usual process of university governance were going to produce an answer to the need they clearly see, it would already have done it. The need, as they see it, is not obscure. So if a better way is to be forthcoming, something has to change. The change they are proposing is that trustees shift their role toward more affirmative educational leadership.

T. Won't the faculty be up in arms about that?

D. The donors think in terms of leadership, not coercion. There is no suggestion that anything be imposed on the faculty. All that is proposed here is that the trustees (as a first step) be offered some money that they cannot give to the faculty. They, the trustees, must take the responsibility to find the answer—how to do the job better. The faculty, students, and administrators can contribute. The only limitation is that they can't be paid for what they do out of the grant of these donors.

T. The donors are challenging our ability to match their minds.

T. I see. You came to us because you think we are good. That implies that we have something going for us, that we really believe in ourselves.

T. But with the resources we now have we are really doing the best that we can. We really believe in what we are doing. Now, you come to us and you offer us some money, and the money is awfully handy. And we've got some ideas of how we would like to do better and the only thing that is holding us back is money. I'm a little skeptical when you come to us and say that you want something entirely new. It makes me want to find out whether the donors feel that money can buy everything.

T. That's nonsense!

T. Look, the spending of the two million is to be given to dedicated people—trustees.

T. Are the donors really saying that a school like ours that is doing such a good job should throw everything out? There must be something in what we are doing that is still good for the years ahead.

D. There is no suggestion in this proposal that anything be changed or thrown out. You can keep your present program as it is if you want to. But if you install a new program alongside of it, one that prepares students to serve and be served by the present society in a substantial way, the program you now have may not long survive the competition.

As the donors see the present state of higher education, it is locked into a set of assumptions that need to be examined in a new way. They are willing to bet two million dollars that if a strong board of trustees would examine the assumptions and get some mechanism engaged other than faculty committees, a better way can be found. Frankly, they do not believe that the institution is as good as you say it is—when judged by what is reasonable and possible with its available resources, human and material. They believe that some strong institution should make a determined effort to break out of what looks to them like a monolithic pattern. And all they are asking is, first, does a trustee board like yours want to try to find a better way? They are sufficiently aware of the inertia in faculty processes and the lack of leadership of administrators not to want to invest the two million with them.

T.   But are they suggesting that we, as trustees, move off in a way that indicates a distrust of our faculty and administrators? I would vote for turning down the proposal—all of it. It would upset the university more than it would help.

D.   I am a little surprised, after this long discussion—and we have been at it for two hours—that none of you has suggested that, as trustees, you take no immediate action but simply circulate the proposal to your faculty, students, and administrators and ask them: "What do you think about this?" Don't submit it to them for decision. Just ask them what they think. Perhaps some of you might sit down with them in small groups and discuss it. You take the role that I have taken here, as the donors' representative. Try to explain to them why a concerned group with money to give might make a proposal like this. And listen carefully, as I have listened to you. Such a procedure might accomplish two things of value to you as trustees.

First, it would alert those of your constituencies that have not gotten the message that there are responsible people who value education but who have come to distrust the capacity of the typical university to govern itself wisely. And of late these people seem to be growing in numbers, among both private donors and public funding bodies. They are still giving support, but they are asking more questions and laying down new conditions. *And these are friends of education.* The university is seen as too anarchistic an institution to be as influential as it is. One hundred years ago, when only about 1 percent of college age young people were actually enrolled, not much note was taken of what kind of institution the university was. But now that 50 percent of the young people are involved in some post-secondary education, the structure of the institution and its impact on values have become a matter of concern. By presenting this proposal to students, faculty, and administrators, you may add some helpful communication— helpful to all who are interested in the university—to the effect that all is not well with the university among those who have the power to turn the money on or off.

Then, second, you may learn some things that will be helpful to you as trustees in deciding how to respond to this proposal. As a representative of the donors, I get around the colleges and universities. And I hear some things that you might not ordinarily hear—things that I believe you will hear if you explore this proposal with your faculty. And what you hear when you engage with your faculty in this way might surprise you.

Some of your faculty, not all—perhaps not a majority—but an important segment, will agree with the donors on the three main arguments I have given as their representative in support of this proposal:

1. The university's present program is not adequately preparing its students to serve and be served by this society and to grow with their opportunities. And it misses it by a wide margin.

2. As the university's governance is now structured, it is not disposed to correct this deficiency.

3. Only the emergence of strong leadership in the governing board, the trustees, will set the university on a sounder course

soon enough to recover the public trust that its survival as a viable institution requires.

The faculty members who support these three contentions will tell you that the fundamental flaw in the structure of the university is that the faculty governs the institution, yet the primary loyalty of too many faculty members as individuals is not to their university or even to their students, but to their discipline, their professional expertise and reputation, and their colleagues that share these in universities generally. Perceptive faculty members know this, and the donors know it. And the donors are wise enough to accept that they cannot, and ought not, use their influence to try to change the predominant loyalty of faculty members. Perhaps this is what a good teacher-scholar has to be. The donors also know that the trustees have given the faculty so much power that the administrators cannot lead them in their educational goals. So the trustees must assume more leadership.

One of the interesting emerging sentiments among faculty is the acceptance that trustees must be strong. They aren't sure what trustees need to do to be strong. But they know they have to be strong in order to maintain the university as an island of freedom in which creative teaching can take place.

What some faculty members now know, what all trustees should know, and what the donors are absolutely convinced of, is that this island of freedom cannot be maintained if the wider public sees trustees as merely acting as a front for a program that does not adequately prepare students to serve and be served by the present society and to grow with their opportunities.

The donors' aim in making their proposal is primarily to give the trustees of a strong university (which means that it has a strong faculty) a way of asserting a new leadership that will build a new public confidence in the university. They are offering you a way (and some means) to rebuild the trustee role as one of, among other things, educational leadership. It is a task for dedicated trustees to build a strong institution to serve the public need in an acceptable way, through the work of a faculty whose predominant loyalty is to its several disciplines. This, in itself, is no small task. Now, if, as is likely, you find a small articulate minority of your faculty urging you to accept this proposal, and if, as is also likely, you have an equally articulate majority arguing against it, you, as trustees, then have a problem of leadership.

It is no challenge to lead when everybody is with you.

LIBERAL ARTS EDUCATION AND THE WORLD OF WORK

In the spring of 1974 I spent ten days in residence as a Senior Woodrow Wilson Fellow at Dickinson College at Carlisle, Pennsylvania. The following is a talk I gave near the end of my stay.

I spent a few days getting acquainted here at Dickinson College before I started to prepare this talk, and I am aware that there is an unusual level of concern, and justifiably so, for the vocational and career outlook of many students. And this concern has raised questions about the adequacy of the college experience as preparation for the conditions that students now face after they leave college. I have been asked many questions in the hope that I could give answers that will give greater assurance for the future. I have no answers to most of these questions, partly because I am of another generation, one that has not experienced the problem as it is seen today, and partly because I believe many of these questions are unanswerable except as one ventures into an experience and learns to respond, in the situation, to the immediate problems one confronts.

I would find it pretentious to talk about the subject "Liberal Arts Education and the World of Work" if the common assumption was how there is, or could be, a close linear relationship between one's experience as a student in a liberal arts college and the subsequent events in the course of any role in society—whether in one's income-earning vocation, or as a parent, or as a citizen. I do not see such a relationship, and I am glad that I live in a world where it does not seem possible. I am not speaking of professional education, such as preparation for careers in engineering, medicine, or law, or about some "bread and butter" subjects that might be offered in an undergraduate college. There, obviously, the student expects an explicit rationale for most of what is learned; it is directly anticipating some later vocational need.

Not very much of a liberal arts education, as it is commonly experienced, can be taken as vocational in this sense. And it is not my intention here to assert that it should be. Rather, I would argue that, in a good society, every person who is capable of being educated at all should be liberally educated first, without direct reference to any specific societal role but with general reference to all of them. Professional or vocational education would be added to that.

Having made that assertion I am in the same trouble as any who assert such things: What do I mean by "liberal education" in this sense, and can what I mean be translated into how faculties might better design a liberal arts education and how students might better cope with what faculties have designed?

Liberal education suffers, in these times, for want of a contemporary definition. Your college catalogue has one of the better definitions I have read: "a quest after knowledge for its own sake, but also as leading to social involvement in practical affairs for the sake of social good and individual dignity." The editorial in the current *Dickinsonian* (which I thought was a very good editorial) quotes a previous president as stating it in these words: "The grand design of education is to excite, rather than pretend to satisfy, an ardent thirst for information; and to enlarge the capacity of the mind, rather than to store it with knowledge, however useful." My own inclination would be to state the goal in more operational terms: "to prepare students to serve, and be served by, the present society." By this I mean that a college, operating through the program its faculty chooses to design, will influence its students to be a more constructive building force in society and to do this in a way that helps them find their own legitimate needs, psychic and material, better served, than if they had not participated in the college program. I state the goal this way because I believe that new sanctions regarding all of education are emerging and that, with regard to private liberal arts colleges especially, the colleges will be better able to sustain what I regard as a vital and necessary role if they state their goals (and shape their implementing programs) in operational terms such as I have suggested—to prepare their students better to serve, and be served by, the present society. This has different connotations from the usual language used in defining the aims of liberal education, and I commend it to your consideration.

If I have anything of value to share with you in how to implement such a goal, it is because I have had an unusual opportunity to observe and participate in a wide range of contemporary institutions. And if a liberal education is to prepare its students better to serve and be served by the present society, it needs, it seems to me, to begin by giving students a realistic view of the institutional structure that students will enter as participating members four to eight years later.

Within my lifetime ours has shifted from a society dominated by small farmers to one dominated by large, urban-based institutions: large government, large business, large university, large philanthropy. This complex structure is so new that we have not yet taken the full measure of it, and, I suspect, we have not yet learned how to prepare people to live in it and to cope with the challenges it presents. Along with this there has been a shattering of many certainties that I grew up with—certainties that made life less threatening, even though some of the assumptions that gave this certainty proved to be questionable.

I want in a few minutes to try to communicate a view of the vagaries of this institution-bound society as I see them from my particular vantage point. I will not do this in a closely reasoned way. That would take too long—and besides, I am not capable of it. Rather, I want to read a brief quotation from the early writing of G. K. Chesterton that sets the mood in which I want to discuss the subject "Liberal Arts Education and the World of Work." Chesterton wrote this in 1924, when I was coming of age and before the era of the computer had overtaken us:

The real trouble with this world of ours is not that it is an unreasonable world, nor even that it is a reasonable one. The commonest kind of trouble is that it is nearly reasonable, but not quite. Life is not an illogicality, yet it is a trap for logicians. It looks just a little more mathematical and regular than it is; its exactitude is obvious, but its inexactitude is hidden; its wildness lies in wait.

As I have participated in the affairs of this world I have found that its wildness *does* lie in wait. I see a world full of ambiguity. But I am also aware that one person's ambiguity is another's regularity. All of us see the world through our own peculiar colored glasses. Let me give you a few examples of what loom as ambiguities through my particular colored glasses.

Coffee, tobacco, alcohol, marijuana, and heroin are all drugs. All, if used excessively, are health impairing. Heroin is so destructive when one becomes addicted (and addiction comes easily) that few would question the strict control of it. Coffee is so relatively mild that few would advocate its restriction. Of the middle three, a case can be made that marijuana is less addictive and possibly less harmful than the others. Yet tobacco and alcohol are freely available, and you can be put in jail for having anything to do with marijuana.

The verbs *correct* and *reform* are frequently used to indicate the function of penal institutions, whereas *crime-inducing* would more accurately label the consequence of the usual imprisonment.

One would think that inspired and creative contributors to society would leave a liberating influence as their legacy. In notable instances, however, a cult ensues that obscures the teaching. It happened to Jesus of Nazareth two thousand years ago and to Kurt Lewin, the great experimental psychologist who died in 1947 leaving in his wake a succession of "groupy" movements: sensitivity training, encounter groups, etc. It even happened to a work that my wife and I originated twenty years ago. A few years after we had left it in other hands it was brought to us for review.

It was codified, manualized, and ready for copyright, thereby to establish a jurisdiction. I will never forget the startled, almost panicked, expression on the face of the person who brought it when I said, "Why don't you just give this away and go do something else?"

A few years ago I was serving as consultant to the trustees of a college. This was a period in which there was considerable pressure from students to relax parietal rules, and I sat in as the trustees discussed the issue. Among the trustees, the conspicuous holdouts for hard-line adherence to the old rules were two who were noted as playboys.

The killing of wild animals is widely accepted as a sport.

In the last few years I had two revealing conversations with the heads of two of our very large institutions. In the first I was in a counseling relationship and was listening to an outpouring of frustrated feeling of a very able chief executive who was trying to lead his institution (a large and influential one) out of a vexing problem. I must have listened for nearly an hour to the details of his unsuccessful effort to get this institution to deal realistically with the problem. When he finally concluded, I made a statement something like this: "I have no answer to your dilemma and, from what you have told me, you have exhausted every avenue open to you to deal with it. In such a situation, with the problem still urgently needing a solution, I see no course open to you but to set in motion an inquiry to get a deeper and more comprehensive understanding of the problem, in the hope that out of this larger understanding will emerge the clue to a new course of action that you haven't thought of." I took a little longer than this to state my position, and while I was doing it I noted the color rising in his neck, and I knew that when I finished my little speech I was going to catch it—and I did. He glared at me as he pounded his desk with his fist and literally shouted. "Damn it," he exploded, "I don't want to understand anything. I just want to know what to do about it!"

In the case of the second top executive, I had come to him with the account of a serious situation, a major flaw, I had uncovered in his institution that I thought was urgently in need of correction. In this case, after stating my position, I got a gentle lecture something like this: "There are a lot of things wrong with this institution that need correcting. At any one time I can deal with only a limited number of them, and the only way I can sleep at night so that I can come back tomorrow and keep working at it is to pretend that most of these problems are not there. And that is what I am going to do with the one you mention. This job of mine is tolerable only because I am capable of living with the illusion that things are a lot better than they really are."

Any who were members of the academic community in the late 1960s must be sharply aware that its wildness lies in wait. Colleges and universities, like other institutions, tend to forget their histories. There have been earlier periods of wildness; the late 1960s was not the first one. Early in 1969 I attended an off-the-record meeting of twenty-five university presidents who met to discuss, among other things, the current student unrest. Two of them were conspicuous by their superior air of "it won't happen at my university." But before June, both their campuses were a shambles and those two presidents had resigned.

I could give you many more anecdotes and illustrations of this kind. These are a representative selection of recent ones out of a wide range of experiences over many years that give meaning to Chesterton's sharp observation fifty years ago.

The world of affairs, as I have experienced it, is a very ambiguous one. The problem of preparing people to serve and be served by this society is, as Chesterton says, that the world is nearly reasonable but not quite. It is not illogical, yet it is a trap for logicians.

Part of the ambiguity that students need to learn to deal with in the course of their preparation to serve and be served by the present society is that it is a high form of art to ask the right questions. But it is also unrealistic to expect that someone else has answers for them. I said at the outset that many of the questions students have asked me during these days I regard as unanswerable except as one ventures into some experience and learns to respond, *in the situation,* to the immediate problems one confronts. And to do this one must have learned how to open one's awareness to receive insight, inspiration, in the moment of need. One must accept that only venturing into uncertainty with faith that if one is adequately prepared to deal with the ambiguity, *in the situation,* the answer to the questions will come. The certainty one needs to face the demanding situations of life does not lie in having answers neatly catalogued in advance of the experience. That, in fact, is a formula for failure—one is surprised, sometimes demoralized, by the unexpected. *Dependable* certainty (which we all need a lot of) lies in confidence that one's preparation is adequate so that one may venture into the experience without pre-set answers but with assurance that creative insight will emerge in the situation when needed, and that it will be right for the situation because it is an answer generated in the situation. A liberal education provides the best context I know of for preparing inexperienced people to venture into the unknown, to face the inexactitude and the wildness, with assurance. *But, having said that the conventional liberal arts curriculum is the best context for such preparation, I must also say that it usually does not contain the preparation—and it should.*

I have said this in a way to lead up to something. The usual assumption about liberal education is that the preparation I am talking about is implicit. I would contend that, as in the song in *Porgy and Bess,* "it ain't necessarily so." I am not judging whether the impact of a liberal education at Dickinson gives the preparation I am urging because I am not close enough to have an informed opinion. I will only say that *it ain't necessarily so.* If you want to assert that it does happen here, or that there is a high probability of its happening here, then I would be interested in hearing a more explicit case for it than I have been aware of in what I have encountered thus far.

Let us assume for the moment that my view of it is correct, that what you have in a conventional liberal arts program is a good context for preparing students to venture into the unknown with assurance, so that students are better able to serve and be served by the present society, but that the preparation itself is lacking. I would like to address the issue thus presented as a student of organization, of how things get done, not as an educator.

As an organization theorist, I am an idealist—as you will find if you read the three essays I have written on the theme of *servant:* one on leadership, one on institutions, and one on trustees. But, as a consultant, I am a gradualist, because I am disposed to work with the ambiguities and not try to impose idealistic solutions. Rather, I try to take the time to understand the ambiguities in order that my own creative processes will respond in constructive ways. So, in addressing the problem as it might be identified here at Dickinson, I am assuming that you are being guided by a consultant who is providing this creative service. With this reservation, here is my advice.

First, I think you need a goal that is stated in operational terms. I have suggested one: *to prepare students to serve and be served by the present society.* You might find a better one, but I urge you to ponder mine for a while before you discard it. I urge your consideration of it because I believe it is on the wave of the future. We are beginning to see our society as one of limited resources and the people who have the power to turn the money on or off are going to scrutinize the goals of all institutions, including colleges and universities, and make critical judgments of performance, more so than they have done in the past. They may continue to support a few elite institutions for scholars (I hope they do), but I am sure that they (the people who have the power to turn the money on or off) are not going to continue to support, on the scale we now have them, institutions that state their goals wholly in scholarly terms.

Second, I would not state the initial operational goal, *prepare students to serve and be served by the present society,* as an immediate substitute for the one you now have. I give this caution because I suspect the college is not prepared to deliver on it. Rather, I advise you, initially, to state it as the goal for a quite limited program for a few students who are immediately attracted to it and for faculty who wish to participate in it. At the start, there probably will not be many of either. But I have met both faculty and students here who I believe would respond to the opportunity.

You need, at the start, at least one strong faculty member (supported by a consultant) who meets these tests:

1. He or she is deeply committed to the goal of helping prepare a few students to serve and be served by the present society. They will probably keep their scholarly involvement, too, but they will be more deeply committed to the new goal.

2. They have prepared themselves by thoroughly understanding the two basic needs: learning to cope with the inevitable ambiguity, and faith in the dependability of one's creative resources to produce, in the situation, answers to one's going-in questions as one ventures into new experience,

3. They are prepared to make their way through the faculty decision process and to keep their colleagues informed and at least acquiescent. This is a formidable task, but I have participated in it, and it is manageable—by even just one strong member of your faculty who wants to do it. And that faculty member can be from any subject-matter field.

With a faculty member thus prepared, the basic approach is to set up a group of close-knit students in a non-credit program soon after they arrive as freshmen. The faculty member would communicate to the entire freshman class somewhat in these terms:

> You are offered the opportunity to become a Dickinson Fellow, the purpose of which is to form a close-knit, highly committed group of students who will accept a discipline at least as exacting as participation in a major sport, and with the following aims and obligations:

1. To learn to understand the college community as a *real* and typical community within which you will become effective in societal roles that are comparable to those you will experience in the next stage of your career, after you leave here.

2. Under the leadership of the faculty adviser, the Fellows will examine together the impact of the total college experience on their growth as persons and will learn to plan and manage their own growth—now and after college.

3. You will be counseled, both by your colleagues and by your faculty adviser, in how you can best be served by the resources of the college in order that you will learn how to relate later to other institutions so that your own legitimate needs will be optimally served by whatever your later participation in society will be.

4. The Fellows as a group will organize and execute missions in the service of others, both for the benefit that you can give to others at this time and so that you can learn how best to organize to serve and to discriminate between good and poor service—in preparation for later stages of your career.

5. The commitment required is that you place this work as the first priority after your academic program—and ahead of social life or other extracurricular activities. The reason for this is that the work of the Fellows program requires it, and it offers an opportunity to establish the habit of voluntary discipline in the use of your time as a preparation for organizing an effective life for the remainder of your career. Periodically the level of commitment of Fellows in the program will be reviewed.

This is a rough suggestion for an extracurricular offering that might be made to all freshmen. I have a little experience with this sort of thing, and I believe that if a strong faculty member undertakes to organize and direct it, there will be some takers, maybe not many at first, but enough to start.

You can see in the way I have stated this that I reject the idea (which I have heard from both faculty and students here at Dickinson) that there is a *real* world outside beyond these walls and that what you have here is something else—a place where you prepare for the *real* world. If I hear you correctly, you have accepted a terrible limitation. This place is just as real as anything its students will ever experience. It is real because the ambiguities are here—as rich an assortment as will be found anywhere.

In the two basic life skills I have mentioned, making one's way in an inexact and ambiguous world and venturing into the unknown with unanswered questions—and I call them skills because both call for rigorous preparation—the chance to learn these skills in a way that makes one both marketable and assured in taking the next step beyond college is actually better in these undergraduate years than it may be at any later stage in one's life. And the context of a liberal arts curriculum, I believe, is a better setting for it than is any other post-secondary opportunity I know about.

This is a long way around to the answer to a question you may have brought with you about the implication of the title of this talk, "Liberal Arts Education and the World of Work," in which you may have assumed that I was going to present some new rationale for liberal arts education, or argue for its relevance to business or some other calling, or give you my judgment about whether any particular vocational emphasis within the college should be expanded or contracted. The great asset of a broad liberal arts education, as I know it, is that it does not have much bearing on any vocation in particular but has great relevance to all vocations in general—*provided* that the college environment within which it is carried out is accepted as real, as real as any chapter in one's life, and *provided* that an explicit effort is made to prepare students to serve and be served by the present society, using the college experience as the working laboratory.

As your uninvited consultant, I have tried to suggest a way that you could move toward making the connection between the liberal arts and the world of work *necessarily* so, with a minimum of claim on the resources of the college and with no disturbance of its present academic program.

As I say this I call to mind the thoughtful face of one of your seniors with whom I discussed some of these ideas this week. "I wish somebody had talked to me like this when I was a freshman," she said.

CAMPUS USE OF RESOURCE PEOPLE

The Woodrow Wilson Foundation, under a grant from the Lilly Endowment, administers a program with about seventy-five colleges (mostly liberal arts) in which visitors from the fields of business, government, and the professions spend periods of one to three weeks on campus as Senior Woodrow Wilson Fellows. In the fall of 1974 the representatives of seventy participating colleges met at Wingspread Conference Center at Racine, Wisconsin, for a discussion and evaluation of their first year of experience with this program. I gave the following talk at the opening of that conference.

I regard the three-year term of the grant that supports the Woodrow Wilson Foundation Senior Fellows program as a testing period for what I believe is a basically sound idea. It also provides an opportunity to learn how best to use such resources as senior fellows for the optimal yield of educational benefit to students, with the hope that there will be valuable by-products for the senior fellows, for the campus coordinators and other faculty, and for the colleges. But service to students is the primary goal.

I have no idea what the priorities of funding agencies will be a year or so from now when the need to refund this program arises. Nor can I predict how their staffs might then view the value of work of this sort. Therefore, the best contribution I can make to your discussion is to exploit my relatively detached, yet somewhat informed position and present a view from my own experience that may suggest ways that service of the senior fellows to students may be made significantly greater than I believe it usually is. This is the best way I know to help assure that this program will continue.

I believe that the senior fellows program has had an auspicious start, that a good beginning has been made; but the evidence of accomplishment that I have seen thus far does not assure me that the best use is being made of senior fellows. If my judgment is correct, the burden of the necessary action in this program rests on the colleges rather than on the Woodrow

Wilson Foundation, which, after all, can only advise. Consequently, I will address what I have to say to the colleges. And I will address the question, How can a college make the visit of a Woodrow Wilson senior fellow of optimal value to students?

As I have assessed the possible contributions to students that are made by visitors of all kinds on college campuses, they are in three categories. (1) There are the "big names" who will draw a crowd and give the students the feeling of being in touch with the controversial issues that make the current news. (2) Then there are those whose primary contribution is to enrich the culture of the campus by reading their poetry, giving concerts, presenting general lectures, and so on. (3) Finally, there are subject-matter specialists, scientists and the like, who may excite little interest outside faculty and student groups that are identified with their specialties. Occasionally a visitor will serve in more than one of these ways. But these, I believe, are the main categories. All of these people make their contributions, and to the extent that the college can afford them, they are a vital part of the college program. Also, the usual college is prepared, administratively, to schedule the use of visitors in these categories in a satisfactory way.

However, the usual Woodrow Wilson senior fellow is not chosen to fit any one of these categories. By chance some of them may do very well in one or more of these ways; if they do, it is a bonus that was not bargained for. And, as I read the reports, it seems to me that the colleges are attempting to use the senior fellows as if they would serve in one or more of these customary ways, and sometimes it works out reasonably well. But even if it does work well in terms of audience response, it is not necessarily evidence that the senior fellows are being used in their strongest roles.

In my own case, the one time I have been a senior fellow, the report sent back by the college suggested that the audience response was good. But, from my standpoint, with some perspective on what a senior fellow like me can do for students (because I have had considerable experience working with them as an outside resource person), I do not believe that I was well used. It was not even close to the kind of educational benefit to students that is easily possible.

As I study the backgrounds of the people who serve as senior fellows, I believe I am fairly typical of them. There is an occasional person on the list, like ex-senator Margaret Chase Smith, who would readily fit into the first of the three categories I mentioned—she would be well known enough to draw a crowd and she would contribute in other ways. But, the credentials of most of us are what the purpose of the program states: we are persons with substantial experience from business, industry, the professions, and government. If the colleges were spending their own money to bring people who fit into one of the three categories, and if the credentials of all of us on the list so far were fully known, very few of us would be invited—because we would not serve well in any of the three ways that resource people usually are expected to contribute. I have had other invitations to be a campus visitor in recent years because, in a few places, there is a fourth category clearly established where my kind of qualifications are readily of service to students. Let me describe the kind of students and the arrangements needed for a resource person like me to be well used.

I know from my own experience that on every campus there is a substantial group of students (perhaps not the majority, but substantial) whose members have the potential to become carriers of responsible roles in society, roles like those most of the senior fellows now occupy or have recently occupied. These students are already committed to a servant ethic; they are willing to work hard (without the incentive of grades, credits, and degrees) to build the competence that is required to act responsibly; and they have the potential to develop that quality of intuitive judgment, the gift of knowing, that sets successful bearers of responsibility apart from others. Usually, in their college years, students are but dimly aware, if at all, of their potential in these regards, nor do they always clearly see the significance of these talents as they enter their careers. Some of them mature their talents, but some of them do not—at a great cost to themselves and to the society they have the potential to serve well. *These are people who may make a quantum leap in their growth as responsible persons while they are in college if someone on the faculty takes an interest in finding and coaching them, much as the athletic department finds and coaches athletes.* And the growth of these students in their college years can be just as spectacular as growth in athletic prowess. I have watched it happen.

It is these students that most of the senior fellows are best qualified to serve. But optimal educational benefit is not likely to result from their interaction with the senior fellows if there is not an ongoing program in the college, however informal, that prepares these particular students to exploit fully the opportunity that the visit of the senior fellow presents. I have served as a visitor in several colleges where this particular type of student has been identified and prepared to connect with my particular experience, and I have visited and met with students where this sort of preparation has not been done. I can assure you that the difference in the service I can render to students is enormous. And, remember, I think I am quite typical of the senior fellows in this program.

There is a hazard, I know, in using the athletic program as a model. But I use it because it is the best way I know to emphasize that potential bearers of responsibility need special help to mature their talents just as athletes do. And it is at least as important that the college concern itself with their growth—as a distinct mission.

I have said that such students need to be identified. In the case of athletes, this is easy. They come to college with a record. In the case of potential bearers of responsibility, it is difficult. The talent is usually latent, not clearly evident, and often not known by the student. What is required is a faculty member who will articulate the concept so that students can see it and respond if they feel they have it. I have talked to enough students to know that if this talent is latent within them, they know what I am talking about.

What I mean by a potential bearer of responsibility—a leader, if you want to use that term—is not a vocational category, and it is quite independent of career choice. It may be latent in the potential lawyer, doctor, engineer, businessman, scientist, or scholar in the classics. And it is not something to be taught about in an academic way. It is a talent to be coached, using the campus as the laboratory for learning to bear responsibility well.

The college should not depend on the senior fellow to awaken the students' awareness of their latent talent. Senior fellows usually are not teachers and do not know how to do this. Furthermore, they do not have the established relationship with students that is required. It is a faculty responsibility to awaken the students' awareness and prepare them to work with the senior fellows. Also, the senior fellows are not there as role models. They are there as a special kind of wisdom source for those students who have a sharpened awareness of what the senior fellows, out of their experience, can give them.

I realize that the assumption has been made that this kind of preparation is implicit in a liberal arts education. It may be, and it may not be. As far as I am aware, it is one of those unexamined assumptions. All I can say is that, in my experience, between those situations where an interested faculty member takes the initiative in finding and coaching these students as consciously and explicitly as the athletic coach does (maybe even in competition with the coach), and where this is not done, the contrast is very great when viewed from the vantage point of a visitor like a senior fellow.

Why have the colleges generally chosen not to make this a part of their established programs? Why do colleges not want to identify and coach those students who have the potential to become exceptional bearers of responsibility? There is a definite reluctance to do it, I can assure you. I have worked at this for the past ten years. In a few cases I, and others who have similar beliefs, have been able to persuade a college to do something— where we helped raise the money to pay a faculty member to do it and invested a lot of our own time. But when we stopped (and the money stopped), the effort stopped.

This has puzzled me. Colleges make a real effort to do the things that they think are important in the education of their students, and they stretch what money they have over all of those things. Yet what I have described is rarely accepted as an obligation by the college. Occasionally there are faculty members who, on their own, wield an influence that has this effect— sometimes, I believe, without being conscious that they are doing it. In one college I know of back at the beginning of the twentieth century, a few professors, one in particular, wielded an influence that lifted the quality of the culture in a whole state. One teacher performed this service for me in a significant way. But why is this not explicitly acknowledged as an obligation to all students in all colleges—and at least a pass made at doing it in a formal way? I have puzzled over this for a long time, and I would like to construct a very speculative theory in answer to that question, using one tiny fragment of evidence.

When I served as a senior fellow last spring, I was watching the process closely because that was partly why I was there. Although I had many ideas about how I might best be used, I did not offer them. I wanted to see what the experience was like when the college handled it its way. And it was handled very well—I was kept enjoyably busy. There was not the preparation of students that I have advocated here. But I doubt that that has been done in many places. My wife and I had a pleasant time, and we valued it as a plus experience. But in the course of going about, I was several times introduced as a representative of the *real* world. Finally, I challenged some faculty members on it. "What are you saying when you say that? This place is as real to me as anywhere I have ever been. And it seems to me terribly important that students see it as real." Folks were startled by my question, and I did not get a good answer to it. Afterward I speculated on whether there were some deep Freudian implications in the frequent use of the word *real* in referring to the nonacademic world, with the suggestion that the college is *unreal*. Is there the possibility that there is the unconscious wish for the colleges not to be seen as *real* because then the institutions may be able to escape the implications of the kind of obligation I have been pressing on them?

The burden of my argument is that these students who are potential bearers of responsibility should see their college years as being as real as anything they will ever experience. Therefore, they should conduct themselves in the college environment in a way that develops to the full their capacity for responsible behavior. *But they need help.*

Even the communication from the Woodrow Wilson Foundation reinforces this *unreal* image when it refers to business, industry, the professions, and government as "the world of *practical* affairs." Does that suggest that the college is the world of impractical affairs?

One hundred years ago, when only 1 percent of the college-age population was actually enrolled, there was not such concern about what kind of place academe was—it could be unreal or impractical, if it wanted to. But now that 50 percent are enrolled, there is much concern with the nature of academe because it is so very influential. It cannot be unreal or impractical in any sense.

Senior fellows may, of course, contribute to the program of the college in many ways, such as giving lectures (if there really is a place for them), visiting classes, meeting with faculty committees, talking with those who want a personal conversation, and socializing with both faculty and students. But these, as I see it, are *peripheral reasons* for their being there. The central reason for the senior fellows' presence is that the college has a sustained program for identifying and coaching those students who are most likely to achieve, in some field, positions like the ones the senior fellows now hold in their own fields, and who will be greatly stimulated by a substantial opportunity to share with the senior fellows *if they are prepared in advance of their coming.* This, I believe, is the strongest case for the senior fellows' presence, and it should not be left to chance that the students will identify their own needs and arrange for this service for themselves. This, it seems to me, is part of what a college is for.

As I have pondered the sad state of leadership in our country in recent months—not just in Washington but everywhere—I have wondered whether there is an other single opportunity in our colleges and universities today that ranks greater in importance than finding and coaching those students who have the potential for being exceptional bearers of responsibility. All of the other great services of higher education may not avail us much in the future if the talents of students with this particular gift do not mature *now*, while they are in college. It is neither difficult nor expensive to do—but it does take the will to serve, clarity of purpose, and determination. Any college that does it and makes it known will find the ablest people from the nonacademic world knocking at its doors eager to help. There is no surer way to guarantee the future than to have strong ethical leaders in the making now.

I was not involved in the decision to make the grant that supports the senior fellows program, but I know that it grew out of conviction that communications between the academic and the nonacademic sectors should be encouraged. It was hoped that in three years we could learn enough about it so that a much better judgment could be made by all concerned about the problems and opportunities in doing this. I am a part of the process of learning, and I welcome the chance to share with you some of my learnings thus far. I want very much for the Woodrow Wilson Senior Fellows program to continue, and I look forward to learning much from you as the conference proceeds.

VI

Servant Leadership in Foundations

The most difficult way to serve may be the giving away of money. If one is to serve, one needs a continuous assessment of how the persons being served are responding. In other kinds of institutions—businesses, universities, churches, hospitals—the recipient of service is prompt and candid in reporting assessments of the value of the service. The givers of money, on the other hand, rarely hear anything but commendation. When, as occasionally happens, a recipient complains, the giver is apt to find it unnerving because complaints from donees are so rare. The giver of money is denied the essential element of criticism without which sustained service is difficult (not impossible, but difficult).

Since people with money to give away, whether individuals or foundations, tend to become preoccupied with reacting to the importunings of grant seekers, there is little opportunity to lead—because leading is initiating rather than reacting. (The opportunity for foundations to lead is limited, but it is there.)

Foundations err, I believe, by regarding their existence as a right, rather than as a privilege. They may have a right, but that is a legal question. If, however, *the people* in foundations—trustees and staffs—wish to be servant-leaders, then they should think of their existence as a privilege rather than a right. Of course, every truly serving institution thinks of its existence as a privilege. In a foundation, the concept of its existence being a privilege needs to be clearer and stronger than in the others.

The two articles that follow were published in *Foundation News*, the journal of philanthropy, in 1973 and 1974. They were written out of my experience as a consultant to foundations, seven of them, ranging from the very large to the quite small. In addition I was trustee for a number of years of a middle-sized one.

215

Out of this experience I have a deep conviction of the potential for service by foundations in our plural society. And, since foundations, of all contemporary institutions, are the most responsive to leadership by trustees, they have a clearer opportunity to become models of servant leadership that others may learn from and emulate.

FOUNDATION TRUSTEES

There is ample literature on the legal, financial, and procedural aspects of foundations. My concern is with less explored dimensions: the impact of foundations on people and institutions, and the opportunity for foundations to become respected examiners of assumptions for the benefit of all of us.

My interest in this subject grows out of a larger concern for the whole gamut of our voluntary (nongovernmental) institutions and for the changing expectations of the times that make imperative a radical advance in their service to society—all of them, that is, universities, businesses, churches, social services, philanthropies. Under the existing organizational arrangements (especially the role of trustees), internal administrators and staffs are not responding adequately to the new imperative. A new trustee initiative will be required, with trustees in a much more affirmative and much less reactive role.

As I see it, there is no other way that so few people can raise the quality of the whole American society as far and as fast as can trustees and directors of our voluntary institutions, *using the strength they now have in the positions they now hold*. It is within the context of this larger concern for voluntary institutions and their trustees that I will discuss the role of foundation trustees.

My bias about foundations as we now have them is that they make a much needed contribution to our plural society—and that they have the potential for a much greater contribution. I believe there is a useful role for the very large and the very small, for the family-dominated and the non-donor-governed, and for the business foundation and the special-purpose fund. It is important that they all continue as significant influences and make the adaptations necessary to survive and grow in stature with enough autonomy to do their work.

Foundations, like other voluntary institutions, exist at the pleasure of the people and their government. But the tenure of foundations is less secure than that of other institutions because they appear to be almost wholly creatures of tax privilege; further, they are secondary institutions in that they are usually not operating philanthropies that render a direct public service.

A foundation is essentially a group of trustees who manage a pool of uncommitted funds that can be used for a wide range of socially beneficial purposes. This is a very privileged role, not just for what can be accomplished by giving money, but for the opportunity for the foundation to make of itself a model of institutional quality, integrity, and effectiveness.

Most of the power that foundations hold is centered in the grant-decision process that is almost exclusively a trustee prerogative. The staff of a foundation, where it has one, usually does not have the autonomous stature of the faculty in a university or the medical staff in a hospital or even the management and technical cadre in a business—because in all three of these the staffs are delivering the service in the marketplace by which the institution is judged.

Furthermore, foundations are a relatively new phenomenon with little tradition to guide them. Because there is no well-defined constituency that provides a continuous market test for their efforts, and because theirs is largely a *giving* rather than a *serving* posture, foundations receive little informed criticism of their work. Recipients of grants, and those who see themselves as potential grantees, rarely criticize. And if they do criticize, usually trustees do not hear it. Thus most of the criticism of foundations that trustees hear is from people who do not get grants, or who do not want them, and this has limited value as a corrective for future decisions.

All institutions, all people, do better when they are guided by informed criticism. Foundations get much criticism, but they suffer for want of this essential kind. Therefore, one should not be surprised that some responsible, well-informed people choose to question whether foundations as we know them should exist at all.

These conditions impose an unusual obligation on foundation trustees, a much more demanding obligation than in other institutions, profit or nonprofit. More than in any other, *foundation trustees are the institution.*

Those who have been deeply involved in foundation staff work, particularly in a large foundation, are aware of the incessant pressure of grant requests. They know how difficult it is to judge the merit of a request, and they know that many meritorious ones must be turned down. Sensitive people have referred to this as "corrupting work" because the grant applicants, no matter how prestigious and powerful they may be, approach the foundation as supplicants. Communication is warped to the extent that a feeling of omniscience is a serious occupational disease of foundation staff work. Not all who are exposed contract the disease, but the incidence is high. An early foundation officer recommended a ten-year limit of tenure in order to reduce the liability.

Dr. Merrimon Cuninggim, former president of The Danforth Foundation, in his book *Private Money and Public Service,* takes a more theological view of it when he suggests that "giving is a potentially immoral act." He continues:

> Its danger lies in its assumption of virtue by the agent, of the virtue of agentry, with an accompanying train of other unvirtuous assumptions. The relatively innocent desire to help is so thinly distinguished from wanting to be the helper. But the latter is capable of all sorts of distortions: wanting to be widely known as the helper, wanting to make some decisions for the helpee, wanting to dictate, to paternalize, to manipulate. It is not likely that a foundation, any more than a person, will escape these faults by thoughtlessness or accident. Only by being conscious of the danger is there a chance to escape. In other words, a foundation must believe in the potential immorality of giving.

These may be debatable positions, but my experience with foundations leads me to accept them. They are cited here not in criticism of foundations but rather to establish how difficult and dangerous their work is, and that it imposes the most exacting level of trust upon those who carry the ultimate responsibility—trustees. Further, the burden of these risks is heaviest on the administrative officers and staff who deal personally with grant applicants, a contact from which trustees usually are shielded—and should be shielded.

Since the officers and staff are the ones who are vulnerable, someone else should stand watch. Thus trustees, directly and personally, become the nurturers and guardians of the integrity of the institution. And to carry this role, even in the smaller foundations, the trustees should have help that their administrative officers and staff, who must deal with grant applicants and grantees, cannot supply. There is no clearer way to acknowledge these critically important dimensions of the trustee obligation than to engage a staff that will serve trustees in their oversight function exclusively, and thus establish a clear delineation between the staff that is solely concerned with the trustees' corporate responsibility and the staff that is solely concerned with grant administration.

As I have known them, foundations generally are adequately competent in their legal, financial, and procedural affairs (or, under the spur of the 1969 Tax Reform Act, they are rapidly becoming so). The question about their future (and there is a question) rests more on whether they build and maintain a level of institutional quality, integrity, and effectiveness that is exceptional.

What would this mean? What would be the evidence of a level of institutional quality, integrity, and effectiveness that is exceptional? As an example, take the issues leading to the Tax Reform Act of 1969. There were many foundations that were, and had long been, clear of most of those practices that the act was designed to remedy. For several years there was ample evidence of restiveness in the Congress about those practices, and this was made known to foundation trustees by questionnaires addressed directly from congressional committees to trustees. The foundations (one or several of them) that were striving for institutional quality and integrity might have done the research and prepared the draft of a comprehensive foundation law and taken it to Congress. The result would probably have been a better law than that which came as a result of waiting for the initiative to come from the Congress.

The moral here is that integrity is partly foresight, anticipating the conditions that must be dealt with and acting while there is freedom to act. It is unlikely that the grant administrative staffs of foundations will take initiative of this kind—or that trustees would take such initiative seriously if they did. This kind of action is a trustee function, and trustees themselves should have a concept of their role that would lead them to originate it, with the help—perhaps the urging—of staff support that is exclusively concerned with the trustee function.

If, as I believe, *foundation trustees are the institution*, more so than in any other corporate form, then the obligation to build integrity in the institution with their own initiatives is greatest with foundation trustees. The pre-1969 opportunity is gone. The next opportunity may be sooner than we think.

In my experience, what is described above is not the prevailing view of their roles among foundation trustees. They invest more time in board meetings in deliberating on grant proposals and discussing policy questions than other types of trustees and directors spend on similar details. But the conventional practice, particularly in a large foundation, is to delegate administration to a hierarchical staff structure, much as a business board would do it. And when bureaucratic inertia takes over, as it does—in time—in all institutions that are so structured, the usual remedy is to install a new top administrator who will build some new life into it.

This approach to board responsibility is coming into question in business corporations, and it never has been appropriate for foundations. Under such a policy, the foundation's grant-making staff does not attract and hold enough of the best people, people who will stand as symbols of quality, integrity, and effectiveness.

Nor do the usual staff arrangements favor their professional growth in other important work before the occupational disease mentioned above overtakes them.

Some very able people find their way into foundation staffs despite this, and some have enough immunity to permit long and fruitful careers. But there is too much chance in the process to assure that it will happen this way. The system does not favor it.

Foundation trustees, with the help of their own trustee staff, are responsible for the design of an appropriate structure for the grant-making staff, one that will attract and hold the best people for that work, and for watching it closely for evidences of bureaucratic inertia and "almoner's disease." A small investment by trustees in this area will yield large results.

Foundations that are seen as institutional models of quality, integrity, and effectiveness have the opportunity to become audible voices of reason and sanity in a confused and despairing world. Where were the foundation voices? Who was examining the assumptions *and being heard* in the twenty-five years after World War II, when we moved the percentage of college-age young people who were enrolled in college from fifteen to over fifty?

To be sure, it was mostly government money that propelled this movement and it is public universities that account for most of the growth. But government is not the best examiner of assumptions for society. The foundation staffs could assist trustees to be respected examiners of assumptions *if* trustees were fully functioning as persons of trust and were consciously working for a respected society-building role that their privileged position makes possible.

Project grants to universities (by government, foundations, corporations, and individuals) since World War II have become a vital source of university support. And, for foundations, they now represent a major use of their funds that go to universities. Some universities became more fragile and vulnerable to assault during this period of great growth partly because project-support donors tend to operate in a way that supersedes university administration.

Individual faculty members, departments, and schools are sometimes entrepreneurs, responsible more to outside funding agencies than to their universities. Thus donors dictate some of the university's program and the administrator's role is to receive the money and account for its disbursement with little responsibility for what is done with it. Therefore, in some situations the donor becomes the administrator.

Faculty grantees, singly or in groups, sometimes move from one university to another, taking their grants with them. The university is reduced to the role of broker in this process—a serious blot on its integrity. Foundations have contributed to this unfortunate state of affairs, and they are the best positioned of all donors to help universities recover from the harm that has been done, *providing that foundation trustees accept this as their problem.*

The above paragraphs summarize a few of the ways in which a direct and personal trustee responsibility might manifest itself. Important in all of this is a new trustee attitude about what the institution is that they hold in trust. It is neither *public* nor *private. In trust* is a more suitable way of saying it—which means, simply, funds to be disbursed, within certain legal limits, at the discretion of trustees. If trustees can cease thinking of their role as *private* and start thinking wholly in terms of *trust*, they have then begun to establish the attitude that should guide their work.

Foundations, along with other institutional forms, are caught up in the pervasive ferment that involves all of us. The whole range of trustee and director roles, whether the institution is for profit or not for profit, is receiving careful scrutiny these days, and the literature is burgeoning.

The cause of this surge of concern, I believe, is a shift in the general public's criteria by which the overall quality of institutions and their performance is judged. Whereas, up to now, an institution was judged "good" if it was seen at or near the top of its field, now the test for each institution is how well it serves society when judged by what is reasonable and possible with its available resources, human and material. When judged this way, some of the best institutions may be seen in greater default to society than the poorest, and none of them come off very well.

This may explain why the revolution of expectations has been so hard on the elite institutions and why the demands of the disadvantaged seem so unceasing. In this context the privilege of foundations—freedom from taxes and market pressures—may place them in a category where societal expectations are the highest, and there really may be no long-run future for foundations as we know them unless the great majority come to stand above all other institutions as models of excellence, probity, dedication, and human sensitivity.

The opportunity to achieve these objectives defines a new role for foundation trustees.

PRUDENCE AND CREATIVITY: A TRUSTEE RESPONSIBILITY

Three conditions sharply distinguish foundations from other kinds of institutions:

● Foundations are the only general category of institution that some responsible, intelligent, and informed citizens have judged should not exist at all. There are many criticisms of other institutions, but there is little sentiment that would support the complete abolition of a whole category—except that of foundations. This anti-foundation attitude is reflected in the Congress.

● Foundations, of all categories of institutions, are the easiest to second-guess. Some intelligent, responsible, and informed people, when they read the report of grants made by a foundation, say, "If I had that money to give away, I could do a lot better with it." They may criticize some aspects of other institutions, but they are unlikely to say that, if put in complete charge, they could run the whole institution better all by themselves. However, they do say this about foundations.

● Foundations are the only category of institution that is wholly without a market test in the sense of clients or customers having immediate and direct sanctions at their disposal. All others—churches, businesses, schools, governments, hospitals, museums—have a market; that is, they have clients or customers whose support, or lack of it, has an immediate effect on the success of the institution. Foundations have only to meet the requirements of the law, and the only recourse of individuals is through the political process.

These conditions mark all foundations, from the very large to the quite small, as requiring a trustee function and a mode of program administration that is distinctly different from what is acceptable elsewhere.

Since foundations, like all other institutions, exist at the pleasure of the people and their government, and since, as I believe, they are capable of rendering an invaluable service in our pluralistic society, there is need for clarity about the tests that should guide the policy of foundations if they are to render, into the indefinite future, the unique service of which they are capable. Two such tests are *prudence* and *creativity*.

First, the test of *prudence*, in the sense of being cautious, circumspect, or discreet. An institution that is subject to an immediate market test can be flamboyant, boisterous, or unconventional if it wants to. The market will send an unmistakable signal—quickly, if these tactics are judged inappropriate—and, usually, if the offense is not too extreme, a recovery can be made with little loss. But a foundation, in the absence of such an immediate market test, does not have this latitude. An offense of imprudence by a foundation, as judged by the public through the political process, may go on the record as a black mark and stay there.

For several years before the passage of the Tax Reform Act of 1969 there was ample evidence of restlessness about the role of foundations, especially in the Congress. It is a reasonable conjecture that some of the particular restrictions that were placed on foundations by the Tax Reform Act were precipitated by a few grants by major foundations that were judged imprudent by a majority in the Congress.

It is not difficult to be prudent; that is, it is not difficult for a prudent person (one who by nature is cautious, circumspect, and discreet) to be prudent. And it is not difficult to staff a foundation with prudent men and women, so as virtually to guarantee prudent actions, like grants to worthy and respectable institutions such as hospitals and united funds. But a foundation for which prudence is the only test is probably contributing to the ultimate demise of foundations generally. Violations of the rule of prudence may bring a quicker public response, but, in the long run, the adverse reaction to nothing but prudence may be just as certain. If foundation programs are seen as little other than a mechanism for delayed contributions to conventionally operating charities, then fewer and fewer people are likely to judge foundations as legitimate institutions, and more determined moves than were threatened in 1969 may be made to curb or end them.

There is yet another test that should be considered, the test of *creativity*, in the sense of bringing into being socially useful ideas and procedures that institutions more harried by market pressures are not likely to produce, or to produce as soon. Creativity involves risk, experiment, and perseverance in the face of failure, somewhat the opposite of prudence. As an example, one thinks of the recent foundation-supported work in the development of plant strains that made possible the Green Revolution in Asia. Foundations may be more creative than they are generally credited with being, but as one scans the reports of the current work of most foundations, there seems to be relatively little that meets the test of creativity—yet the need for such activity is great, and one senses, among some intelligent, responsible people who are informed about foundations, a deep-seated criticism that foundations are not sufficiently creative. What test is being applied when this judgment is made? I believe that the critics are saying, "Some foundation work is constructive, but not much of it goes beyond conventional wisdom." An exception: when the reader of the foundation report notes the work leading up to the Green Revolution in Asia (especially after it was successful), the reader is likely to comment, "I wouldn't have thought of that!" In other words, the critic is not likely to second-guess foundation work that is seen as truly creative.

In the case of the food need in Asia, conventional wisdom would have prescribed, "Give them our food management technology plus our fertilizer, seeds, tools, and the means to get water." That was tried, but it did not work. What actually unlocked the situation was a new invention, extending our knowledge of plant genetics and hybridization to a problem that was outside our experience and anybody else's. This is probably the test of creativity that the responsible foundation critic would apply: Does it extend existing technology to critical social problems in a way that brings solutions that are beyond conventional wisdom? This test of creativity urges foundations to produce new solutions. The test of prudence suggests that foundations probably should not use their funds to influence the *choice* of a solution.

I have said that it is not hard for a prudent person to be prudent. Neither is it hard for truly creative persons to be creative, providing they are given support, resources, and freedom from the restraints of convention. But the actions that follow a creative development are sometimes seen as imprudent. *Thus it may be said that the survival of foundations as useful institutions depends on the majority of influential citizens judging them to be both prudent and creative.* To meet these two tests simultaneously is really difficult. Perhaps it is the most difficult problem that any major institution faces, maybe more difficult than meeting a tough, competitive market test. Moreover, it is just as tough a test for the very large as for the quite small foundation.

Trustees of small foundations are apt to say, "If we had the staff of big foundations, we could be more creative." But it is not a problem of staff or of size. It is a problem of structure. There is a structural flaw in most foundations—large and small—because trustees have not generally accepted the idea that it is *their obligation as trustees* to design an institution that meets the tests of both prudence and creativity. The basic problem in doing this is the same in a small foundation as in a big one.

This is suggested as a prime trustee concern: to act as trustees, directly and on their own initiative, to assure that the program of the foundation will be accepted by the majority of influential citizens as both prudent and creative. For reasons given below, trustees will need their own source of counsel, independent of the advice of their professional operating staff, which they will, of course, also heed.

The chief reason that trustees will need independent counsel on the matter of a balance between prudence and creativity grows out of one of the peculiar conditions of life in a foundation: the incessant pressure of requests for grants from needy nonprofit institutions, and the fact that practically all operating philanthropies that are not fully endowed (and that is the great majority) are needy. Their adequate funding depends in part on the art of grantsmanship; that is, it depends on handling their relations with foundations so as to maximize their support from that source. Grantsmanship has become a highly refined art. In large institutions there may be staffs of several people who spend all of their time studying, calculating strategy, writing grant proposals, and cultivating their relationships with foundation staffs. Smaller institutions that cannot afford such elaborate resources have access to consulting firms that advise them on how to deal with foundations. The volume of input to foundation offices, both large and small, that all of this generates is very great, and even well-staffed foundations are hard pressed to deal with it.

This incessant pressure from people who stand as supplicants has a corrupting influence on foundation personnel who are long exposed to it, and this risk presents the same obligation to trustees as would any occupational hazard in any kind of institution. This unceasing pressure from grant seekers seems to build a reactive response that dulls creativity of both the professional staff and the trustees (if the latter are exposed directly to grant seekers). Creativity, we know, thrives best when people can maintain a perspective of detachment from the problem before them. Foundation personnel, and sometimes trustees, who are constantly bombarded with letters, phone calls, visits from prospective grantees, and end runs through their friends, have difficulty in maintaining an outlook that favors creativity. They are too busy simply reacting to grant-seeking pressures to do that. This is not an argument that a foundation should try to avoid exposure to this constant importuning. Somebody has to maintain this interface with the grant seekers, because among their proposals are some that the foundation will want to support. Small foundations can retain a consultant to serve as their staff for this purpose. The important rule is that trustees of all foundations, large and small, should be shielded, by staff or consultants, from direct importuning by grant applicants. Trustees will, of course, be deeply involved in grant decisions, but they ought to avoid personal involvement with people seeking grants.

All grant seekers should be dealt with thoughtfully and courteously and their proposals should be carefully evaluated. The point here is that very few grant applicants bring proposals that meet the tests of both prudence and creativity, and trustees should not expect that their operating staffs, who must deal with this mass of grant applications, will be likely to originate creative courses of action for the foundation. That, as I have said, requires more detachment from the unending pressure of dealing with grant seekers than the operating staff of a foundation can be expected to have.

If, as I have argued, all foundations have the obligation to be creative in the use of a substantial part of their funds, then trustees have the further obligation to set apart some staff members or consultants who are independent of the staff that deals with grant applicants. This separate staff should work on foundation-originated, creative projects exclusively, with complete insulation from involvement with grant applications and the decision process regarding them. In a large foundation this might work best if two wholly separate staffs were to report independently to the trustees.

To the immediate objection, "This costs money," the obvious answer is, "Of course it does, but can you afford *not* to do it?" If a foundation, large or small, is to meet the tests of both prudence and creativity, then the trustees must maintain a separate staff that works only on foundation-originated, creative projects. This is part of the cost of doing what only foundations have a unique opportunity to do.

This suggestion for trustees to maintain a staff reporting directly to them for work on foundation-originated, creative projects is made in the belief that foundations may better serve society if they ignore the conventional organizational structures that are common among institutions that must meet immediate market tests to survive. Foundations should have a structure that will facilitate their optimal performance, in which the tests of both prudence and creativity are met. Such innovations in market-oriented institutions (that is, just about everything except foundations) are undertaken at considerable risk, if they are substantial. But organizational experimentation in foundations is low risk because there is no market to lose. This fact of life suggests that, if foundation trustees accept the idea that part of their obligation to society is to invest in creative projects that take them beyond conventional wisdom, then perhaps the first step is to become creative with respect to their own organizational structures—even in the smallest foundations.

The suggestion that trustees and directors of all institutions should be supported by their own staffs in order to function fully as trustees requires an enlargement of the usual concept of trusteeship as well as an adjustment in the leadership roles of both trustees and administrators. This concept deviates from conventional organizational wisdom, which posits that trustees should function so as to fit in with the way administrative hierarchies prefer to work. The new wisdom may stipulate that the administration should be organized to fit in with the way trustees believe they must work if their trust obligation is to be fulfilled. Foundations are in the best position to test such theories, for the benefit of all institutions.

There is a tendency in all speculative organizational thinking to deal with large institutions because of the obvious differences between small- and large-scale operations. However,

foundations are an exception. The larger ones are more conspicuous, but the smaller ones, no matter how small, have all of the
problems and all of the opportunities and bear all of the risks of
being further circumscribed or disowned that large ones have.
The obligation to be prudently creative is the same, as are the
organizational steps necessary to accomplish it.

At the outset of this article, three conditions were listed that
sharply distinguish foundations from other kinds of institutions.
These render foundations substantially different from all other
categories and leave them more vulnerable to curtailment of
their opportunity to serve.

If foundations were substantially more creative, the first
two of these conditions—the sentiment that foundations should
be dispensed with and the ease of second-guessing their decisions—might be reduced to insignificance. This would leave
foundations with only one major distinguishing characteristic—
absence of a market test. Foundations might be able to live with
that one condition and have a long and useful existence with
great benefit to society. But since they are now seen as not being
sufficiently creative, and with all three conditions in full force,
the responsible, intelligent, and informed people who now feel
that foundations should be abolished or drastically restricted may
one day prevail.

The tragedy in this prospect, for trustees, is twofold: (1) if
foundations disappear or are severely restricted in their options,
there will be a breach of trust on the consciences of those trustees
who might have managed them to a long and distinguished history, and (2) the personal lives of the foundation trustees who
might have given leadership to a prudently creative role for their
foundation will be poorer through this lost opportunity.

VII

Servant Leadership in Churches

As stated earlier, I am a student of organization—how things get done—and of wisdom—what works best. Religion is seen in the root meaning of that term—*religio*, "to rebind." The thing to be done with religious concern is to rebind humankind to the cosmos, to heal the pervasive alienation.

My view of religion is relatively non-theological. I am content to stand in awe and wonder before the ineffable mystery. I do not feel called upon to invent explanations of the mystery. I meet with others, whose religious concerns are expressed differently, at the level of the mystical. In this mood there is much common ground with those of quite differing theological positions.

I view the churches, as I have said, as the institutionalization of humankind's religious concern. As an institution, it seems not unlike other institutions with other missions. The churches, too, seem troubled to find how best to do what they have set out to do.

Two of the three pieces that follow appeared in *Friends Journal*. The third was a talk given to The School Sisters of St. Francis, a Catholic women's religious order. I see all three of these as dealing with how to do what churches have set out to do, as sharpening and strengthening their capacity to heal the pervasive alienation—an ever present struggle.

In addressing the subject of servant leadership and the churches, I am bringing to bear my wider concern for institutions and their service to society. Churches are needed to serve the large numbers of people who need mediative help if their alienation is to be healed and wholeness of life achieved, but I regret that, for the most part, churches do not seem to be serving well. They can be helped to do much better. And they can be helped to become servant-leaders—by being examplars for other institutions.

ON BEING A SEEKER IN THE LATE TWENTIETH CENTURY

There is a theory of prophecy which holds that prophetic voices of great clarity, and with a quality of insight equal to that of any age, are speaking cogently all of the time. Men and women of a stature equal to the greatest of the past are with us now addressing the problems of the day and pointing to a better way and to a personeity better able to live fully and serenely in these times.

The variable that marks some periods as barren and some as rich in prophetic vision is in the interest, the level of seeking, the responsiveness of the hearers. The variable is *not* in the presence or absence or the relative quality and force of the prophetic voices. Prophets grow in stature as people respond to their message. If their early attempts are ignored or spurned, their talent may wither away.

It is *seekers*, then, who make the prophets, and the initiative of any one of us in searching for and responding to the voices of contemporary prophets may mark the turning point in their growth and service.

Some who have difficulty with this theory assert that their faith rests on one or more of the prophets of old having given the "word" for all time and that the contemporary ones do not speak to their condition as the older ones do. But if one really believes that the "word" has been given for all time, how can one be a seeker? How can one hear the contemporary voice when one has decided not to live in the present and has turned that voice off?

Neither this hypothesis nor its opposite can be proved. But I submit that the one given here is the more hopeful choice, one that offers a significant role in prophecy to every individual. One cannot interact with and build strength in a dead prophet, but one can do it with a living one. "Faith," Dean Inge has said, "is the choice of the nobler hypothesis."

This thesis seems to be supported by the record of the times of George Fox, the first leader of the Quaker movement. For many years before the start of his mission there had been an unusual stirring of seekers who were expectantly watching for a new vision with new leadership. Without that sustained readiness, Fox might not have found the response to his initiative that was necessary for his mission to become strong.

The times we live in appear in sharp contrast. Many are seeking, but there is a confusing bombardment of communications from those who would satisfy the seeking hunger. Within the last twenty-five years the number and variety of offerings from those asking the support of seekers, usually for a fee, has grown enormously. To name only a few of the better known of these in vogue now, there are transcendental meditation, sensitivity and encounter groups, a resurgence of intentional communities, healing seminars, transactional analysis, biofeedback, a substantial enlargement of services from the field of psychotherapy, reevaluation counseling, and expanded programs of churches plus some new churches. Standing conspicuously apart is a slightly older offering, Alcoholics Anonymous, which over forty years ago resolved that it would be poor, it would own no real property, no one but a participating alcoholic could contribute to its modest budget, and the essential work of one recovered or partly recovered alcoholic helping another would not be done for money. Some who are close to the problem hold that AA has helped more to recover from this dreadful illness than all other approaches (mostly for a fee) combined.

The seeker in these times can be bewildered by the scope and attractiveness of what is available, and unfortunately some have been tempted into a lifelong pursuit of wholeness, in one's personal terms, to the exclusion of coming to grips with what should be (and in Fox's day was) a fruit of seeking: effective involvement with the ethical dilemmas of one's times.

What made George Fox's service to seekers (and their response to him) so exemplary was the significant move to new and more exacting ethical standards, the force of which carries to this day. Fox's major contribution was not his theology, nor even his encouragement to care for suffering, important as these were. Rather, it seems to me, what gave durability to the Quaker tradition was the practical result that so many of those who called themselves Friends *behaved more lovingly toward all creatures and assumed an impressive level of responsibility for their society and its institutions.* Perhaps the most innovative result was that, by the effort of those whom Fox inspired, the quality of some contemporary institutions, notably commerce, was markedly improved.

We live in a time that is much more dominated by institutions, both public and private, than was true in Fox's day. And these institutions—all of them, including the very best—are crying out for a new mission to them that would raise their stature as servants of society and drastically reduce their impact as sources of suffering and injustice. I see little disposition toward this outcome in most current offerings to seekers.

Richard B. Gregg, writing in an early Pendle Hill pamphlet forty years ago, observed: "Christianity needs a means of implementing its ideals of human unity into a social program." The need seems even more urgent today, with little evidence of movement to serve it.

What may be needed, and perhaps now it is a possibility, is a new initiative from some seekers in which (1) they take responsibility for finding and responding to the contemporary prophet who will help them find their ways out of their individual and collective wildernesses so that they will become more effective servants of society, and (2) they respond less to the kinds of cafeteria offerings enumerated above which seem not to dispose them to become servants. How would Seekers Anonymous do for a name? And could the model be taken from AA: no one will be paid, and only funds contributed from active seekers will be used? For those who participate, *healing*, in the sense of being made whole, will come from deep involvement with creative work on the structural flaws in our society, work that has both meliorative *and* society-building consequences.

Seekers Anonymous will be religious in the root meaning of that word, *religio*, "to rebind," to bridge the separation between persons and the cosmos, to heal the widespread alienation, and to reestablish men and women in the role of servants—*healers*—of society.

Some people (it could be just one) who have the strength, the vision, the integrity, the competence, and the youthful vigor *right now* are actively testing our responsiveness to their leadership and our capacity to be religious in this sense. And what is being said to us may seem as strange and disturbing—and as compelling, if we will listen—as Fox's message did in his day. Are enough of us really listening with a readiness to respond? Are we diligently trying to sort the truly prophetic voices of our time, those that would lead us to constructive service, from the veritable babble of communication that engulfs us all? Are enough of us prepared—emotionally, intellectually, and with physical stamina—for the new demands that may be made upon us? Are we adequately reinforcing one another as seekers in order to build, in each of us, the required competence, clarity, and strength to serve?

Albert Camus wrote in the last paragraph of his last public lecture: "Great ideas, it has been said, come into the world as gently as doves. Perhaps, then, if we listen attentively, we shall hear, amid the uproar of empires and nations, a faint flutter of wings, the gentle stirring of life and hope."

Those who see themselves as part of Seekers Anonymous will learn to listen attentively and respond to that faint flutter of wings, that gentle stirring of life and hope. *By their intense and sustained listening they will make the new prophet who will help them find that wholeness that is only achieved by serving.* And out of that wholeness will come the singleness of aim and the capacity to bear suffering that a confrontation with a basic malaise of our time, the failure of our many institutions to serve, may demand.

Do not seek to follow the footsteps of men of old. Seek what they sought!

—BASHO

Take from the altar of the past the fire, not the ashes!
—JEAN JAURES

THE ART OF KNOWING

*The article that follows appeared in the October 15, 1974,
issue of* Friends Journal—Quaker Thought and Life Today. *It
deals with what I believe to be the central element in the leadership of
George Fox in founding the Religious Society of Friends in England
in the seventeenth century. Aldous Huxley, writing in* The Perennial Philosophy, *says of Fox: "The Mystical tradition, perpetuated
by the Protestant Spiritual Reformers, had become diffused, as it
were, in the religious atmosphere of the time when George Fox had
his first great opening and knew by direct experience."*

*Fox, an earnest seeker after truth when quite young, records
the early event in his Journal: "I had forsaken all priests…and
those called the most experienced people; for I saw that there was
none among them all that could speak to my condition. And when
all my hopes in them and in all men were gone, so that I had nothing outwardly to help me, nor could tell what to do, then, oh then, I
heard a voice which said, 'There is one, even Christ Jesus, that can
speak to thy condition.' And when I heard it my heart did leap for
joy…And this I knew experimentally."*

*The ensuing forty years of Fox's leadership and ministry were
turbulent ones in which there was much persecution of Fox and his
followers. Thousands of them were jailed and over one hundred died
in the awful prisons of that time. Fox himself spent a total of over
six years in prison. During a later incarceration he was offered a
pardon by the king, but he refused it on the ground that acceptance
of a pardon was an admission of guilt. He preferred jail.*

*The principal impact of Fox, in my judgment, was upon eth-
ical practice, immediately and permanently, in all walks of life.
The impact was impressive: a new commercial ethic, equal status of
women, education for all, and, in America, the Quakers were the
first religious society to denounce slavery and forbid the holding of
slaves among members—one hundred years before the Civil War.*

While my article was addressed to "those working out of the Quaker tradition," it may serve any who sense power in the words "This I knew experimentally."

This I knew experimentally. These are the words George Fox used to explain how he received, early in his ministry, what may have been his greatest insight, an insight that led to his decision to depend almost wholly on his own reading of scripture and what was revealed directly to him, rather than to be guided by the views of contemporary authorities—civil, military, scholarly, or ecclesiastical. All of what I see as Quakerism (and there is, of course, much beyond my perception) flows out of the image that these four words create—*This I knew experimentally.* These words are best understood, I believe, in the total context of George Fox's life and thought. The Quaker tradition, as distinct from other contemporary religious traditions, therefore, is not to be succinctly defined; rather, I suggest, the heart of the tradition is to be found in the symbolic meaning of these four words from Fox's journal.

What does the tradition, so viewed, point to as the special opportunity for Friends now? I will address this question as a student of organization, of how things get done, not as an educator or a theologian.

There is a high probability that this great gift of knowing experimentally is what gave Fox his extraordinary leadership with which he guided his seventeenth-century followers to a sharp return to the spirit and substance of early Christianity. Without this unmistakable mark of a truly inspired man, Fox, a man of many gifts, might have been just another impassioned preacher, one with a following perhaps, but not with the power to found and lead a significant new movement and raise a new moral standard for his times.

George Fox was ruled by an ethic that was rooted in his solid Judeo-Christian origins. Without that ethic, or with its opposite, he might have been a destructive force—perhaps a Hitler. His awesome power would have been used for something. But what was new about Fox was not the ethic; rather, it was his ability to know experimentally in a way that moved the ethic along so that a new and cogent meaning, a superior wisdom for his times, could emerge. The traditional ethic gave him his direction, not his force. Pure original inspiration was the propelling force.

What inspiration gave to Fox is not necessarily what we would get today from knowing experimentally. Leadership, as demonstrated by Fox, is knowing experimentally what is superior wisdom—*now*. It is for us to say, from our own experimental knowledge, what that is in the late twentieth century. Superior wisdom might be defined as competence and expertise plus the experimental knowledge that tells one what to do with these *now*. And with such superior wisdom one is empowered to go out ahead and show the way—to lead. One is given this power by others who believe that that particular individual knows better where to go and what to do now. And those who bestow the power to lead can take it away if they change their minds.

There is, and should be, much concern with competence and expertise, but the responsibility for educating in these ways is widely shared, and they need not be the special obligation of Friends. The traditional ethic and the many social positions of Friends are also common knowledge, although they may not be widely adhered to in practice. But teaching how to know experimentally may be a special opportunity for those who understand the Friends' tradition, because so few among our literate and well-motivated contemporaries understand it, or seem to want to understand it.

As I think of my own life in this regard, I am reminded of the poignant words that comprise the title of John Masefield's story of his early life, *So Long to Learn!* I feel now that I entered adulthood with a modest potential for knowing experimentally, but that it has been but meagerly realized. What a treasure it would have been to know as a youth that I had this unrealized gift, the cultivation and use of which was to be the overshadowing priority of my life. Fox apparently matured his gift without a mentor. Most of us need some help. I did. Is this not what most of education is about—the more experienced doing for the moderately gifted what the exceptional ones sometimes do for themselves?

Twelve years ago I spent a year as visiting lecturer at the Sloan School of Management at the Massachusetts Institute of Technology. Among other things, with no model I knew of to draw on, I offered a course called "Intuition in Strategy and Decision Making." My course was oversubscribed, and I had to offer it in two sections. This was not so much because the study of intuition was popular as it was the desire of some of those highly trained analytical minds to heckle the fellow who had the temerity to offer such a course in that bastion of conscious rationality. But we had a great time and, at the conclusion, some of my students admitted to a substantially enlarged view of their human potential.

In the intervening years, while knowledge of the full range of our mental powers has expanded, I sense that schools of administration—schools generally, in fact—have moved even further to emphasize objective knowledge and formal analysis, with still less attention to how one can strengthen one's ability to intuit the gap between the limit of what objective knowledge will do in a situation and what is required for a good plan or decision; and there usually is such a gap, sometimes a very wide one. This neglect in the formal training of administrators and others, both in explicit attention to their intuitive powers and in the ethic that might guide their professional lives, may substantially limit their fulfillment as persons—one of their greatest gifts may lie with them useless; such a lack may pose a hazard to the society they presume to serve.

What may be most needed now, from those working out of the Quaker tradition, is help—however it may be given—in alerting young people to their potential for knowing experimentally so that they will be aware of the many signals, some from the "accidental" and the "irrational," which have the possibility, ultimately, of "making sense." For example, the amazingly creative contemporary artist Juan Miro, who is still producing with zest in his eighties, was eating his lunch while working on a sketch for a painting. A drop of strawberry jam fell on his drawing. After contemplating it for a moment, he enlarged it with his

finger and incorporated it into his design. George Fox might not
have understood this, as he might not have understood what I did
in my course on intuition. But I would resist the contention that
these examples (Fox's, Miro's, and mine) are not all the same
thing—in different contexts.

What makes the tradition from Fox so terribly relevant
today is the urgent need, around the world, for leadership by
strong ethical persons—those who by nature are disposed to be
servants (in the sense of helping others to become healthier,
wiser, freer, more autonomous and more likely themselves to be
servants) and who therefore can help others to move in constructive directions. Servant-leaders are *healers* in the sense of *making
whole* by helping others to a larger and nobler vision and purpose
than they would be likely to attain for themselves. This, in
essence, is how Fox served—as a *healer.*

The growth of servant-leaders is urged as a prime concern
for those who work in the Friends tradition and who have a special interest in education. We are not wanting for knowledge of
how to do things better or (in the United States) for material
resources to work with. But we are sorely in need of strong ethical
leaders to go out ahead to show the way so that the moral standards and the perceptions of the many will be raised, and so that
they will serve better with what they have and what they know.

The path of those who heed this advice will not be easy
because, much as we need strong ethical leaders, we have the
misfortune to live in the age of the *anti-leader.* Some intelligent
and serious-minded people denigrate leadership and urge a leaderless society. Others simply ignore leadership as a critical problem. There is a widespread, naive assumption that great
institutions just build themselves. As one perceptive observer has
put it: "The academic world appears to be approaching the point
at which everyone wants to educate the technical expert who
advises the leader, or the intellectual who stands off and criticizes
the leader, but no one wants to educate the leader."

As I contemplate the national scene in this summer of 1974,
we seem to be reaping the grim harvest of this clear and calculated

policy to neglect leadership. By default, far too much of the inevitable leadership is in the hands of the gross, the self-seeking, and the corrupt. The evident consequences of all of this on the whole range of the complex institutional life in which we are all enmeshed are devastating. It is a losing battle for persons of good will to devote so much of their interest and energy to rescuing individuals from the hurt of their involvement in the "system" when so many of these institutions are grinding them down faster than our most diligent saving efforts can rescue them. One may analyze, criticize, protest, beat upon the system, castigate the holders of power, but most of this is wasted breath if there are not, somewhere within the structures of these discrete institutions, persons with the will and the competence and the vision to lead them to better performance as servants of society. These institutions can be circumscribed by law, and they can be pressured into some kind of conformity by criticism from the outside, but they can be built to servant stature only by strong ethical leadership operating inside. Who is preparing the next generation of leaders —institution builders—to do this?

Not only do we live in the age of the anti-leader, we are burdened with an *anti-innovative* attitude as well. There is innovation aplenty—sometimes too much—in our enveloping gadgetry, in individual lifestyles, in the trivialities that concern us so much; but the essential structures of the institutions that should serve us—governments, churches, schools, businesses, hospitals, philanthropies—are seriously hobbled with rigid, obsolete, and retrogressive patterns. It seems as if those to whom ultimate responsibility has been entrusted—trustees and administrators—would prefer that the institutions they hold in trust fail completely, operating in the conventional way, rather than risk an innovation that would have a chance to modify for the better the traditional structure of power and authority—and thus to build a more serving institution.

The concerned person who accepts this statement of the problem may ask: "I have no competence for this; how can I help these non-serving institutions that dominate us to become better servants of society?"

The obvious first answer to such questions is that if we lack competence, we had better get some. Institutions are the stuff this society is made of, and if we feel responsible, we will either get some competence regarding institutions or we will follow the leadership of someone who has it. Everyone, at some time and in some areas, is a follower, and it is just as important to be discriminating in choosing whom to follow as it is to prepare to lead.

But there is a deeper answer, as I see it, that is central to the tradition of Friends; it is for competent moral persons to learn to know experimentally so that they can effectively discriminate when they *follow*, and so that when they lead they can dependably illuminate, with a superior wisdom, the path for others to follow so that those others will trust, and be justified in trusting. The problem is how to assist the growth of more and stronger persons to do this through an educational process. One must, I think, begin with a new, contemporary meaning of *knowing experimentally*. But, if that term is not to be defined (as I prefer), how then is one to know its meaning? We are faced with a reflexive dilemma, of finding that meaning in our own individual consciousnesses.

I once asked Robert Frost the meaning of his most symbolic poem, "Directive." His answer was, "Read it and read it and read it and it means what it says to you." My advice regarding the meaning of *knowing experimentally* is the same: Go back to George Fox's journal and read it and read it and read it until meaning comes through. And, if one is open as a seeker, contemporary meaning will come if one lives with that remarkable document long enough. Something will come that is unique and personal to each seeker.

But don't try to be like George! The question in seeking from his journal is not "What was he like?" or "What did he say?" or "What did he do?" but, rather, "How did he learn?" *What he said and did* was appropriate and effective in his times. It might not be in ours. But *how he learned* is timeless. Learn from

Fox how to learn what is superior wisdom for these times. Then one is ready to teach.

The late Rabbi Abraham Joshua Heschel must have learned some of this in his early life in the closed world of Jewish piety in Warsaw, where he grew up. His voice and manner of speaking had the authentic ring of the Old Testament prophet. Once when he addressed a student audience, he alluded to the false prophets and the true prophets. In the question period a student asked him how one could tell the difference. His answer, in the mood of the prophet, was, "There—is—no—way!" Later, with a gentle smile, he elaborated. "My friend, if there were a way, if we had a gauge that we could slip over the head of the prophet and say with certainty that he is or is not a true prophet, there would be no human dilemma and life would have no meaning—it would not be worth living. *Yet it is terribly important that we know the difference!*"

I am with Frost and Heschel. There—is—no—way for competent persons to gain superior wisdom for these times—*and to serve by leading*—except to immerse themselves in the record of a person like George Fox, who had it to a remarkable degree, and then wait with wonder and expectancy for new insight. They will go along the path of objective knowledge and analysis as far as these will take them—which sometimes is not very far. Then they will have a process, a learnable process, one that is unique to them, by which they will receive, experimentally, the dependable insight that will guide them the rest of the way. And they do not ask what that insight is or whence it comes. They simply accept it, welcome it with gratitude, believe it, act on it. And its dependability does not rest upon conformity with custom or even with their own previous experience. Both may be contradicted. Dependability, and the faith it engenders, is in the inner mysterious process that is rooted in the congruity of one's life (between what one says and what one is), within the context of the ethic one embraces.

The hazards of this approach are the same as they were in George Fox's time. Commitment to one's inner guidance is the consummate achievement, but the line that separates that commitment from fanaticism is fuzzy, and the first Quakers were not always aware of it. But fanaticism or not, the early years of Fox's ministry and teaching had a profound effect upon his times *because he could lead*, and he left a rich legacy for us to learn from.

The need for a service like his is as urgent now as it was in his times.

And we are able to learn as Fox did, to know experimentally, and to lead in the way that is appropriate and effective for our times.

And we can teach others. Each of us who is willing to learn can teach. *We can have great schools* if we will help inspired and skillful institution builders to evolve as their leaders!

We are all limited. But each of us is also gifted—and our gifts are various. Among the young of today are some who are committed to a servant ethic, who are willing to work hard to acquire the competence to serve and be served by the present society, and who have a potential to know experimentally. Whether their gifts seem great or small, let us help all of those who meet these three tests to be on with it!

Allons! the road is before us!
It is safe, I have tried it, my own feet have tried it well.
—Be not detained!

—WALT WHITMAN

ORGANIZING TO SERVE

Following is a talk given on the occasion of the 100th anniversary of the School Sisters of Saint Francis at Alverno College in Milwaukee on August 12, 1974. In the tradition of Saint Francis (when the members of his order convened, they brought their mats for sleeping) this conference was called "Chapter of Mats."

I sense that a feeling of urgency will pervade your meeting as you review the past and project the future of your order. You are gathered at a time when all institutions seem precarious, traditional values are in doubt, customary ways of serving no longer seem adequate, and the future appears more uncertain and harder to predict than at any time within my memory.

Recently I visited an old friend who is the senior person in a house of a religious order of your church. In response to my rather casual question, "How are things going?" I received this reply: "How are things going? In this house, pretty well. In our provincial office in so-and-so, fair. Beyond that in the church, all is confusion!"

If this judgment strikes you as accurate, I would like to discuss it with you as an opportunity rather than solely as a threat. I will speak out of nearly fifty years of institution watching—and this is what it has been, watching and participating, rather than studying or reading about. I am not suggesting that mine is the best, or the only view of the problem. But watching and working with a wide range of institutions are the source of such competence as I have. The best I can do for you here is to share, from my particular perspective, how I view your problem of making an opportunity out of a threat. I will share what I have in the hope that this will be helpful when it is added to your own much more detailed understanding.

Let me tell you why I think that the judgment, *all is confusion*, may be seen as describing an opportunity. It presents an opportunity because it *is* a threat. I have watched closely many able leaders in all sorts of institutions. The best of them feel that a prolonged period of calm and stability is a greater threat to viability than is an occasional state of confusion. So, when appropriate, they will do something deliberately to create confusion—not so much that the institution founders, but enough that it will be challenged to new life. There may be better ways to maintain viability, but this is one of the more common ones.

I like that great line from Wait Whitman, "From any fruition of success, no matter what, shall come forth something to make a greater struggle necessary." To an institution watcher like me, struggle is of the very essence; it is life-giving; therefore it is necessary. I look upon the struggle to recover from confusion as a necessary condition for viability.

I once asked the head of a prestigious school whether his was really a good school. His reply startled me. "There are no good schools," he said, "but mine is as good as schools are." When pressed for an explanation he took this position: "Teaching is one of the highest forms of art, and one can no more successfully set up an institution to teach than one can institutionalize the painting of pictures or the composing of symphonies. The constraints of institutions and the aims of education are incompatible."

Such a sweeping generalization is arguable, but in my experience with many quite different institutions I would say that it is true of all of them. The optimal contributions of the most gifted persons are restrained by life in institutions—everywhere. Possibly this may be an important source of the widespread confusion that we all are experiencing—and your church has no monopoly on this condition.

The endemic confusion may have its source in a profound change in the attitudes of people toward the restraints that participation in institutions imposes on the contributions of the gifted (and these, in effect, are restraints on all of us, because limited though each of us is, we are all also gifted).

Within the last fifteen years we have seen a growing intolerance of these restraints. The most dramatic, because the tradition that was challenged was so hallowed, was in our universities in the 1960s. Students became aware that they were being used too much to support universities that seemed to be operating primarily for the benefit of faculties. Some of the student reactions were brutal and costly. But I cannot accept, as some hold, that these student revolts were irrational. In other areas those who find their gifts to be restrained and their contributions less than optimal are reacting in more subtle ways. Everywhere I sense a general tendency, in sharp contrast to the world I grew up in, to reject restraints on our fulfillment as persons and to take some action, covert or overt, to this end. It is a new attitude toward restraints that pervades everything.

If we could accurately assess the causes of this shift, I suspect that lovable old John XXIII, in those four short years that he was pope, had as much to do with this as anybody. For a brief moment in history, many literate persons in the Western world felt a lift of spirit, they became more significant as persons, they gathered strength to contend with the forces that were grinding them down. And although John has been gone for twelve years now, the force of his presence seems undiminished. The confusion that we all feel may be that the institutions in which most of us are deeply involved have not caught up with the new vision that so many of us have of our unrealized potentials as persons. And our sustained determination to reach much closer to our potential has not yet been fully reckoned with by the power structures of institutions generally. All institutions—business, government, school, church—are deeply troubled as a result of this failure of leaders to function under these new conditions.

Some lament that John had so few years for his great work. I do not share this view. The day he died I was teaching a class of bright, young, ambitious, hard-driving business executives. We took half of our class period to talk about the implications of John's life for the work of the world. We noted a remark that he was quoted as having made a few days before he died, but after death was imminent: "Any day is a good day to be born; any day is a good day to die." And I took occasion to comment on the uses of old people (since I was the only one there over thirty-five), and I noted that a young person, in any field, would not be likely to exert the influence that John did at eighty—this was part of the total rightness of his role. In the course of the discussion on the shortness of his period of leadership I quoted one of my favorite poems, "The Noble Nature" by Ben Jonson:

> It is not growing like a tree
> In bulk, doth make man better be;
> Or standing long an oak, three hundred year,
> To fall a log at last, dry, bald, and sere:
> A lily of a day is fairer far in May
> Although it fall and die that night—

It was the plant and flower of light.
In small proportions we just beauties see;
And in short measures life may perfect be.

We have much to account for in how lives might be lived
more effectively, in how to achieve these short measures of perfection—as John seemed to do. Perhaps what is required of us is
that we must face realistically the conditions we must deal with as
the first step in this accounting.

Recently when I was in Europe I had conversations with
Catholic lay leaders, clergy, and women and men in religious
orders. In the course of these conversations an outstanding
layperson asked me how I assessed the situation of the Catholic
Church in the United States. I had to think about this for a while,
and this is how I answered.

The Catholic Church in the United States is a minority
religion, but I regard it as, potentially, our largest single force for
good. It fails to realize its potential for good in the society as a
whole because, I believe, it is seen as predominantly a negative
force. The issues on which the church is in opposition, such as
birth control, abortion, euthanasia, divorce, and communism,
are specific and precisely defined, and the actions of the church
are vigorous and sustained. The issues on which the church is
affirmative, such as peace, justice, and charity, are broad idealistic
generalities, and the actions are sporadic and imprecise. To be
sure, many positive goods can be cited, but they do not stand on a
par—as social influences—with those areas of opposition. I
respect the church for opposing those social practices that it
believes to be wrong, even though I may not always agree with its
judgments. But, unfortunately, all that one can do with opposition is to stop or prevent something. One must oppose those
things that one believes to be wrong, but one cannot *lead* from a
predominantly negative posture. One can lead an institution or a
total society only by strong, specific, sharply aimed affirmative
actions. As a non-Catholic, I was lifted by Pope John's regime
because an affirmative building leadership seemed to be emerging, and this gave a new hope for the world.

This was my brief answer to the request to assess the church as I saw it in the United States at this time. Had the request concerned business, government, philanthropy, or education, the answer, in substance, would have been much the same: too much defense of something, too little building of a better order of things.

The reality we need to face, I believe, is that it is so much easier for a person of good will to be negative than to be affirmative. This is not that human nature is preponderately negative. It is simply that, in a negative posture, someone else has defined an issue and taken an initiative that we believe is wrong and all that is required of us is to react against that initiative. And this is much, much easier to do than it is to define an issue responsibly and take the initiative. Since, in a hyperactive society such as the one we live in, there is a plethora of initiatives being taken that we are impelled to oppose, if we do not watch it, all of our energy can be consumed in reacting through moves of opposition. The tragedy of being swallowed up in these negative actions is that it may leave the leadership of society to others; or, if one is successful in checking all other initiatives, it creates a leaderless society. Sometimes I feel that this is our present dilemma: so many of the forces of good are trying to cancel out what they regard as error, and too few are attending to the quality of the institutions that dominate us all. Within these institutions one finds, again, a preoccupation with defending the status quo or simply yielding to the revolt against repression by letting people do their own things—with an ultimate result that is likely to be about as bad as repression. Sustained or augmented confusion is the inevitable result of both responses.

I realize there is a problem with the word *institution*. I have studied the etymology of that word, and it does have a rather checkered history. Tucked away among the many historical meanings is "something that enlarges and liberates." Can you think of another single word that has that connotation?

We have the habit in this country, when something goes wrong, to abandon the word that names it. Wouldn't it be a better idea, especially if we have the right word, to change the offending practice and keep the word? I want to keep the word *institution* and build a far greater substance in what that word refers to. Let me suggest a definition for our purposes: "An institution is a gathering of persons who have accepted a common purpose, and a common discipline to guide the pursuit of that purpose, to the end that each involved person reaches higher fulfillment as a person, through *serving and being served* by the common venture, than would be achieved alone or in a less committed relationship." This is what I am thinking about when I use the word *institution*.

There is sufficient discussion elsewhere of the dimensions of the new urge for self-fulfillment—and most of you who are young may understand it better in your own experience than I can delineate it. What I would like to share with you is my feeling of optimism that new institutions can be built—*not* renewal of old ones but building ones that are so different that they will be regarded as *totally* new. The quality of the new institution itself will be regarded as a positive social force.

The hope for the future that the prospect of building such institutions generates (and I see real grounds for hope) lies in building with what we now have—in your case, first, your religious order, and then your church. The aim is to make institutions of both of them that stand out in the world as exceptional because those who work in them, or are involved with them, find, through their participation, that their gifts are recognized, enlarged, and fulfilled in a way that they could not find by acting independently—*even under a benevolent shelter.* What I am suggesting to you is that you make a primary mission of refuting, by a practical demonstration, the contention of the old schoolmaster who said that the constraints of institutions and the aims of education are incompatible. And you will not do this, I believe, by abolishing all constraints in an avant-garde manner. Your successful demonstration may involve more constraints, more exacting discipline, than you have ever known. But what you design will be a great institution for all who are involved with it—because personal significance, selfhood, will reach a level heretofore not achieved by individuals working singly or in concert. *I see this as the overshadowing challenge of our times,* and I believe it must be met first by those two absolutely basic institutions, the church and the school, before we can expect that governments, businesses, hospitals, and philanthropies will accept the challenge. Churches and schools, using the initiatives now available to them, must make of themselves exceptional institutions in which *all* of the people participating in them in *all* roles (and this includes everybody from the janitor to the most esoteric scholar) can find in their participation conditions that favor fulfillment of their potentialities as persons. Unless the churches and the schools can do this, I see little hope that the remainder of our institutions, whose pretensions are less noble, will have reason to strive to improve. This is different from the traditional view in which the church and the school purveyed knowledge and values for the use of individuals in their separate lives. Now we are saying that in a society dominated by a complex of institutions, the first such in the history of the world, the quality of life achieved *within* churches and schools may have more to do with their influence on society than what they teach or advocate.

Most charitable institutions, of which the church is one, have tended to view the problems of society as "out there," and it was assumed that service to the "out there" was the sole justification for their existence. Now the view is emerging that one begins "in here," inside the serving institution, and makes of *it* a model institution. This model, *because it is a thing of beauty, in itself,* becomes a powerful serving force.

This may sound like strange doctrine to those of you in the School Sisters of St. Francis who might not easily think of your order as an institution. But by denying that you are an institution, functioning in the larger society like all other institutions, you may be cutting yourselves off from the most creative society-supporting role that is available to you. Inherent in the attitude of love is tremendous creativity. Some people must refute, with creative new inventions, the assertion of the old schoolmaster by replacing the type of institution they thought of as inevitable with one in which teaching or any other high form of art can be practiced with greater creative effect than if the artists did their work entirely outside the framework of the institution. As I see it, whoever brings the influence that establishes this *in practice* must have learned how to deal with the necessary constraints of institutions so as to make assets rather than liabilities of them. This poses the crucial question that I would put before any association of persons who wish to perform at their best as servants of society: Can you make of yours an institution in which the conditions of life in that institution raise *all of those* involved in it to a higher achievement as fulfilled persons than if they did their own things without the benefit of those conditions? Can you devise a disciplined participation that raises people's sights to nobler purposes than they would embrace if they were not constrained by that discipline? Discipline, in the past, has been viewed, unfortunately in too many places, as the price one must pay for the privilege of belonging. In the university field with which I have had a close association these past years, "discipline" seems almost synonymous with "hazing." Can you make of discipline the means whereby larger achievement *for the person—for every involved person*—is assured?

I have not come here to tell you that this will be easy. But I have come with the hope that I can suggest a general strategy for doing this, that you will be encouraged to make one of your goals to build a model institution out of your religious order, and that the accomplishment of this goal will be the most challenging and rewarding adventure you have ever embarked upon.

Briefly stated, here is a suggested general strategy for building such a model institution:

1. *First, there must be a goal, a concept of a distinguished serving institution* in which *all* who accept its discipline are lifted up to nobler stature and greater effectiveness than they are likely to achieve on their own or with a less demanding discipline. And *all* means *all*, not *most* or *almost all*. Since the institution is made up of human beings, there will be some error. But a single failure to lift an involved individual to greater stature *should be judged to be an unwarranted exception*, and the experience of such failure should be

carefully analyzed to learn from it with the intent of avoiding it in the future. It seems to me that, in these times, a goal short of this is inadequate for a church or a school, and that it is doubly important for an institution such as yours, which is both.

2. The second part of a general strategy of institution building is *an understanding of leadership and followership* that is essential for movement toward a goal such as this. Everyone in an institution is part leader, part follower. If an institution is to achieve distinction as servant, then only those who are natural servants should be empowered to lead. There is no magic in a serving institution, one that lifts everyone involved to nobler stature. At base, its form is shaped by the incremental actions of persons who are natural servants, those who, by nature, want to lift others so that others become healthier, wiser, freer, more autonomous, and more likely themselves to become servants. The servant operates by a theory of justice in which the least favored in society always benefits, or, at least, is not further deprived. I have written an essay, "The Servant as Leader," in which I discuss several of the aspects of such a person (see chapter 1 herein).

3. The third major element is *organization-structure-modus operandi.* On this, too, I have written an essay, "The Institution as Servant" (see chapter 2 herein). The key question is how power and authority are handled. If the institution has a discipline, as I have argued it must have if it is to help individuals accomplish for themselves and others what only an institutionalized relationship can do in the modern world, then how administration is to be structured becomes critical. The major conclusion I have reached after much searching is that we have at long last come to grips with the liabilities in the obsolete idea of the single chief atop a pyramidal structure, and that henceforth the ultimate authority should be placed in a balanced team of equals under the leadership of a true servant who serves as *primus inter pares,* first among equals.

4. This arrangement, however, calls for the fourth, and final element in the strategy of institution building, *the need for trustees.* Trustees are what the term implies, persons in whom

ultimate trust is placed and who stand outside the institution, apart from the administration and with more detachment and objectivity than insiders can summon. The trustee role is to monitor closely the movement of the institution toward its goals and to act both as critic and advocate, defender and court of last resort. Such an arrangement is essential, I believe, if the internal leadership, the administration, is to be placed with a council of equals rather than with a single chief. I have written a third essay, "Trustees as Servants," for those who wish to pursue this idea further (see chapter 3 herein).

Thus the strategy of institution building I suggest is in four steps: (1) goals-concept, which only you can supply, then (2) leadership, (3) structure, (4) trustees. The last three of these fall within the purview of my experience as an institution watcher, and in these you share the common problem of all institutions. In saying all of this I hope that I have encouraged you to be thoughtful about yourselves as an institution, even though we live in a climate where the label *institution* is sometimes in disfavor. Institutions—not just the word but the entities themselves— are in disfavor, and should be, because so many of them have not been managed well and the consequences of their existence are far too much in the negative.

If we are to move out of this situation, we have only three choices, as I see it. (1) We can let things go on as they are and accept the woeful inadequacy that pervades all of our institutions in the hope that some miraculous intervention will rescue us. (2) We can center our concern on conformity and discipline and other such offending elements and relax them so that individuals may comfortably go their own ways under the shelter of an institution that gives little more than housekeeping. I have suggested earlier that the consequences of this will be anarchy, and neither those serving nor those served by the institution will find this a happy arrangement for long. (3) We can set out with hope and courage to build a new institution in which the essential constraints of discipline and conformity will be converted into assets rather than liabilities. This is a large order, and you will be venturing into

uncharted lands if you undertake it. But I have seen enough fragments of accomplishment to be confident that if you really want it,
you can achieve it. However, you will need a total strategy of institution building such as I have suggested. If you set out only to treat
the symptoms of malaise, such as the irritations of conformity and
discipline, and leave old ideas of goals, leadership, structure, and
trusteeship intact, your efforts will have only a short-lived aspirin
effect. The disease is more fundamental; the whole institutional
arrangement of our society is flawed, and no aspirin-like treatment
will deal with it. Nothing short of a comprehensive rebuilding,
according to a deep yearning for a true and warm humanity, will do
it. This is not a new idea but rather a new realization that age-old
wisdom of how people best relate as individual human beings must
be applied with painstaking care to the vast institutional structures
in which all of us are now inextricably involved.

Caring is the essential motive. What we have learned about
caring for individual persons we must now learn to give to institutions. Have you ever noted how much less qualm of conscience
some people have about cheating an institution than they have
for cheating an individual person? We must change that.

Caring, we know, is an exacting and demanding business. It
requires not only interest and compassion and concern; it
demands self-sacrifice and wisdom and tough-mindedness and
discipline. It is sometimes difficult to care enough for the immediate person one loves and respects. It is much more difficult to
care for an institution, especially a big one, which can look cold
and impersonal and seem to have an autonomy of its own.

Yet a commanding majority of people must care for the
institutions if we are to have a society worth living in. If one
thinks of oneself as responsible, one must care for every institution one touches; and for those one touches intimately, one must
care deeply.

You may be asking yourselves at this point: What does it
mean for a member of the School Sisters of St. Francis, for one
who touches this institution intimately? How does one care
deeply for this particular institution? I know a little bit about

your order but not enough to suggest a particular answer for any one of you. But in what I have already said there are some suggestions for a general answer. Let me share what I feel it is.

Caring deeply for this institution, the School Sisters of St. Francis, means that you are personally dedicated to making of it a thing of beauty—in contemporary terms—something that raises you as a person to a stature you would not achieve alone or in a less committed relationship. These are the things it will require of you as individuals: when it is appropriate for you to lead, you will lead; where it is appropriate for you to follow, you will follow.

Leadership means that one individual has a better than average sense of what should be done now and is willing to take the risk to say, "Let us do *this now*." The process of consensus is followed up to the point where some individual must take this risk— this leap of faith. Spontaneous consensus rarely goes to the point of clearly indicating action. Inspiration is usually received by the best prepared individual who, for this immediate act, is the leader.

Followership is an equally responsible role because it means that the individual must take the risk to empower the leader and to say, in the matter at hand, "I will trust your insight." *Followership* implies another preparation in order that trusting, empowering the leader, will be a strength-giving element in the institution.

Both *leading* and *following*, in an institution that becomes a thing of beauty because of the serving power that is generated, require of all a common purpose and a clear definition of obligations. Where the obligations are not precisely defined and willingly accepted, the basis for trust cannot exist.

Leadership in such an institution will be a different thing from what we customarily assume. There will still be a titular leader, but such a person will not be seen as "chief." Rather, it will be a role from which oversight is given to a much more fluid arrangement in which leaders and followers change places as multifaceted missions are undertaken and move into phases that call for different deployments of talent. My suggested four-point strategy for institution building is a design for the generation of a high level of trust that this approach to leadership requires.

The institution that becomes distinguished as servant in the contemporary world—as I hope the School Sisters of St. Francis will become—will have learned to act in a serving way with great economy of resources, both human and material. You will have learned how to be preponderantly affirmative as an institution. And this requires, I believe, that, guided by your common purpose—however you define it—you will learn to act one step at a time as you see your way clear. You will take each step, sometimes at considerable risk, with confidence that such an act of faith opens one for insights on which the next step is taken. The path to a better society is never laid out before us as a safe journey. We move from one insight to another—every step being a risk. It requires little faith to take a step that involves little risk.

What makes an institution a thing of beauty is the demonstration of faith at work. And when a large institution, such as yours is, accomplishes this, I would choose to see it as a distinguished serving institution.

The application of this point of view is not difficult conceptually. We have known for several millennia what the individual is like who becomes distinguished as servant. But in large, complex institutions, we have yet to learn how to work together to achieve what individuals have long been able to do. This we must learn. We have no other options.

Earlier I noted that there was sufficient discussion elsewhere of the new urge for self-fulfillment and that most of you who are young may understand it better in your own experience than I can delineate it for you. I am not underestimating what individuals must do for themselves in finding their own significance as persons as they go along, even when powerful forces may operate to deny it. What I have tried to share with you is some of the fruit of my own experience with a variety of institutions because I sense that in this Chapter of Mats you will be confronting some of the very real problems of your own organizational existence. As I see it, the overarching issue is: Will you accept the challenge to build of your religious order an entity of such commanding distinction as servant in the late twentieth century that the force of the model you present will move your church—and the world? You will lead with your example.

A number of years ago I attended a lecture in New York by the South African writer Laurens van der Post. It was a disturbing lecture about the vexing problems of that part of the world. In the discussion period a questioner asked, "Colonel van der Post, I am deeply moved by what you say about the plight of your country. What can we over here do to help?" I will never forget the answer in that beautiful clipped English speech: "Cultivate your own garden and its fragrance will be wafted across the ocean to us."

Fifty years ago the great leader of my religious society, Rufus M. Jones, in addressing a gathering of his people similar to yours here today, put it in one succinct sentence. "We stand in a crisis and we can be bearers of the torch or we can carefully husband a little flame and keep it from going out a little longer."

In the few minutes I have had to talk with you I have tried to hand you a torch. Will you accept it?

THE GROWING EDGE CHURCH

As I reflect on these three pieces and what was said in Chapter 2, "The Institution as Servant," about the growing edge church, I have a feeling of the imminence of a new prophecy being received, one that will come from among the young who have a fresh view of things. Not that I am expecting a new messiah, but I believe that voices that are speaking now, but not being heard, will gradually come to be heard. These voices are speaking in minute particulars about the contemporary alienation and are offering precise and disturbing solutions. The imminence I sense is not that they will speak where they have not been speaking, but that some of those who have not been hearing will begin to hear.

There is now seeking on an unprecedented scale, and the land abounds with gurus who are feeding the hunger of the seekers. The change that I anticipate is a new awareness among seekers in which those whose needs will be met *only* as they serve others will separate themselves from those who are satisfied to remain committed almost wholly to meeting their own needs—which, in the nature of things, will probably never be met because one is rarely satisfied with what one seeks only for oneself.

Where will such newly aware seekers turn? What will be the direction of the search when one gives up centeredness on the exclusive service of self with only vague generalities about the good of humankind? Will not such aware seekers turn to listening to (or generating) prophecy that is rooted in a realistic understanding of the human dilemma in the late twentieth century, with service to others defined in minute particulars? Will not whatever institution shelters the new teachers and husbands the new teaching become the growing edge church in these times? And will not such a growing edge church have a unique chance to rise conspicuously above the level of mediocrity in which so many of our institutions seem mired?

What is mediocrity? Is it not anything that is substantially less in quality than what is reasonable and possible with available resources, human and material? "Mediocrity is the truly diabolical force in the world," said Burckhardt.

In the Western world I believe that this all too common fault, settling for mediocrity, derives from a flaw that is right at the heart of traditional moral law. When Moses came down the mountain carrying the law, chiseled in stone and bearing God's imprimatur, he may have laid the groundwork for our present condition. If we view Moses as a human leader, subject to error like the rest of us (in Chapter 2, "The Institution as Servant," I pointed to one such), he may have yielded to the temptation, common to this day, to attribute the law to "those higher up" rather than to assume the burden of justification himself. We do not know his conditions; he may have felt that he could not be sufficiently persuasive as a mere rational man.

But how much better it would be for us today, if, as the inspired man he obviously was, he had presented the law as a reasonable codification of experience and wisdom, a summary of those sensible rules to guide individual conduct, and as the basis for a good society. This would have opened the way for continued growth of the law with further experience and would have made the rational justification of the law always a contemporary concern. The law, thus derived, would still have been essentially religious in the root meaning of *religio*, "to rebind." Human beings are rebound to the cosmos so that, as intellectual individuals, probably estranged by their intellectuality, they can belong in this world and be at home in it.

There may have been two further flaws in the original concept of the law. Most of it was "thou shalt not's" and they are quite categorical. The few affirmations are general, and conformity with them is difficult to establish. This allows the interpretation that if one obeys the prohibitions, one is virtuous.

Then, by stating the law as uniform for all persons, regardless of their capacities, rather than placing the greater obligation on the more able, the better endowed persons are relieved of the obligation to measure up to their opportunities and their potentials. This permits many to be seen as law abiding when, in fact, their performance is far below what it might be.

In the shadow of this view of the shortcomings of the traditional moral law, I have tried to delineate the *servant* as one who meets the test of a higher law whose requirements of both persons and institutions are proportional to their opportunity to serve. While I would like to see more non-servants converted to servanthood, my greater hope is that more of those who are natural servants, who get joy out of serving, will become aggressive builders of serving institutions. Within these institutions the opportunity may seem larger for those in higher status positions, but as more and more people, regardless of their status, are asserting their autonomy and articulating their beliefs, literally everyone who is inside and who has some force as a person can be an institution builder.

Those outside can criticize, flagellate, and disrupt, but only those who are inside can build.

For the servant who has the capacity to be a builder, the greatest joy in this world is in building.

Will not the growing edge church become the chief nurturer of servant-leaders, institution builders for the future?

VIII

Servant-Leaders

It has been my privilege to have had a close friendship with several great exemplars as servant-leaders. For only two of them have I written my appreciation. Donald J. Cowling, of my father's generation, was president of my college. In his political and economic views he was a far-out conservative. The other, Rabbi Abraham Joshua Heschel, was of my generation. He was a liberal activist. In my estimation both of them were of the truly great.

Superficially, these two men had very little in common. Donald Cowling wielded his influence on me when I was young. Rabbi Heschel and I did not become friends until I was nearly sixty, but it was a close friendship for his last years.

The memoir on Dr. Cowling was published by Carleton College, and Rabbi Heschel's appeared in *Friends Journal*. When these two pieces were written, about ten years apart, I did not think of putting them side by side and reflecting on how these two extraordinary people wielded their separate influences on me. But on thinking on it now, it was most fortunate for me to have had these two friendships separated by thirty years.

Deep down, I believe these two men, had they known one another, would have had a feeling of kinship, different as they were. They shared two inestimable qualities: great integrity and a profound sense of the mystical—each was guided by the heart.

There was an interesting reaction to the memoir on Dr. Cowling from old friends. "You have made him out to be an autocrat," they said, "and we don't like that."

My reply was, "Let's face it; he *was* an autocrat." But that fact would not justify the emphasis on that quality that I have given. This memoir will be distributed to contemporary students at the college. And as you know, we are in a period in which strong leadership is denigrated in the colleges. Students today should know that the quality of institution they now enjoy did not build itself; it was built by the dedicated effort of a very strong man, so strong that, to his contemporaries, he was seen as autocratic, as I have portrayed him. Once a quality institution like Carleton is built, a more meliorative type of person can maintain it, perhaps better than the one who built it. But to build a place such as Carleton is today, starting with the feeble institution Dr. Cowling took over in 1909, and under the conditions of those times, required a very dominating leader. I do not want today's students to miss this important bit of history.

My memoir on Rabbi Heschel was written out of a mood of a different relationship, a recent close friendship with a contemporary.

I am grateful for the influence of these two great men on me. Both of them are as alive in my memory, and the resonant qualities of their voices are as distinct as if they were here with me now.

ABRAHAM JOSHUA HESCHEL: BUILD A LIFE LIKE A WORK OF ART

"What message have you for young people?" asked Carl Stern of NBC in concluding a television interview with Rabbi Abraham Joshua Heschel shortly before his death on December 23, 1972.

Rabbi Heschel replied: "I would say: Let them remember that there is a meaning beyond absurdity. Let them be sure that every little deed counts, that every word has power, and that we can—every one—do our share to redeem the world in spite of all absurdities and all frustrations and all disappointments. And above all, remember that the meaning of life is to build a life as if it were a work of art."

His academic title at Jewish Theological Seminary was Professor of Ethics and Mysticism. And the title bespoke the man. He was ethical to the core of his being, in the deepest religious sense. And he was a thoroughgoing mystic in his insistence on the primacy of unique present existence, no two moments ever alike. "True insight," he once wrote, "is a moment of perceiving a situation before it freezes into similarity with something else."

My friendship with Abraham Heschel began many years ago when I went to his office at the seminary to invite him to address a group of young business executives with whom I would be working the following summer at Dartmouth College. We wanted our students to explore the subject of ethics through a firsthand examination of the thinking of Protestant, Catholic, and Jewish theologians. After a long, absorbing discussion he accepted—because it was a new challenge, not like the many invitations to speak that came his way. He wanted to learn about the ethical involvement of these executives. And he wanted to learn much of it before he met with them. To satisfy his need, and to my own great profit, there were three or four long sessions in his office that spring. An enduring friendship was forged in those discussions.

Our guests were asked to speak as long as they wished at an evening session, with discussion held for a leisurely seminar the next morning. Abraham talked for two hours and held this group of sharp, ambitious young executives on the edges of their chairs. When he closed there was polite applause, and he and I said goodnight. The next morning one of the group said to me, "You did not see what happened when you and the rabbi left. We sat there glued to our chairs in silence for five full minutes. Finally one of us broke the spell with, 'Well, fellows, we've had it. The prophet Amos was here. He stepped right out of the Old Testament.'" Such was my introduction to Abraham Heschel.

In the succeeding years there were many meetings: some with our families, with his gracious wife, Sylvia, and their lovely daughter, Susannah, at their home and ours. Occasionally there was a family event at the seminary when he would loan me a yarmulke, and we would all meet around the festive table with the faculty for one of the great Jewish celebrations. Then there was a memorable visit to a Benedictine monastery where the abbot was his special friend, and Abraham and I spent the day having our meals and participating in the religious services with the brothers.

Abraham Heschel was born in Warsaw in 1907, descendant, on both father's and mother's sides, from a long line of Hasidic leaders. He grew up in the closed world of Jewish piety. A biographer writes that "at the age of ten he was at home in the world of the Bible, he had acquired competence in the subtle dialectic of the Talmud, and he had also been introduced to the world of Jewish mysticism, the *Kabbalah*. The understanding for the realness of the spirit and for the holy dimension of all existence was not primarily the result of book learning but the cumulative effect of life lived among people who 'were sure that everything hinted at something transcendent; that the presence of God was a daily experience and the sanctification of life a daily task.'"

At twenty he entered the University of Berlin. By 1936 he had earned the Ph.D. and established himself as a scholar, writer, and teacher. He was then chosen by Martin Buber as his successor at the Judische Lehrhaus. In 1938 he was expelled by the Nazis to Warsaw, and in 1939 he escaped to London where he established the Institute for Jewish Learning. In 1940 he joined the faculty of Hebrew Union College in Cincinnati where he stayed for five years before coming to New York.

Rabbi Heschel wrote extensive scholarly works in four languages and was fluent in two others. When asked how he knew when he was at home in a language, he replied, "When I dream in it."

One of his most widely known writings in English is an impressive book entitled *The Prophets*. In his last television interview he said of this work:

> I spent many years on it. And, really, this book changed my life. Because, early in my life, my great love was for learning, studying—the place where I preferred to live was in my study with books and writing and thinking. I've learned from the prophets that I have to be involved in the affairs of man, in the affairs of suffering man...I think that everyone who reads the

prophets will discover that the prophets really were the most disturbing people who ever lived…If I were to say what challenges me most in the Hebrew tradition it is the high view it takes of the nature of man…The tragedy of our education today is that we are giving some easy solutions: Be complacent, have peace of mind…No! Wrestling is the issue; facing the challenge is the issue.

His activist life after his book on the prophets was a remarkable transformation. He marched with Martin Luther King Jr. at Selma. A news account quotes him as saying: "I prayed with my legs as I walked." He was co-chair of Clergy Concerned About Vietnam and participated in demonstrations in Washington and elsewhere. Wherever the action was these last ten years, there you were likely to find Abraham Heschel. The protesting Old Testament prophet really came alive in him.

All the while, though, there was a steady outpouring of theological writing. And he also found time for his friends, especially his non-Jewish friends, who learned to call on the Sabbath when he would be at home with his family. He was a "fun" man, stimulating to be with. There were always Hasidic stories. I will never lose the sound of his voice in: "My friend, let me tell you a story—"

One of Abraham Heschel's later accomplishments was his intervention in the Vatican Council to question Catholic positions regarding Jews. He wanted to end once and for all the Catholic mission to convert the Jews and their position on Jewish guilt in the crucifixion. He worked closely with Cardinal Bea and had audiences on these matters with Pope Paul VI. Shortly after Heschel's death, Pope Paul quoted him in a sermon.

In 1965 he became the first Jew ever to be appointed visiting professor at Union Theological Seminary. There his classes drew more students than any previous visiting professor in the school's history.

His theological writing was judged unique by critics. He had compared Judaism to "a messenger who forgot the message" and to "a well-guarded secret surrounded by an impenetrable wall." His writing was a determined effort to recover the message and to breach the wall. This comes through and gives his writing a prophetic quality to Jew and non-Jew alike. "The root of religion is what to do with the feeling for the mystery of living, what to do with awe, wonder, and amazement. Religion begins with a consciousness that something is asked of us...It is in the awareness that the mystery we face is incomparably deeper than we know that all creative thinking begins."

His lifelong credo was simply expressed: "Just to be is a blessing. Just to live is holy."

I have often wondered what was the bond between him and me. I shared neither his scholarship nor his exclusively Jewish theology. We did meet at the level of social concern: he with his political activism and I with my efforts to reconstruct within the system. Each was interested in and respected the other's involvement, and both realized that these were separate paths that could not be merged.

But the firmer bond, and one of profound meaning to me, was the shared belief that the highest level of religious experience is awareness of oneness with the mystery—as he would say, the feeling of awe and wonder and amazement. When I was in the presence of this good and gentle rabbi and was suffused by the warmth of this feeling, I was lifted above all the differences that divide people, differences that divided the two of us when we descended into the realm of concepts, language, and practice. What kept our friendship close was a common need, a shared feeling of not being supported in this sense of the mystical by the religious sentiment of our times.

His was the more poignant feeling of need because he was the more disturbed—as one would expect of any European Jew who survived the Nazi regime. And in our last meeting, which I left feeling that I would not see him again because he seemed so frail, we covered ground that we had explored many times before. This time he asked, plaintively, "Why do so many of the great religions which had their origins in the mystery come ultimately to be social service agencies, or in their religious life to be preoccupied with form and concerned more with the container than the content?" My considered reply at that last meeting was, "In the Quaker tradition, the answer to that question lies beyond the mystery where one does not ask. In the face of these conditions, one simply builds anew. We are called to listen for the prophetic voices who have the rebuilding message for these times so that we can support and encourage them." I believe that Abraham in his later years was listening—really listening for a new prophecy for these times.

On Monday of his last week Abraham hand-delivered to his publisher the manuscript of his book *A Passion for Truth*. On Wednesday, despite his ailing heart, he journeyed to Danbury, Connecticut, where he waited in the snow and rain to greet his friend, Philip Berrigan, on his release from prison. He returned to his last class at the seminary and came home Friday evening utterly exhausted. He died quietly in his sleep early on the Sabbath—as any devout Jew would wish to do.

His friends were consoled to recall his often quoted words, "For a pious man it is a privilege to die."

DONALD JOHN COWLING: LIFESTYLE OF GREATNESS

What does it mean to be *great?* What lifestyle, cultivated when one is young, augurs for greatness over a life span? When I was young I was stirred by Daniel Burnham's dictum, "Make no little plans, they have no magic to stir men's blood and probably themselves will not be realized." Then I had the good fortune to be an undergraduate at Carleton College (class of 1926) when Donald John Cowling was president and in his prime. Later I knew him intimately over a period of years. As I saw him, he became one of the *truly great* because, as a young adult, he chose a lifestyle that was congruent with his own unique personality, a lifestyle that brought the best of his strong character to bear upon the situations he faced; and he stayed with it consistently over a long and impressively constructive life.

The example of this man marked me in a particular way, and I welcome this opportunity to record my appreciation because I would like to share my estimate of him with those who knew him, as well as with those of this student generation whose lifestyles may yet be shaped by conscious choices. Dr. Cowling was the model of the *responsible human* whose heart guided his actions.

Because personal greatness cannot be categorically defined, and because it is not synonymous with perfection, I will try to convey my appreciation in a way that will make more accessible that meaning about greatness that is beyond definition. "No language can be anything but elliptical," wrote Alfred North Whitehead, "requiring a leap of the imagination to understand its meaning in its relevance to immediate experience."

Dr. Cowling was president of Carleton College for thirty-six years, from 1909 to 1945. He was twenty-eight when he was named president, and he retired from that position at sixty-five. Over those years he was approached many times about the presidencies of other institutions, some forty of them, but he discouraged them all. There was always a good reason—he was in the midst of a fund-raising campaign, or there was the emergency of a war or a depression. The truth was that he had really committed his life to the building of Carleton from a little struggling denominational institution with a half-dozen old buildings to a model for small liberal arts colleges. His two successors have carried on with distinction, but if ever there was a demonstration of the truth in Emerson's declaration, "An institution is but the lengthened shadow of a man," Carleton College is the lengthened shadow of the man I knew as Prexy.

Not many really knew Donald Cowling. To the students of my generation he was Prexy, and I shall refer to him thus, though in addressing him it was always Dr. Cowling. He was an aloof, reserved man, not unfriendly—but restrained, and on a first-name basis with very few. He seemed to many of us students, and perhaps to faculty as well, to be preoccupied with raising money and building buildings and dropping cliches about Carleton being a Christian college.

I would not have known him beyond this image had I not been a student who occasionally got into trouble and found myself in his office with some explaining to do. There I discovered the man few knew, a man with deep and dependable understanding and compassion and with an unequivocal belief in freedom for the human spirit to flower. I was too young to understand it all at the time, but it is an influence that has grown through the years and continues to grow.

I am sorry for those who have never gotten into trouble because they really cannot share my experience. It is one thing to understand compassion intellectually, or even to give it. It is quite another thing to receive compassion when one knows that all one is entitled to is justice. There is no one best way to live a life, I have concluded. There are penalties and compensations for being "good" as well as for being "bad." Paradoxically, one must be both good and bad to enjoy this life to the full or to comprehend its meaning. This I discovered at Carleton, and from Prexy personally.

Shortly after I came to New York in 1929 I met him at an alumni gathering and a friendship began in which we got together in New York once or twice a year until the war, which interrupted so many things. Usually we would settle down with a bottle of wine in a quiet corner of a restaurant for an evening of conversation. Once when Prexy was quite mellow he remarked slyly, "You know, I can't do this in Northfield."

These were often spirited conversations. After 1932 were the New Deal days and he was a staunch conservative while I was a mild New Dealer. He was absolutely dedicated to Carleton and I, being something of a maverick who didn't fit the established ways of colleges, was sharply critical of all collegiate education. My point in mentioning it is that Prexy grappled tenaciously for better than ten years with the issues I pressed on him.

With the passing of years I have come to realize that adult performance in all fields is pretty mediocre when judged by what is reasonably possible, and I am now less critical of the performance of educators and more critical of their pretensions. But in those days I was more critical of performance. One night I got under Prexy's skin and he came back at me with, "See here, now, you are doing pretty well. You must have gotten something out of your education at Carleton." I thought a minute while the gremlin in me went to work. Then I said, "Yes, now that I think of it, there is something." "Please tell me something good," he said. "I've taken a lot of criticism." Screwing up my courage I said, "I learned how to make a little bit of work look like a whole lot or I would never have graduated from Carleton and wouldn't get along now." Prexy did not reply to that. He just looked at the ceiling and changed the subject. For a minute I thought it was the end of our friendship.

Then one evening he almost lost me when I pressed him to define what democracy meant to him. His reply, in about these exact words, was, "Democracy is a state of affairs in which the more able who emerge in the lower classes can get into the upper classes." This time I looked at the ceiling and changed the subject. But as I thought it over, no, brooded about it, his reply seemed a part of the internal consistency of this man. Prexy thought of everything in terms of what he was trying to do at Carleton. He was operating an escalator for those whom be regarded as talented people. It was a part of his basic belief in freedom, which held that the way should be open for people to succeed or fail, and he wanted to help those who had the makings of success.

Conservative that he was, he respected ability regardless of how ideologically different others were from himself. My class of '26 arrived at Carleton near the end of the witch-hunting period after World War I. During that period, if an able professor was fired for his political beliefs, Prexy tried to hire him. John Gray, a distinguished economics professor at Carleton in my day, was one of these. I shudder to think what would have happened had Prexy been the active president during the McCarthy era. He would have hired any good professor he could use, who would be dedicated to his work at Carleton, if he was in trouble where he was because of his beliefs or affiliations. And he would have done it even if the trustees threatened to fire him summarily. One had to know him well to sense his intense passion for freedom in general and academic freedom in particular. I developed a tremendous respect for the deep, solid character of this man, and it led me to overlook things I would have found fault with in lesser men. He did well to retire in 1945, before institutional loyalty had all but disappeared in academic people and before the teaching of students ceased to be the prime value among many college faculty members. This state of affairs is hard on many college presidents today, but Prexy would have suffered deeply because his quality of dedication and institutional loyalty was rare even in his day. I venture the opinion that many careers today, in education and elsewhere, would be more significant if institutional loyalty were a stronger motive.

I often wondered why Prexy wanted to spend those evenings with me. He was a busy man. I was anything but a distinguished product of his school. One reason he stayed with these talks, I think, was that he was a builder in more ways than just physical assets. He was trying to build an institution of quality at a time when quality in education was not the common pursuit it is today. He was seeking quality by current standards (he sometimes spoke of building "the Dartmouth of the West"), but he was groping to go beyond that, too.

He stayed with me, even though I made him uncomfortable at times by my insistence, because I constantly pressed him to examine his assumptions about meaning and process in education and what alternatives might make a better college. Prexy was the model of the responsible man. He felt the obligation to do his best. But he kept putting me off because these were the depression years and the college was broke. Any innovative effort would cost money, so we always left it there. Then one visit he appeared with a broad smile. He had just received a gift of a half million dollars. Now he could do something; what should he do? We spent an evening at it but the conclusion was—nothing! He would do the conventional thing and endow a chair. He was sixty, and he had spent too many years enmeshed in a monolithic educational ideology. He had let go too long the full examination of the assumptions he operated by. He must settle, he conceded, for what he had; he must continue to run his college as colleges were conventionally run, much as the thought of advancing the growing edge excited him. It was a sad evening, which both of us acknowledged. This was the last of those conversations. I didn't see Prexy again until the twenty-fifth reunion of my class in 1951 when he came to speak to us—six years after his retirement. We vowed then that we would get together to renew our conversations. And they were renewed, as I will note later.

In an exchange of correspondence with my classmate, President John Nason, shortly after Dr. Cowling's death on November 27, 1965, Dr. Nason wrote:

> I sit here at Dr. Cowling's desk meditating on how the mighty have fallen. Here is the man who, more than any other person, built the modern Carleton. Without his devotion and labors over thirty-six years (too long a time in my judgment for anyone to be president of one college) Carleton would not be the kind of college it is today. There was an heroic quality to the man which makes pygmies of the rest of us. I am not much given to belittling myself, but I sometimes sit here in an office which D.J.C. still haunts wondering how I can ever measure up to the standards set and carry forward the enterprise to which he gave his life.

Donald John Cowling was born in Trevalga, Cornwall, England, on August 21, 1880, the son of John P. and Mary K. (Stephens) Cowling. John Cowling was a shoemaker, and in the stratified society of his Cornish village, his status was below that of his wife, whose family were prosperous farmers. This class difference is thought to have led to the family's emigration to the United States in 1882; they settled in Pennsylvania. There was a move to Canada, where John Cowling worked in the slate quarries and served as lay minister. Then back to Pennsylvania, where he had country parishes. The family was so poor that one winter in Canada they lived on rutabagas. Later, Prexy's daughters recall, he always wished rutabaga served at Thanksgiving. Pennsylvania was home to the family. In addition to Donald, there was a brother, Roy, later a lawyer in Minneapolis, and sisters, Maude, Bertha, Blanche, and Lillian.

John Cowling was deeply religious with a simple untrained faith and was a boy preacher in England. He was devoted to his family, but he had a quick temper that interfered with his work. His son Donald had great respect for his father and was strongly influenced by his religious convictions. At the age of eight he was leading prayer in his father's church. But he also developed a reserve and a control that may have been a reaction against his father's temper. The family was poor, and there was no way for the children to be educated without working their way; this no doubt brought the pattern of hard work into Donald's lifestyle. He worked in a factory in all of his spare time during his high school years, and at the age of eighteen he was assistant foreman in charge of one hundred men.

Clearly from his father's influence came his passion for freedom (no other word than *passion* adequately labels it) and his strong sense of responsibility. Also his father gave him a buoyant spirit that stayed with him to the end. It was often expressed as "This is a wonderful world," and he awoke every morning glad to be alive. He always brought this buoyant spirit with him when I saw him during the depression years when he was terribly pressed just to keep the college alive.

Little is known of the character of Donald's boyhood or the influence of mother, brother, and sisters. He spoke often and warmly of his mother, saying that the first dollar he ever earned he gave to her. His father's identification with the United Brethren Church probably directed Donald to Lebanon Valley College with the help of loans arranged by his father. There he received his B.A. degree in 1902. A B.A. from Yale followed in 1903, which was succeeded by an M.A. in 1904, a B.D. in 1906, and the Ph.D. in 1909. He was enrolled in the two graduate schools simultaneously and received top grades in both.

These were demanding years in which he was working to pay his way and studying intensively. Among other duties he was pastor of a little church in Connecticut. There probably was not much student life and a larger than ordinary seriousness of purpose. But whatever the demands of this period and the resulting lifelong pattern of unremitting work, an essential gaiety and good humor survived. Also the influence of the Yale theological training seems to have had a liberalizing influence on his early more primitive religious training. He held to a simple Christian faith throughout his life, but there was nothing doctrinaire about him. The marks of the early religious influences may have stayed with him—in a deep emotional way if not in conscious theology. We are all the creatures of our experience—not necessarily the servants or the prisoners of it. If a coherent lifestyle emerges, as it certainly did with Donald Cowling, every significant experience is somehow woven into the fabric of it.

The invitation to Baker University in Kansas came in 1906 to be assistant professor of philosophy and biblical literature, and this was quickly followed, in 1907, by advancement to full professor. It was from this position that he was invited in December 1908 to become president of Carleton College. He took over the post in July 1909. He had been married in June 1907 to Elizabeth L. Stehman, of whom more will be said later.

His unusual record at Yale had brought him to the attention of trustees who were searching for a new president to lead Carleton out of the shadow of some administrative misadventures. It was a brave decision to hand over the reins of a college in trouble to this twenty-eight year old. This was probably suggested by Dr. Marion Leroy Burton (Carleton 1900), and a classmate and roommate at Yale. Dr. Burton was then becoming president of Smith College. Later he was president of the University of Minnesota and the University of Michigan. As a young adult Prexy kept good company.

There must have been some qualms about his appointment when Prexy announced promptly to the trustees that if he were to do anything at Carleton he had to be the boss. If anything was clear about Prexy from the day he took office to the day he retired, it was that *he was in charge*. And everybody—trustees, faculty, staff, students—knew this. He was involved in every detail of building buildings, maintaining the grounds, running the farm, hiring and firing of faculty and staff, and issues with students. He had tremendous capacity for detail. Correspondence with the architect on the design of a new milk house on the college farm reveals his careful research on the attributes of a good milk house. I sat in the balcony of Skinner Memorial Chapel one sunny winter afternoon and read the files of correspondence with the architect on the design of the chapel. Much of it concerned the large stained-glass window which I faced at the end of the chancel. And what careful thought Prexy lavishly devoted to the design of that window! I wish that every student who sits in the chapel and looks at that window could see beyond its literal beauty to the loving care devoted *just to that window.* The Italian tile on the chapel floor was an issue with the trustees who wanted a less expensive domestic tile. But Prexy persuaded them to let him use his judgment—and the Italian tile went in. Later the trustee who had led the fight for cheaper tile admitted his error.

This attention to detail, this complete "in charge" approach to his job, is illustrated further by two anecdotes on small matters. Walking across the campus one day at trustee meeting time, shortly after he became president, he came upon a groundsman in the act of cutting down a tree. "Who told you to cut down that tree?" Prexy asked the groundsman. "Trustee so-and-so," was the reply. "Hereafter," ordered Prexy, "I decide when trees shall be cut down." He then confronted the assembled trustees with his decision and they conceded that he should manage the buildings and grounds.

A young botany instructor reported that one afternoon he was working with saw and hammer building some small cases for exhibits when Prexy walked through his place, stopped, and asked what he was doing. On being told, Prexy produced a rule from his pocket, carefully measured each case and, being satisfied that they were all right, walked on with no comment.

How did such a man deal with his faculty? He had unbounded respect for the integrity of teaching and the freedom of the individual teacher for independence of thought. A considerable controversy arose around a distinguished professor of my time, Dr. Albert Parker Fitch, who was a liberal theologian. The Baptists, who were then supporting the college, took out after him and several others. In particular, a hard-shell fundamentalist preacher in Minneapolis was after his scalp. I recall going to the local armory in Northfield to hear this rampant preacher speak, and he was wild in his attacks. But Prexy stood his ground. He made a great effort to mollify the Baptists, but he stood by Dr. Fitch and others under attack for their liberal views. When Dr. Fitch decided to resign to accept the pastorate of Park Avenue Presbyterian Church in New York, his letter to Prexy contained the following:

> You were so kind, in our previous conversation, as to express your regret that I contemplated severing my official connection with the College and to express the opinion that my teaching and public representation of the College, during these three and one-half years, had been distinguished service to the institution.
>
> I was deeply touched by so generous an appreciation and it should be added, now, on my part, that, if this be true, it is in no small measure due to your own administration. You have given and maintained for me, sometimes under trying circumstances, absolute freedom of teaching in my classrooms; I have found a never deviating loyalty and sympathetic support from you throughout these years.

A year later (October 26, 1928) the following resolution was introduced by Professor Karl Schmidt at a faculty meeting and approved by the faculty:

> The Faculty of Carleton College wishes to express its regret at the action of the Minnesota State Baptist Convention severing relations with Carleton College. As this action is really based on a criticism of the faculty

and its "liberal" teaching, we feel impelled to express our sincere appreciation of the fact that neither the Board of Trustees nor the administration has in any way attempted to obtain a continuance of this relation with the Minnesota State Baptist Convention by any surrender of academic freedom. Neither you nor anyone else in authority at Carleton has even suggested that a member of the faculty teach anything which his scientific training, his best insight, and his conscience did not dictate.

We take this opportunity of stating our faith in academic freedom as a fundamental condition of all advance in human endeavor, as the right of a citizen in a free country, and as the principle underlying and defining the *protestant* form of Christianity. This faith involves a belief in the fundamental right of reason to decide questions of truth, and a conviction that science, and religion are not intrinsically irreconcilable; that a clash of dogmas in a science with those in a religion cannot be settled by ignoring or attempting to annihilate the one or the other; that, like clashes in science itself, discrepancies should provoke a critical examination of all claims and a fundamental re-examination of our faiths. We believe that thought should not be obstructed and that revelation has not terminated. We believe, therefore, neither in a college in which an outside authority dictates convictions preliminary to investigation, nor in a college divorced from religion.

This was a period of considerable controversy on matters of religious liberalism. The Scopes trial in Tennessee had stirred quite a storm, and Dr. Harry Emerson Fosdick of New York, a famous preacher of that period, left his denomination over that issue.

In defending the college against the fundamentalists in the 1920s, Prexy was unequivocal. Speaking in Minneapolis at the time he said:

What does orthodoxy mean? It all depends on the man whom you ask. Orthodoxy is what he believes—as though anyone had a monopoly on the love of God and alone were the recipient of all the wisdom of the ages. Is that the Church? If it is I would not hold it up to the youth of America as an institution to follow.— Orthodoxy is a dam that is built by persons who think they have reached the ultimate in human thought, and that there will never be anything as good. They are finding that it is easier to become interested in the dam than in the great current that it is holding back.

These were brave words in 1926, and one knows why the faculty would pass a resolution praising his stand.

Prexy had a high regard for the faculty as a corporate body, too, and he encouraged its committee process. But he was also a man of action, and sometimes he moved ahead of them. There was the incident with a faculty committee that was charged with promulgating a curriculum revision. The chair of the committee got a brilliant idea, but it was rather radical. Knowing Prexy's *in charge* tendencies, he decided to test the idea on Prexy before proposing it to the committee. Prexy thought it was a fine idea. "Put it into effect," he told the chair. "But," protested the chair, "I haven't even told the committee. Don't you think I ought to have their concurrence?" "If they are the people they ought to be," replied Prexy firmly, "they will agree. Put it into effect!"

There were faculty meetings, and they were long and tedious. But these meetings were not where the decisions were made that moved the college along.

Prexy wrote an interesting letter in 1941 to the president of another college that was revising its by-laws. In this he outlined his views on authority within the college. The fact that the trustees of Carleton had twice set up by-law revision committees during Prexy's tenure suggests that there may have been some restiveness with Prexy's use of authority. Both times, apparently, they decided to leave well enough alone. There is an old adage that one does not argue with success.

Our by-laws at Carleton have not been revised since I came here. We have considered doing so many times and have twice appointed a committee for this purpose. However, these committees have never made any formal report to the Board.

The entire authority for managing the College is invested in the Board of Trustees by our Articles of Incorporation. Without any formal action on the part of the Board I have always assumed that the Board wished me to exercise its authority between meetings. I have always assumed that, subject to approval by the Board, I had authority to organize the entire administration of the College in accordance with my best judgment. In coming to decisions, one naturally consults many members of the faculty.

On the other hand, I have never assumed that it was wise for me to attempt to supervise the teaching of the College. We have tried to select responsible people who are in sympathy with the purposes of the College. Once an appointment is made a teacher is expected to assume the responsibility of teaching in his own right. I have coveted for our teachers the same kind of freedom which a minister in our free Protestant churches is given when he speaks from his pulpit. Obviously, if a teacher should be disloyal to his trust and exercise an influence resulting in tearing down the College rather than building it up, it would create a problem which would have to be dealt with as an individual case. No such case has developed in all the years I have been here.

This plan is two-sided. (1) The President is responsible for the administration of the College subject only to the authority of the Board of Trustees but in frequent conference with individual members of the faculty best informed regarding particular questions and with the cooperation of the faculty as a whole, which he should be wise and tactful enough to secure. (2) All teachers teach in their own right and are responsible only to professional standards, to their own conception of the truth and to the purposes and ideals of the institution, subject of course to such suggestions and counsel (not supervision) as the President may be able to give, especially to the younger teachers. This plan has seemed to work out very well in our case. As far as I know, the faculty have never desired a more official part in the administration of the College.

Being made president at twenty-eight may have encouraged his *take charge* style. He was aware, no doubt, that faculties and other constituents of colleges have been known to eat up administrators; thus, being young and untried, Prexy may have chosen a bold offensive with everybody and, finding success in it, he may have liked the role and decided to adopt it permanently. But I am inclined to the belief that this was his natural stance, and it evolved with the opportunity. He was a determined builder; he said so in his inaugural address. Looking back over his active years at Carleton, much was predictable from that address.

Not every institution in our land is sure of a future...

The processes of history are merciless and irresistible, cutting down with a hand apparently ruthless all that is inadequate or ill-adapted to meet the ever-changing and ever-increasing demands of the times, a process apparently without heart and yet in the long run beneficent, for only what is best is preserved...If the Christian college is to continue to appeal successfully to those of money and sound business judgment, it must be able to show a reason for its existence and adequate grounds for its claim upon life in the future...Carleton...will need at least to double her present income...The raising of this money is the task of the immediate future...Carleton does not hope to become a large university. It is not her desire to add materially to her numbers. But she does aim at such educational efficiency as will enable her to give to those she undertakes to train a preparation for life that is excelled by no other institution in the land. This is her dream and her vision.

This was not just appropriate oratory for the occasion. The only error in his prophecy was his use of the words *immediate future* in referring to the task of raising money. *Indefinite future* proved to be more accurate. Raising money overshadowed his life from that day to the onset of his final illness.

A contemporary of mine who graduated from the University of Minnesota tells this story from his undergraduate days.

In about 1923 or 1924 a new president was inaugurated at the University of Minnesota. As a waiter at the Minnesota Union I "served" at the inaugural banquet. Governor Olson was the master of ceremonies. College presidents and university presidents from all over the continent were there. Governor Olson was the president of the Board of Regents. He was a superb after-dinner speaker but he could not hold a candle to Dr. Cowling. In introducing President Cowling as one of the speakers, Governor Olson pretended that he did not know him very well. He said that he felt obliged, however, to try to secure some relevant information about the man. He said that he had asked his dinner partner, Justice Pierce Butler (of the U.S. Supreme Court and a member of the Board of Regents), if he could tell him anything about Dr. Cowling. The governor reported that Justice Butler responded, "No, I don't know him very well, either. I can only say that five minutes after I sat down here with him at dinner he was asking me for a contribution to his college!" Dr. Cowling's reputation as a money raiser being what it was, the assembled college presidents roared with laughter. Finally, after the laughter had abated, President Cowling opened up. He said that the situation reminded him of a story from the back-woods farming country. Joe, the father of fourteen children, brought suit for divorce in the local court. The judge at one point tried to cut away the formalities. He asked Joe to come directly before the bench and to answer a simple question. "Joe, you and this woman have lived together for forty years and you have brought up a fine family of fourteen children. Now why, all of a sudden, are you asking for a divorce? Just tell me straight out what is the trouble." "I tell you, judge, I can't stand her always asking me for money. It's give me money for this, give me money for that, give me money for this. She always asks me for money, money, money, more money." Then the judge asked, "Joe, that is a real nuisance, a real bother. It's hard to stand it. Joe, would you just tell the court roughly how much money you usually give her?" Joe replied, "Oh, judge, I ain't give her nothin' yet!" You can imagine the roar of laughter that followed upon this story. Justice Butler was so embarrassed that he had to take off his spectacles half a dozen times to wipe off the steam.

The chair of another large meeting where Prexy was to speak had the temerity to advise him to "make it interesting." So Prexy opened with the story of a young man who sent a manuscript to a publisher. It was returned with a rejection slip that implied his stuff was too dull to publish. So the young man revised it and sent it back with a first sentence that read, "'Oh, hell,' said Henry who up to that point had taken no part in the conversation."

Prexy was truly gifted in his ability to produce the right story to give an over-serious occasion a light touch or to get himself off the spot. That my friend from the University of Minnesota would remember this occasion for forty years and tell the story with such delight in recalling the event attests to Prexy's presence as a public speaker.

At the Memorial Convocation held in Skinner Memorial Chapel in January 1966, Dean Merrill E. Jarchow delivered the address, in which he said:

> Dr. Cowling was buoyancy disposed. His dreams of what Carleton might become were expansive. Some seemed fanciful—until they came true. For Dr. Cowling all clouds were flecked with silver. His radical optimism afforded balm to the president and a lift to his associates. A losing football season was good for college morale and forestalled suspicion of professionalism. A drive for funds which fell short of its mark was "a pretty successful failure." So long as student enrollment was difficult to maintain, small numbers spelled out the virtues of a small college. After it became evident that the stadium was overbuilt—only Dwight Eisenhower in 1952 ever filled it—Dr. Cowling explained that the structure was really a field house and what happened on its roof was inconsequential.

Despite the humor and the capacity for the light touch, Prexy was all business. His work day began early and ended about 10 P.M., when he would smoke his one cigar for the day, Mrs. Cowling would read to him for a while, and he would go to bed—for eight hours of sound sleep, every night. He had a formula for good health (and he was never sick except once when he got the mumps, and even then he dictated to his secretary through the open window). The formula was plenty of sleep; not too much food; drink lots of water; a nap after lunch; moderate exercise—he walked three or four miles every day when he could, often in connection with his work. He gave up golf early—"Too much time," he said.

He seldom took vacations and every day was a work day. There was one mild family rebellion when he scheduled an important piece of work for the afternoon of Christmas Eve, but for the most part the family accepted that here was a man who worked all the time. "I learned to work hard in college; I had to," he once said, "and I have just kept at it. I find relaxation in turning from one type of work to another." (This may explain why executives generally seem to have more energy available than other people. They have more choice of where to expend energy and when.) Prexy enjoyed his work. He once said, "A properly put together college statement is as enjoyable a construction as a sonnet." The thought would make a poet cringe, but this was Prexy. He really loved what many would regard as the drudgery of administration. And his abundant physical and psychological health may have had its roots in this attitude.

He was blessed with a wife who found her constructive place in a home where there was much entertaining. Mrs. Cowling was a warm, lovely person, easier to talk to about the simpler things of life than her husband. She centered her life on her home and the care of her husband and four daughters rather than on the college. She died in 1951. The new Women's Recreation Center was named for her.

There were four daughters, all of whom graduated from Carleton: Mrs. John A. Guice (Mary Ellen) of Kansas City, Missouri; Miss Elizabeth Cowling of Greensboro, North Carolina; Mrs. Cameron B. Newell (Margaret) of Minneapolis, Minnesota; and Mrs. Cyrus H. Burgstahler (Dorothy) of Birmingham, Michigan.

Their father was too busy for the daughters to have the usual father image. He was busy working when he was at home and he traveled much. One day when one of the girls caught sight of him at home she asked her mother, "Why is Daddy at home?"

Elizabeth recalls that in second grade there was a questionnaire to fill out that asked, "What does your father do?" Elizabeth didn't know and turned to the girl next to her and asked. The girl answered, "He's president of Carleton College." "How do you spell president?" asked Elizabeth.

The story of the family that interested me most concerns an occasion when the father decided that it was time for a paternal talk on the nature of the universe, in which he stressed honesty. So the three older daughters came in and stood in a row while their father stood with his back to the fireplace fire and delivered a lecture—as if he were speaking to a class. This story has special significance for me because I have a vivid recollection of Prexy standing before that fire and lecturing *me*. I don't recall anything else in the Cowling household, but that study is etched in my memory. And I take special delight in those three little girls standing there in a row being lectured on honesty.

Despite his business and travel, Northfield was home to Prexy. He knew the town and its people well, was regular in attendance at church services when he was in Northfield, and maintained an active status in the local Masonic Lodge. One alumnus tells of spending the summer there, during the depression years, with a group of students working with the grounds-maintenance crew. Prexy, he said, was interested in these boys who were there in this country town and cut off from their normal contacts with family and friends, so he conducted a little class in philosophy for them.

The depression years were difficult in Northfield, and Prexy's ability to meet problems realistically was never better demonstrated than it was then. There wasn't much money, so there was some barter with parents, faculty, suppliers, everybody. Faculty members were paid part of the time with promissory notes, which were all ultimately redeemed with interest. In the depth of the depression everybody's credit was stretched to the limit. And Prexy was right in the middle of all of these deals trying to work it out so that the college survived and justice was done for individuals.

The college, under his leadership, had pioneered boldly in building new dormitories by creating a separate corporation that owned and managed all dormitories on the theory that they should not be subsidized but should be income producing, paying a fair return on investment and providing for depreciation.

This made it possible for the trustees to invest endowment funds in dormitories and service facilities as a sound investment. His argument was that if students needed aid they should be given work or scholarships. He also argued that if the dormitories were vacant, the college would be in trouble anyway and the endowment money was safe if they were kept full. He saw to it that the Carleton Corporation operated this way, and this proved to be the best investment the college had through all of the depression of the 1930s. He often said that this income from investment in dormitories kept the college from going under because so much of investments generally were in default during that period. But earlier he had a difficult time to convince the General Education Board, which had contributed to the college's endowment, that this was a legitimate use of endowment funds. This use of endowment in college income-producing property has now been widely adopted by other endowed institutions.

Prexy, having helped to found it, was the first chair of the American Council on Education in 1919. In addition, he served as president of the Association of American Colleges, as chair of the Board of Advisors of the National Student Federation, and as a member of the Executive Committee of the National Research Council. In 1918 he served as chair of the committee that inaugurated the exchange of students with France, for which he was decorated by the French government. He also served as president of the Religious Education Association of the United States and Canada and was a member of numerous committees and commissions on educational matters. For many years, especially during the 1920s, he was the educator's educator in America. He was an educator and a builder, but he was not an educational innovator. I think he really believed that everything an education needed to be would flow out of a Christian environment if good, dedicated scholars and teachers manned the faculty, and if the facilities were what they should be. The building of the chapel must have symbolized this. A more utilitarian educator would probably have put other physical needs ahead of the chapel, but not Prexy. When I was a student a daily

half-hour chapel service and Vespers (a full-length church service) on Sunday evening were all required. And I am not aware
that any of my student generation questioned these requirements. I would not recommend this for today, but as a student
forty years ago it seemed good—and I was not then, am not
now, a pious Christian.

In the inaugural ceremony on October 18, 1909, Prexy's
formal statement of acceptance of office was as follows:

> It is with a deep sense of the duties and responsibilities
> involved that I accept the office to which you have
> called me. I assure you of my earnest purpose to devote
> myself unreservedly to the service of the college, to
> maintain its standards of scholarship, its interest in
> teaching, and its distinctively Christian atmosphere;
> and I pray the blessing of Almighty God may rest upon
> the relationship into which we now enter.

Later, in a talk on the business of the church, he said:

> When I was a student at Yale it was the custom to hold
> a Communion service once each month after the Sun-
> day morning service. The invitation to join in this
> sacrament was always given in these words: "All who
> confess or would confess their love for the Lord Jesus
> Christ are invited to remain." That invitation seems to
> me to represent all the creed any Christian Church
> should have, and there is in it all that the New Testa-
> ment prescribes as essential.

Forty years after his inaugural address, after he had retired,
he preached a sermon in New York in which he said: "The problems that so sorely trouble the world today—the problems of
management and labor, problems of race, of social levels and special privileges, of nationalism and international relations—all of
these and other problems will be solved eventually in accordance
with the essential teachings of Jesus, for the simple reason that
the universe was built that way."

This may seem a little naive to the existential individuals of this student generation. If Prexy were alive today and were confronted with Kazantzakis's injunction to young people to remake the world and bring it more in accord with virtue and justice, more in accord with their own hearts, I think he would say, "Certainly! And the Carleton I know was built to prepare young people to do just that." But he would not have bought Kazantzakis's advice if the last phrase "with your own hearts" had been omitted. Justice and virtue were cold abstractions to him. The "distinctively Christian atmosphere" from the inaugural ceremonies in 1909 and the "essential teachings of Jesus" from his old man's sermon forty years later establish his consistent belief in the influence that shapes the heart, the spirit, and prepares a man or woman to deal with the practical obstacles and attitudes that block the road to remaking the world.

He set high standards and was often uncompromising in his demands on people, an attribute that on occasion sent his secretary scurrying to the ladies' room in tears. But he did not get mad and create obstacles. He realized as a young man, and he carried it throughout his life, that any important influence on this complex organized society must be wielded through persuasion. It must be persuasion that has the effect of shaping the institutions that are the real forces in the modern world. As he saw it, the simple teachings of Jesus must be carried into the work of the world and made practical through schools, businesses, governments, and churches. The Christian atmosphere he sought to establish at Carleton was the best means he knew to prepare young people to do this. This is why, I think, the chapel was the center of his building program and why the north window was designed with such loving care.

Prexy's educational theory, in essence, had these main elements: (1) the conventional liberal arts curriculum, (2) carried on in a pervasive Christian atmosphere, (3) with excellent teacher-scholars who are dedicated to these ideals and who are given freedom to hold and advocate truth as they see it and teach as best they know how, and (4) housed in attractive facilities that encourage good work by both faculty and students. It was a simple formula. No important educational innovations flowed from it, but a great institution emerged, one that an innovator could exploit. And his successor, Dr. Laurence M. Gould, did exploit it, promptly. The foundations were well laid; the time was ripe for change in 1945; and Dr. Gould seized the opportunity, with characteristic imagination and verve, and handed over to Dr. Nason in 1962 a vastly different college from the one he took leadership of in 1945.

Prexy's interest in international affairs would not have been unusual for someone in his position except that so many who shared his general conservative position did not share his international interests.

Beginning in 1918, he was a member of the Executive Committee of the League to Enforce Peace, later The League of Nations Non-Partisan Association, and was vice-president of the Minnesota branch of that organization.

He was vice-chair (presiding at most sessions) of a special conference in Chicago in June 1926 made up of representatives of the various peace organizations of the country. This resulted in a declaration urging the "outlawing of war," membership of the United States in the permanent court of international justice, opposition to military education in colleges, and cooperation with the League of Nations.

He was a member of a special commission organized by Professor John Dewey in cooperation with the American Society for the Promotion of Cultural Relations with Russia that visited Russia in the summer of 1928 to study its educational system. On his return he gave a talk in which he made an appraisal that surprised his friends. In summary he commended the Russian drive to end illiteracy and their concern for the lives of the people. He deplored the lack of freedom but felt that their drama, music, and literature were not decadent. He would make no prediction about the future of Russia, but he felt they should have the chance to work out their own salvation within their own country, and in time he thought that they would modify many of their extremist ideas.

During World War II he was a sponsor of a University Committee on Post-War International Problems and later was chair of the Minnesota United Nations Committee. There were numerous memberships on committees and boards dealing with specific international questions.

The United Nations and the best role for it continued to be an active interest throughout his life. In 1954, in a letter to Dr. Gould, he said: "What I have in mind as a possible future role for the United Nations is a good deal more than a 'debate society.' This function seems valuable although some believe it is a means of spreading Communism...The possibilities of the United Nations organization seem to me almost limitless if there is a clear understanding that it has only moral leadership and that no physical force whatever is at its command." He was fearful of world government or the use of force in connection with the work of the United Nations. Basically he was an educator and a persuader, and he saw the great opportunities for the United Nations in this light. In 1954 he wrote a carefully reasoned eight-page memorandum analyzing the major courses of action open to the United Nations and arguing his position for persuasion and leadership rather than force.

I have spoken of Prexy's intense passion for freedom of the individual. Collections of people, even Carleton College in that sense, seemed abstractions to him. Only individual persons in all of their uniqueness and individuality were real. He was at his best when confronted with the problem of an individual person. I was fortunate, as I have said, to have been such a person alone in his presence, because the full depth of his compassion and his consuming interest in the individual were best revealed there. He was pleasant and gracious when in groups, but he was not a Mr. Chips, not to the students of my generation. He did not wear his feelings on his sleeve.

His concern for the individual led to considerable distrust of the expansion of government, particularly with the trends started by the New Deal in the 1930s. It was clear in the years that I knew him that he did not want the level of freedom for the individual, as it existed when he came of age, to be tampered with. Beginning with the income-tax amendment to the Federal Constitution in 1913, he was on the defensive.

A friend sent me a tape of a talk by Prexy before a conservative group when he was quite old. It was wonderful to hear his rich vibrant voice and to be refreshed on his style of argument. It was a classic example of tight syllogistic reasoning from the broad principles of the Declaration of Independence and the Constitution to present-day affairs without the intervention of two hundred years of history. This was the less constructive side of his conservatism, because he tended, as he grew older, toward idealistic positions from which he could not deal realistically with the issues of the day. At one point he was urged to be candidate for the United States Senate. His wife discouraged him, saying he was too idealistic for politics. I agree. Prexy was a builder, and he needed the stones in his own hands. When he departed from this, his idealistic tendencies led him to become identified as a spokesperson for the far right which barred him, in his old age, from the role of the eminent elder statesman in education that might have been his.

The position he espoused did serve to mark one of the outer limits in the arena of ideas, and one can only see the center in perspective when the outer limits are clearly marked on *all* sides. But his was not a posture from which he could lead the mainstream of American education in his later years. At one time he had the stature and the record of accomplishment that qualified him for this leadership, but he did not influence the course of higher education the way he might have at a time when leadership to new horizons was sorely needed.

As noted earlier, Prexy was not an innovator; he was a builder of quality from conventional plans. With Dr. Carter Davidson he wrote a book entitled *Colleges and Freedom*, published in 1947. It is a good practical compendium of administrative wisdom, but it was not destined to lead to new levels of influence, although Prexy's counsel was widely sought by college administrators. However, in terms of achievement, his was an active and significantly useful old age, as I will note later. Few would match it.

The more constructive side of Prexy's conservatism, on which his claim to distinction rests, was the soundness with which he met the issues faced in building Carleton as an institution of stature. This, too, had its roots in the same idealistic concern for freedom of the individual. As distinguished from his political and economic idealism pertaining to people in societies, in building Carleton he was laboring to bring a dream to concrete reality, and his passion for freedom found its expression in meeting specific issues with "real" individual persons.

The common root of idealism that nourished such different manifestations in Prexy's extraordinary career had its origin in his father's influence. In a talk in 1939 he said: "I was brought up in a home that was almost electric with devotion and loyalty to this country—and by 'this country' I mean the ideas, the principles, the ideals that are at its foundations...The most important of all of those ideas is the interpretation which our forefathers put upon the life of men and women as individuals." When he brought this intensity of belief to bear upon a concrete human problem of an individual he was a "situationist" in the most modern sense— utterly human, practical, realistic, and goal centered. When he applied it to the abstraction called society, in its economic and political dimensions—even to the educational philosophy of the college, he was a "traditionalist"—he lived by principles to which recent history and experience seemed to contribute little.

Standing somewhere between these two poles, or possibly on a different axis, was an interesting position taken by Prexy on the responsibilities of achievers in a free society. The following is from an address to the Community Fund Committee of Minneapolis in 1936:

> I am no socialist. I am exactly the opposite of a socialist. I believe in privileges and advantages of all sorts in the hands of individuals—advantages of wealth, of education, of social position, and in many other forms. I would not flatten out society if I could. If I had the

power to level everything down by a mere gesture of the hand, I would not do it. I believe in individual initiative and that the rewards of one's efforts should be in proportion to the social value of what one does. The working of any such theory inevitably results in different levels of advantages according to the ability, resourcefulness, and industry of each individual. However, I do not believe that anyone is justified in having any advantage, whether of wealth, or education, or position, whatever it may be—except as one uses it to further the interests of the common life. The private possession of advantages is justified when they are regarded as a social trust, and on no other theory— when they are thought of as creating opportunities and a responsibility to contribute to the common good.

I do not believe it will ever be possible to construct a social order that will mete out even-handed justice to everybody. Such a possibility seems to me to be altogether a dream. Therefore the necessity for people who have advantages to share them with those who do not would seem to be a part of what will be required continuously for all time to come.

There are many facets to us all, and able people are not simple. A lifestyle that favors optimal accomplishment probably includes an assumption about the world that is in harmony with what one is, deep down inside—below the level of the differentiated aspects that make the individual. Such a lifestyle provides the overarching consistency that gives direction and purpose to the obvious disparate tendencies, and, if well chosen, it makes possible the optimal use of one's resources, whatever they are. The choice of a lifestyle thus foreshadows the life accomplishment. With Prexy I am quite sure it did.

One of the laudable aspects of Prexy's retirement was that, despite the complete dedication of so many years of his life, his consuming interest in his work, and his abundant good health, he knew when to quit and change his role to one better suiting an old man. When he retired he cut his ties completely, moved to Minneapolis and didn't set foot on the campus for four years—and then an invitation had to be pressed on him to receive an honorary degree.

One of his active interests, which I know about personally and which I shall refer to later, was at the Menninger Foundation in Topeka, Kansas. He was a member of the Board of Governors and an active money raiser for the Foundation. His special interest there was in the Children's Hospital, where he devoted unstinting effort, always spending time there when he went to Topeka. The library of the Children's Hospital is dedicated to him and a photograph of him hangs on the wall. Dr. William Menninger tells of a meeting of the Foundation Board that was called to discuss raising money for the Foundation. "For two hours," he said, "there was talk of dinners, letter-writing campaigns, cocktail hours, et cetera, et cetera, with everyone being more confused as to how to go about it. Then the chairman remembered Dr. Cowling and asked him. In that humble, warm, but positive way he made a short speech that concluded with: 'There is only one way to raise money: find the people who have it and ask for some.'"

He was clear in his concept of roles of educational institutions in Minnesota, and he did not feel that the state university had any claim on the private resources which, after his retirement, he helped to cultivate for all of the private colleges in the state. There was one exception, the field of medicine. Here, he argued, the university, because it was the only one in this field, deserved his help, and he worked valiantly. For his effort in building the Mayo Memorial he received the Regent's Award of the university at a special ceremony jointly sponsored by Carleton College and the University of Minnesota on December 10, 1958. Earlier, in 1954, he had received The Builder of the Name Award at the university. The university had given him an honorary degree in 1945.

He had served as chair of the Committee of Founders of the Mayo Memorial. Dean Diehl of the medical school wrote: "To me the privilege of working with Dr. Cowling during the vicissitudes of this endeavor was an inspiring and gratifying experience…This was a unique and magnificent achievement on the part of Dr. Cowling. Yet it was only a beginning, for the interest Dr. Cowling developed in the medical school as a result of this experience led him to devote a large proportion of his time and efforts, after retiring from the presidency of Carleton College, to the development of the medical school." The result of this effort was a substantial rise in facilities, staff, and quality of the program in medicine at the university.

There were many other causes to which he devoted his talents in his retirement years. Among them were the Masonic Memorial Hospital, Minnesota Tuberculosis and Health Association, Minnesota Medical Foundation, National Citizens Committee for the Hoover Report, the Minneapolis Symphony Orchestra, and the Walker Art Center.

Most of his efforts, and the raising of money for these many causes, resulted in tangibles like buildings and programs, except in his retirement there evolved more variety and less administrative responsibility. For all of this the real center of his twenty years of retirement was, I believe, Plymouth Congregational Church and his relationship with Dr. Howard Conn, the minister. There he served in 1948–50 as the first moderator of the congregation after the change to a layperson as the chief officer of the church. Speaking of him in the memorial service, Dr. Conn said:

> Throughout all his years Dr. Cowling attended Sunday worship with regularity, never missing a Sunday except on rare occasions of necessity. Yet for him worship was no magic ritual. Formality and liturgy had little appeal to him. Worship was important because it keeps a man sensitive and open to the creative spontaneity of the God behind creation and provides an opportunity to express gratitude for the magnificence and mystery of life. Worship is part of man's search for truth and of his expression of ultimate concern. This view of churchmanship is illustrated by the two periods in his life when Dr. Cowling deviated from his practice of regular attendance. One was in the last two

years when his hearing in large groups failed, and he saw no merit in sitting through a service in the intellectual stimulation of which he could not share. The other was during the final illness of President Lars Boe of St. Olaf College. While his colleague and friend was bedridden, Dr. Cowling spent each Sunday morning visiting with him and reading to him. Affectionate concern for a beloved brother in Christian fellowship was in itself to him an act of worship to the common Father who had made them neighbors and friendly rivals in Northfield.

Prexy, as I saw him, was a problem-centered man. Either problems came to him in the normal course of events or he created them by setting goals and making commitments. Often when asked the secret of his success he would answer, "I keep myself in hot water!" His best effort came, and the best in him came out, when he faced an issue or moved in on a problem. He was industrious, worked all of the time, thought a lot, made many speeches; but his real strengths emerged in the confrontation with a problem and with the persons involved in the problem. In dealing with a problem there was an extraordinary harmony between what he believed and what he did. This was part of the consistency in his lifestyle.

I once went to him with a problem of a student organization of which I was president. We were in a bad snarl because of the performance of a faculty member who was at the heart of our difficulty. I laid out the alternatives as I saw them while Prexy listened patiently. Any way out of this difficulty, as I saw it, was going to hurt this faculty member. When I finished he looked at the ceiling for a couple of minutes and puffed at his evening cigar (I had interrupted his quiet time at the close of the evening). Then he turned to me with a smile of reassurance and said, "Well this is one of those situations where we are going to be damned if we do and damned if we don't, and we had better do what is best for the college." Sparks flew, but that was the way it came out.

In one of my conversations in the 1930s when I was pressing Prexy in an argument, I brought up the case of a football player of my day, a giant of a man and a powerful athlete, but no scholar— and one who would not have made it on his own without a good deal of help from his classmates and some indulgent teachers. With all of this he barely got along through four football seasons only to be dropped for poor academic performance at the end of the fall term in his fourth year. I told this story to Prexy with my conclusion that it must have been as evident after the first two weeks as it was after four football seasons that this fellow shouldn't be in college at all. "Was this a good use of a man?" I asked.

Prexy really winced at this. Clearly, he acknowledged, this was not a good use of a man. There was something wrong with student morale that students would do what we did; something was more wrong with faculty standards if they permitted it to go on; and after three and one-half years and four football seasons this student should have been given a degree, somehow. Then I got a gentle lecture from Prexy on the realities of administrative life. And he told me of the things that go wrong in a college that I didn't know about. He really laid his soul bare. Human institutions are weak and full of error because individuals are weak and full of error. Knowing what went on in colleges, he said, he shuddered to think what other institutions were like that probably weren't as good. But, he asked, what is a person with strength and ability and integrity to do? Should one live like a hermit in a cave and be uncontaminated by the world and free from being compromised by other people's errors? Or should one take a responsible institutional role and put as much goodness into it as one can, realizing that one must compromise on occasion and that the total effort may not be very good—but still a little better than if someone had not tried? It was a long and thoughtful lecture, and I have given only the gist of it. I went home wiser. Later I wondered why such a valuable piece of wisdom should come to me by chance ten years after I graduated from college. A distinguished research chemist once told me, "We don't know how to introduce people to my field without teaching them a lot that is only half true." This may be the dilemma of all of education.

This talk with Prexy was thirty years ago, and in the meantime knowledge in general has multiplied several times. But do we do any better at helping young people to start close to where the experience of the race is on many crucially important matters? I think Prexy, in the quiet of his study and in a one-to-one encounter, would say, "No, we really haven't come very far on the matters of importance. More good strong people need to devote their lives to the effort. What is required of the good and the strong is dedication to something that commands their complete loyalty."

The years I was at Carleton were busy ones for Prexy. While he was on hand to meet issues, he was not around much where students had contact with him. He must have felt this and thought he should do something about it; one Sunday evening after Vespers he decided to make a pastoral call, unannounced, in the men's dormitory.

The room he chose for his first call just happened to be one in which there was a big crap game going. There were a half-dozen fellows on their knees in a ring rolling the dice, and perhaps a dozen others looking on. I was sitting on a desk in the corner. The game was going at a lively pace when there was a soft knock on the door. "Come in," somebody yelled. And as one of my esteemed contemporaries rattled the dice in one hand, held two dollar bills aloft in the other and shouted, "Shoot the two, all or any part," the door slowly opened and there was Prexy's benign face. "Excuse me," he said softly, closed the door, and went away. After a pause of silence somebody asked, "Now what's going to happen?"

Well, nothing happened. Prexy knew who he was. He was the president, not the dean. He had come for a social call, not to supervise our morals. As far as I know, he said nothing to anyone about it.

As I said earlier, Prexy and I met at my twenty-fifth reunion in 1951 and vowed that we would get together for another conversation. Several years went by and then it came about in a most unusual way. I had become interested in a program in industrial psychiatry at the Menninger Foundation at Topeka, Kansas. I knew vaguely that Prexy was a member of the Board of Governors of the Foundation, but that august body was quite remote from the center of my interests. Then at the Foundation's annual meeting in September of 1957 1 was asked to participate in a panel discussion of the industrial psychiatry project. It was a big meeting, six or seven hundred people, and when I was seated with my colleagues on the platform I looked over the audience and there, out in the middle of it, was Prexy. I was the last to speak on the panel of four, and I fear that I didn't listen too attentively to my colleagues because I got the idea that this was the opportunity I had been waiting for to express some of my feelings of admiration for Prexy. It was a little irregular and I had precious little time for the portion of the subject assigned to me, but the impulse to say something to Prexy won out.

When I read the notice of his death and decided to write this appreciation of Prexy, I thought of that occasion. I got the Menninger Foundation on the phone and asked whether, by chance, they had a tape on that meeting. Wonderful people that they are, they found the tape and a transcription of my statement on Prexy was on the way. Without editing, here is what I said:

> Before getting into the subject, I would like to take a moment to acknowledge the presence here of Dr. Donald J. Cowling, a valued governor of the Menninger Foundation, president emeritus of Carleton College, and active president during my undergraduate days.
>
> Dr. Cowling, for the better part of the thirty-one years since I accepted my diploma from you, I have been waiting for an opportunity like this to acknowledge my debt of gratitude on two main counts: one is that your model of devotion to your calling, which you have so ably demonstrated and which I only dimly appreciated as an undergraduate, has grown to monumental proportions through the years. The second is, if your memory is good, and I think it is, you will recall

me as a restless undergraduate who found some difficulty in conforming to the well-laid plans of the administration and faculty. And so I made some plans of my own, and, to the extent that I qualify for the chairman's designation of me as an innovator for this group, I think maybe that is where I learned it. But some of our best learning is accidental.

But the important part of this is that on a couple of occasions I got caught, and I found myself in your presence as an erring student held to account for his sins. On those occasions you demonstrated a deftness and an understanding of a young person in trouble which I am sure would draw the admiration of the best and most modern psychiatrists, and which to me now, as a parent of undergraduate children, has served as a very valuable object lesson. I didn't realize when I set off for Topeka the other day that this was to be a bonus added to my experience here, and I am grateful for the opportunity to say this to you. Thank you.

This audience gave Prexy a great ovation.

We had a good visit afterward in which I discovered something about Prexy. His had been a long life, full of accomplishment, for which he had received much recognition, but it was mostly recognition for his external achievement. Prexy's highest values were what he was deep down inside; *he knew who he was.* Somehow in my little statement at the Menninger Foundation meeting I touched something deep in him—or perhaps he let something come through to him that he generally screened out with that reserve of his. Or maybe the educator who deals with undergraduates doesn't hear much appreciation from students. I recall once asking a college professor who was teaching a course to business executives what the differences were between undergraduate teaching and working with mature, successful men. His answer was prompt and clear. "*These* students express appreciation," he said. The capacity for appreciation is a gift of maturity and young people often do not have it—not sensitive appreciation that recognizes the deep and essential human qualities. I was saddened when I realized that, well as I had known Prexy in the years after my graduation, I had not expressed my *real* appreciation before that night at the Menninger Foundation meeting.

I cherish my memories of Prexy. I give him kudos for the institutions he built at Carleton; it was a notable achievement. But this alone would not qualify him for greatness. Achievement is essential, but it is not enough. It is *the quality of people*, seen over a life span within the context of their particular achievements, that must be weighed.

In these few pages I have tried to weigh the quality of the man I knew as Prexy: as I have experienced it myself, as others have told me, and as I have found it in the record. Clearly the evidence requires that he be placed in history with the *truly great*.

Stephen Spender gave us a poem entitled "The Truly Great":

> I think continually of those who were truly great.
> Who, from the womb, remembered the soul's history
> Through corridors of light where the hours are suns,
> Endless and singing. Whose lovely ambition
> Was that their lips, still touched with fire,
> Should tell of the Spirit, clothed from head to foot in song.
> And who hoarded from the Spring branches
> The desires falling across their bodies like blossoms.
>
> What is precious is never to forget
> The essential delight of the blood drawn from ageless
>   springs
> Breaking through rocks in worlds before our earth.
> Never to deny its pleasure in the morning simple light
> Nor in its grave evening demand for love.
> Never to allow gradually the traffic to smother
> With noise and fog, the flowering of the Spirit.

Near the snow, near the sun, in the highest fields,
See how these names are feted by the waving grass
And by the streamers of white cloud
And whispers of wind in the listening sky.
The names of those who in their lives fought for life,
Born of the sun, they traveled a short while toward the
     sun
And left the vivid air signed with their honor.

This was Prexy as I knew him, he left the vivid air signed with his honor. His absolute dedication to his calling, the building of Carleton; his passion for freedom, for the flowering of the spirit; and his impressive humanity are marks of greatness that I bow before in reverence. I hope that somehow the nurturing of qualities like these can become his legacy to Carleton—and to the world.

IX

Servant Responsibility in a Bureaucratic Society

Convocation Address
University of Redlands
1966

The best way I know to build a bridge from your experience to mine is to read one of my favorite stories from James Thurber's *Fables for Our Time:*

> Once upon a sunny morning a man who sat in a breakfast nook looked up from his scrambled eggs to see a white unicorn with a golden horn quietly cropping the roses in the garden. The man went to the bedroom where his wife was asleep and woke her. "There's a unicorn in the garden," he said, "eating roses." She opened one unfriendly eye and looked at him. "The unicorn is a mythical animal," she said, and turned her back on him. The man walked slowly downstairs and out into the garden. The unicorn was still there; he was now browsing among the tulips. "Here, unicorn," said the man as he pulled up a lily and gave it to him. The unicorn ate it gravely. With a high heart, because there was a unicorn in his garden, the man went upstairs and roused his wife again. "The unicorn," he said, "ate a lily." His wife sat up in bed and looked at him coldly. "You're a booby," she said, "and I am going to have you put in the boobyhatch." The man, who never liked the words "booby" and "booby-hatch," and who liked them even less on a shining morning when there was a

unicorn in the garden, thought for a moment. "We'll
see about that," he said. He walked over to the door.
"He has a golden horn in the middle of his forehead,"
he told her. Then he went back to the garden to watch
the unicorn, but the unicorn had gone away. The man
sat down among the roses and went to sleep.

As soon as the husband had gone out of the
house, the wife got up and dressed as fast as she could.
She was very excited and there was a gloat in her eye.
She telephoned the police and she telephoned a psychiatrist; she told them to hurry to her house and
bring a strait-jacket. When the police and the psychiatrist arrived they sat down in chairs and looked at her,
with great interest. "My husband," she said, "saw a
unicorn this morning." The police looked at the psychiatrist and the psychiatrist looked at the police. "He
told me it ate a lily," she said. The psychiatrist looked
at the police and the police looked at the psychiatrist.
"He told me it had a golden horn in the middle of its
forehead," she said. At a solemn signal from the psychiatrist, the police leaped from their chairs and seized
the wife. They had a hard time subduing her, for she
put up a terrific struggle, but they finally subdued her.
Just as they got her into the strait-jacket, the husband
came back into the house.

"Did you tell your wife you saw a unicorn?"
asked the police. "Of course not," said the husband.
"The unicorn is a mythical beast." "That's all I wanted
to know," said the psychiatrist. "Take her away. I'm
sorry. sir, but your wife is as crazy as a jay bird!" So
they took her away, cursing and screaming, and shut
her up in an institution. The husband lived happily
ever after.

We read this fable in our home many years ago, and it has
become the custom in our family to ask of the first who looks
out the window in the morning to greet the day, "Do you see

the unicorn?" Within the spirit of this fable and the imagery it conveys, I want to discuss what may seem a quite ponderous subject: "Responsibility in a Bureaucratic Society."

Responsibility is a difficult thing to talk about. It is often seen as that which others should have more of. Few of us think of ourselves as irresponsible; the admission would be too devastating. We all do pretty well at rationalizing our own acts of commission and omission that bear on responsibility.

Most definitions of responsibility imply conformity with conventional expectations, conventional morality, or being deterred by consideration of known sanctions or consequences. Such definitions imply that the rules and penalties are all set and the responsible person is one who carefully stays within bounds. I prefer not to use the word *responsibility* to mean conformity to expectations (although a sensible person always does some of that). Rather, I think of responsibility as beginning with a concern for self, to receive that inward growth that gives serenity of spirit without which someone cannot truly say, "I am free." One moves, then, to a response to one's environment, whatever it is, so as to make a pertinent force of one's concern for one's neighbor—as a member of a family, a work group, a community, a world society. The outward and the inward are seen as parts of the same fabric. Responsible persons have both. They are the ones who, when they greet the day, see the unicorn in their garden. They have wonder in their hearts. This is the way they *choose* to respond.

You of this college generation have a much better chance of responding so as to make your life optimal, outwardly and inwardly, because you are so much more aware than were many of my generation at your age. It will be much more difficult for you to find some comfortable little niche, knit yourself into a cocoon of complacency, and ride through life undisturbed by the misery and the suffering and the confusion around you. It is more difficult to insulate oneself from the world and limit one's response to it than it was forty years ago when I graduated from college. But some still make it if they try hard. One of my purposes in talking to you is to discourage that effort.

I must admit that I am enough the creature of my generation that the goings-on in your generation shake me occasionally. But I am glad that yours is not like my generation. I am even more disturbed by them. Many of my generation are beyond hope, but *you* I am hopeful about. I was delighted to come across this little bit from Nikos Kazantzakis in his *Report to Greco:* "Happy the youth who believes that his duty is to remake the world and bring it more in accord with virtue and justice, more in accord with his own heart. Woe to whoever commences his life without lunacy."

But what are you going to do with the world as you find it, which I have chosen to call a bureaucratic society? How can one live responsibly in a bureaucratic society?

Bureaucracy is defined as a system that has become narrow, rigid, and formal, depends on precedent, and lacks initiative and resourcefulness—a pretty bad state of affairs. It is the feet of clay that seem to encumber everything that is organized. As I see it, this is the way all institutions tend to become as they grow old, large, or respectable. *All* institutions—churches, schools, governments, businesses, hospitals, social agencies, families—all tend to become bureaucracies, regardless of the sheltering ideologies or the specific goals. They may do some good in the world; in fact, they are all we have. But they still tend to become bureaucracies—given size, age, and respectability. Because we need the good they do, we tend to overlook the harm done because they are bureaucracies.

Vatican Council II gave a rare insight into the momentous struggle going on within one of the oldest and largest and most respectable of institutions, a struggle to unshackle itself from the worst fetters of bureaucracy. The revolutionary impact of this great step has yet to be assessed. That this was initiated by lovable old Pope John in his eighties suggests that *all* of my generation are not hopeless—just some. Don't write us all off. Rather, make note that some crucial roles in remaking the world to bring it more in accord with virtue and justice, with our own hearts, can best be carried on by *old* people. If you really want to use your life well, if remaking the world concerns you *now*, file a little mental ticket to the effect that *some* of what you can do about it can best be done when *you* are old, and some whose leadership you should now be following are old. Why would I make this assertion? Because I believe that old people can better cope with some aspects of bureaucracy than can young people. There comes a time when one no longer cares a damn about a lot of things that are important concerns of young or even mid-career people. Whatever reputation or status people may have aspired to, when they are old they have whatever they are going to get and (if they are sensible) they withdraw from the struggle. Then, in old age, they can do what striving people cannot do. Had John been made pope at fifty rather than at eighty, he might not have left his great mark upon the world. He might have been too enmeshed in the bureaucracy, too concerned with his place in it. He would have had to think of living with his mistakes for another thirty years. At eighty he could rise above these concerns.

But the sensitivity, the strength, the mature humanity needed to play his great role were not suddenly bestowed upon John at eighty. These attributes were the fulfillment of a lifestyle that was set in his youth, and he nourished them, kept them alive, through sixty years of bureaucratic participation. He was a great human being all of his long life because he made some important choices when he was young.

Why does bureaucracy seem the fate of all institutions that grow old, large, or respectable? Why? Because there are too few Pope Johns, too few when they are young greet the day by seeing the unicorn in the garden. They grow old in the wrong ways before they ever start. They don't affirmatively cultivate a lifestyle that will enable them to perform responsibly within the inevitable bureaucratic strictures that will confront them on every side once they are launched upon their careers. While they are young and have the best chance, they do not build that inward radiance that will sustain an outward anti-bureaucratic influence over a long life span. If you cannot judge yourself (few of us can), look around among your contemporaries, among the young people you know, and see for yourself how many of the tendencies to be narrow, rigid, and formal there are, tendencies which, if unchecked, will inevitably help perpetuate bureaucratic rigidity by building or reinforcing systems that depend on precedent, and lack initiative and resourcefulness.

One of the differences between the present generation and mine when I was of college age in the 1920s, is that this generation does a lot more complaining about how those who are in charge manage the world today. Some of this generation, as a few of mine did, even advocate pulling the whole structure down and starting all over. Maybe you share this view.

I am inclined to agree with the judgments of the severest of the young critics: the world of adult practice in all fields is pretty mediocre when judged by what is reasonably possible. On every side the best of the flowering of the human spirit is hemmed in by bureaucracy. Too many of my generation have settled for the status quo and have lost their awareness of the condition. They unfortunately accept it as their way of life. The number of free people who do not suffer from these constrictions is diminishing by the minute. We are well on our way to becoming a completely administered society in which the weight of bureaucracy rests on everyone. This is how I judge the work of my generation. And I am not disowning them because I am one of them. We have done as well as might have been expected of us, groping as we have been in our particular kind of darkness. But my chief disappointment with my generation is that so few seem capable or disposed to exert a leavening influence on bureaucracy. For the most part they tend, as you well know, to reinforce it.

But this question I would raise with the present generation—especially the outspoken critics: What will the state of affairs be twenty to thirty years from now when this generation will be in control and mine will be gone? What will someone viewing the scene from a vantage point like mine say, someone who has ended his active bureaucratic career and now stands aside with more objectivity? Will such an observer say of *your* generation, then in control: "Adult practice in all fields is pretty mediocre when judged by what is reasonably possible"? I regret to say that I fear the judgment will be the same. It may even be more harshly stated because the disparity between the level of awareness you now have and the performance you then demonstrate may be greater. You may be in greater trouble with the youngsters than my generation is with you. I hold this view because I do not see the preparation by your generation for coping with the growing bureaucratic tendencies. You are better educated than my generation was at your age. You have worked harder. You are more aware of the symptoms and you are more critical. But are you any better prepared to deal with the causes than we were? Do more of you greet the day by seeing the unicorn in the garden? *This is how I would really know.*

The more literal minded among you may be wondering at this point what on earth seeing the unicorn in the garden has to do with preparing to deal realistically with bureaucracy. And maybe you are chafing under the patent injustice in this fable in which the wife who clearly knows that the unicorn is a mythical beast is carted away in a strait-jacket cursing and screaming while the husband who sees the unicorn and is obviously loony lives happily ever after.

When James Thurber called this story a fable he was choosing his term carefully, for a fable is in the realm of the supernatural, usually has animals speak or act like human beings, and is intended to enforce a useful truth or precept. It is also told to excite wonder. What do you wonder about when you hear this fable? What truth or precept comes to mind? I wish there were only twelve of us seated in a lounge, because I would like to have a couple of hours to hear you respond to these questions. But let me leave them with you while I go back to an earlier point in answer to the question: "Why does bureaucracy seem the inevitable fate of all institutions that grow old, large, or respectable?" I answered the question by saying: "Because young people do not affirmatively cultivate the lifestyle that will enable them to perform responsibly within the inevitable bureaucratic constrictions that will confront them on every side once they are launched on their careers."

If you believe with Kazantzakis that your duty is to remake the world and bring it more in accord with virtue and justice, more in accord with your own heart, then you have the obligation to prepare yourself *now* by cultivating the lifestyle that will make it a reasonable expectation that you will do your share. Don't think that, when you are forty and have achieved a position of power and influence, an adequate lifestyle will be bestowed upon you because your motives are good and you are able. You need good motives; you need ability. I assume you have them. But these are not enough; our oldest, our most tested wisdom has always said they are not enough. "Not by my might, nor by my power, but by my spirit, saith the Lord."

The word *spirit* has been overused and has lost much of its force. For want of a better term, I use *lifestyle*—and a lifestyle adequate to cope with bureaucracy does not automatically follow from good motives, ability, and opportunity. I have spent too many years trying to help successful, well-motivated, mid-career people to reconstruct their lifestyles to offer any hope that you will find it *then*, when it counts the most. You get a lifestyle, one which augurs for optimum response, while you are young, or it is unlikely that you will ever get it. I do not say it is impossible, only that it is unlikely. Do not bet on it.

What are the dimensions of an optimum lifestyle? What is the best frame of reference through which to regard ourselves and the world? I do not have a categorical list. This is one of those areas where I feel the importance and the urgency but I "see through a glass darkly." There is no formula, no set of commandments; we must each find our own path. I will give five words that may suggest a way of thinking about it and try to put some meaning behind those words. They are *beauty*, *momentaneity*, *openness*, *humor*, and *tolerance*. These imply some dimensions of the lifestyle that I believe build both the will and the strength to deal creatively with bureaucracy and help one to find the best way of working with teams and groups and societies. Let us examine the five words that are suggestive of an optimum lifestyle.

Beauty. Few words have excited the imagination of poets as much as the word *beauty*. And what a range of responses there are: from Shakespeare's "Beauty is a vain but doubtful good" to Robert Bridges's "Beauty being the best of all we know/Sums up the unsearchable and secret aims of nature." But the aspect of beauty that best serves the use I am making of it is the use mathematicians make of the word. A mathematical solution is called beautiful when it penetrates the unknown, opens up new insights, advances knowledge.

A science writer recently commented on the failure of a noted physicist to capitalize on an important insight because it looked unreasonable in the light of present knowledge, thus losing for himself the credit for a major discovery. The writer observed: "It is more important to have beauty in equations than to have them fit the experiment." There is more wisdom in these sixteen words than first meets the eye. This science writer is saying what Robert Bridges is saying, in a way. One needs a lifestyle that keeps one in touch with "the unsearchable and secret aims of nature."

One can cultivate beauty. If music speaks to you, get a good recording of Beethoven's C Sharp Minor Quartet Opus 131. Listen and listen and listen. There is a story behind this work, now regarded by some musicologists as the greatest piece of music ever written. This is one of the "later" quartets. Most of the music upon which Beethoven's reputation as a contemporary composer was built had already been written. According to this legend, when he began to write this series of quartets, a close friend said to Beethoven, "Ludwig, what has happened? We don't understand you any more." Beethoven is reported to have replied, "I have said all I have to say to my contemporaries; now I am speaking to the future." Whether true or not, this story checks with history. A century went by before this particular part of Beethoven's music was appreciated, and then only by a few. Perhaps those who would be moved by beauty must constantly strive to cultivate the uncertain ground by reaching for a response to that which is not yet generally appreciated—or understood.

Momentaneity. The psalmist of old proclaimed, "This is the day which the Lord has made; rejoice and be glad in it." More recently Emerson has said, "He only is rich who owns the day."

A central attitude for those who believe it their duty to remake the world and bring it more in accord with virtue and justice, with their own hearts, is, "This is the day!" So many able people I have known have nullified their effectiveness by living in a past that will never return or in a visionary future that may never materialize, and the opportunity to be grasped here and now slips by them. Too many able young people entering business today stumble on their first jobs because they are so preoccupied with where this first job will lead them that they fail on what is in hand to do.

There are moments that contain eternity. Try to see the moment "now" not as an instantaneous fraction of clock time but as a focus of intensity in which the bright intense center *is* this instant of clock time but which, as the intensity of the light recedes from the center, extends back into historic events and forward into the indefinite future—a sort of moving average, as the statisticians see it.

Even if the present center of this span of time carries for you illness, suffering, and loss, *this is the day*. It is what you have now!

Openness. An old Italian proverb runs, "From listening comes wisdom, from speaking comes repentance." *Listening*, as I use it here, is not just keeping still, or even remembering what is said. Listening is an attitude, an attitude toward other people and what they are trying to express. It begins with a genuine interest that is manifest in close attention, and it goes on to understanding in depth—whence cometh wisdom. It is openness to communication—openness within the widest possible frame of reference—openness to hear the prophetic voices that are trying to speak to us all of the time.

A few years ago in my old company we made some studies of the effectiveness of managers and discovered that sometimes managers did not manage well because they did not listen to their people. So we devised a little training course in listening—three intensive days of it. Because it was a rather novel thing to do, our course on listening got a little publicity.

Then one day I received a call from a professor in a local medical school who said he had heard of our course on listening and had a problem he wanted to come and talk about. This is what it was. The medical school had made a study of doctors in practice. Researchers put on long white coats, posed as doctors' assistants, and closely noted everything that went on in medical consultations. Strangely enough, they found that many doctors didn't listen to their patients. They were so busy making tests and records and *asking questions* that the patients were unable to express how they experienced the symptoms. As a result, the patients were frustrated and resentful and the doctors didn't fully understand their cases.

So the medical school decided that doctors in training should be taught to listen. But when they tried, they had a problem. The young medical students rebelled because a professor of psychiatry undertook to teach them to listen within the *psychiatrist's* frame of reference. The medical students in their fourth year knew that what they needed was not what the patient was saying as seen within the *doctor's* frame of reference, but what the meaning and significance was to the patient. My guest, the medical professor, asked, "We hear that you teach managers how to listen within their subordinates' frame of reference. How do you do that?" It was an interesting session. It confirmed that very bright people can make pretty stupid mistakes. Don't assume, because you are intelligent, able, and well-motivated, that you are open to communication, that you know how to listen. Make a motto on your wall of that great line from the prayer of Saint Francis, "Lord, grant that I may seek not so much to be understood as to understand."

Humor. "True humor," said Thomas Carlyle, "springs not more from the head than from the heart; it is not contempt, its essence is love, it issues not in laughter, but in still smiles, which lie far deeper. It is a sort of inverse sublimity that draws down into our affections what is above us." Let us look at humor this way, drawing down into our affections what we must learn to love.

How can we grow to respond to the opportunities to remake the world and bring it more in accord with virtue and justice, more in accord with our own hearts, unless we can have that quiet inward smile called humor when we regard the silly little half-made creatures that we are? But, as Carlyle said, it is a loving smile.

The relevance of humor to growth in responsibility is that we can have this loving, indulgent, inward smile about ourselves—self-acceptance, some call it. I would rather say love of self, of the self as it is when laid bare only to our inward seeing in moments of quiet introspection.

Scripture says, "Love your neighbor as yourself." How, then, can you love your neighbor *unless* you love yourself? And how can you love yourself without humor?

Tolerance. I use this word in an older meaning—the ability to bear suffering with serenity.

You are young, and if you have not yet suffered much, you will one day. "We must die young or suffer much," runs a Portuguese proverb. There is a poignant line in Marc Connelly's play "The Green Pastures" in which the Lord in his great frustration with the waywardness of his people cries out, "Even God must suffer." The ultimate of suffering is to suffer through the pain of others.

Robert Frost, whose poetry has meant much to me, writes in his poem "New Hampshire":

> I make a virtue of my suffering
> From nearly everything that goes on round me.
> In other words, I know wherever I am,
> Being the creature of literature I am,
> I shall not lack for pain to keep me awake.

And, in his little poem, "The Night Light," he admits of the haunting fears that few of us talk about when he describes the girl who needed a light while she slept to reassure her even though it disturbed her sleep. But, he concludes,

Good gloom on her was thrown away.
It is on me by night or day,
Who have, as I suppose, ahead
The darkest of it still to dread.

In these two poems Robert Frost states the problem of tolerance, serenity in the face of suffering, as well as I know how to state it: to acknowledge that we do not want for pain to keep us awake, but to make a virtue of it—learn from it—and to see the darkest of it still ahead (as it is for most of us) and cut away the gloom.

This is deep in our tradition. In Sophocles' account of the great tragic figure of Oedipus, blind and desperate with the only bond linking him to the world the hand of his daughter Antigone, he proclaims, "Despite so many ordeals, my advanced age and the nobility of my soul make me conclude that all is well."

I suggest these five words—*beauty, momentaneity, openness, humor,* and *tolerance*—as marking some dimensions of a lifestyle that is rooted in an inward grace: sensitive and aware, concerned for the ever-present neighbor, both the well-fed one next door and the hungry one on the other side of the earth, seeing and feeling what is right in the situation.

I assume that you are resolved to use your lives well and to contribute more than you take out of life because you are among the more favored, and any civilized society requires that the more favored carry more than their share of the burdens; and because life is more worth living this way. Furthermore, since you are creatures of this highly complex organized age, I assume that you are not seeking some isolated ivory tower existence but rather are prepared to make your contributions through bureaucratic institutions, pretty much as they are—through societies and groups and teams *as well as on your own!* Thus responsible persons are the ones who, while recognizing the pervasive bureaucratic nature of the world in which they will live and do their work, cultivate, as a conscious discipline, a lifestyle that favors their optimal performance as an anti-bureaucratic influence, over a life span of mature living. They bring their own unique meliorative influence to bear on the pervasive bureaucracy.

I wish I could share with you the fruits of my own experience with the problems of our bureaucratic institutional life as I have watched governments, businesses, churches, universities, and foundations on both sides of the world struggle to find able, well-motivated people who can carry the responsible roles and limit the bureaucratic tendencies. As John Gardner put it recently, we do well at growing critics and experts, but we do not produce enough people for the responsible roles.

At the heart of every constructive action are responsible persons, those who reach out to engage with real-life issues where the going may be rough, lay out alternatives (invent some if necessary), assess their relative merits, choose one that accords with virtue and justice—with their own hearts—make the choice knowing they may be wrong and suffer for it, *and bear the risk bravely.* But at every level from the family to world society we are tragically short of such people. We have plenty of able people who are only critics, plenty who are only experts, and too few responsible people. And we are in this dilemma because not enough of my generation, when they were your age, thought it their duty to remake the world and bring it more in accord with virtue and justice, more in accord with their own hearts, and too few consciously sought a lifestyle that would prepare them for responsible roles that would make a difference. If they were able, too many settled for being experts and critics. They had the chance to be exceptional, by adding responsibility to good motives and ability, but they settled for the ordinary.

If you have a chance to be exceptional, and the fact that you are here today suggests that you have that chance, it is not important that you make a lot of money, achieve high status, write books, or receive medals or honors. But it is important that the quality of your life be extraordinary and that you carry this quality into the work of the world, take on the bureaucracy with spirit, and accept the bumps, and, as Harvey Cox says in *The Secular City*, you "may discover that, even in the age of organization, precisely he who loses his life gains it!"

Let me urge, then, while you are young and your lifestyle may still be formed by conscious choices, that you cultivate sensitivity to beauty, that you live in the moment to the full, that you be open to receive what those around you have to give, that you enjoy the delights of objectivity that only humor will bring, and that you be serene in that suffering without which you will not truly grow.

To return to Kazantzakis—I would not have used his injunction to remake the world in accord with virtue and justice had he not added "in accord with your own heart." Great destructive violence has been done in the name of virtue and justice. Ideas about virtue and justice, when validated by experience, are useful guides and not to be ignored. But, at best, they are abstractions. In the ultimate test, the only reality to be trusted, that which shelters decision-making with sensitivity and compassion so that one sees and feels what fits the situation, is the prompting of the human spirit—from the heart.

This must have been deeply rooted in Kazantzakis because of the influence on his life of his study of Albert Schweitzer and Saint Francis. "These two poor men of God," he said, "were able to help me in only a single respect, the inestimable one of showing me that man is able, and has the duty, to reach the furtherest point on the road he has chosen. Thus they became models for me, lofty examples of persistence, patience, and hope. God bless them, for these two heroes of exploit taught me that only by means of hope can we attain what is beyond hope."

This, to me, is the symbolic significance of the unicorn in the garden. Look for him tomorrow morning when you greet the day.

The unicorn is a fabulous creature of good omen, and the symbol of longevity, grandeur, felicity, illustrious offspring, and wise administration. —The predominant characteristic of the Unicorn is its perfect goodwill, gentleness, and benevolence to all living creatures. —It is said to be the noblest form of animal creation, the emblem of perfect good. (From the *Encyclopedia of Chinese Symbolism and Art Motives* by C. A. S. Williams. Copyright 1960 by The Julian Press.)

X

America and World Leadership

In January 1976 1 attended an International Symposium on Leadership Development. In responding to the charge of arrogance by Americans, I made the following statement.

Our African friend has said that we Americans are arrogant. It hurts—but I accept the charge.

Our arrogance stems, I believe, from the fact of our great power. In the years that the British were the great power, they were seen as arrogant. When the next shift comes, the nation that emerges into that unfortunate spot will quite likely be seen as arrogant. Civilization, it seems, has not advanced to a point where, as a natural gift of grace, either individuals, institutions, or governments are likely to be both powerful and humble without some basic changes in public thinking that are not yet evident. Some may make it, but the odds are against it.

In this conference I have learned from Father Benjamin Tonna of Malta that humility in the more powerful is ultimately tested by their ability to learn from and gratefully to receive the gifts of the less powerful. It is in my experience to know this, but sometimes one needs to be taught before one understands one's own experience.

When I retired from my active business career twelve years ago, I was asked by an American foundation to take an assignment for it in India. The first school of administration to be set up there after independence in 1947 was a close copy of an English model that, by 1964, had proved not to be a sound idea for India. And the foundation had been asked to give technical assistance and a grant of money to help develop a new program for that school that would better serve the development needs of India. I took on the staff work on that project and made four long

320

visits over the ensuing four years. I found the top cut of Indian society with which I dealt, both in and out of government, to be highly sophisticated. Yet I was treated as if I had a level of expertise far beyond what my old colleagues at home who knew me well would concede. This is heady stuff, a fertile breeding ground for arrogance, and the several thousand who participated in aid programs in India, both private and governmental, in the heyday of technical assistance, were all exposed to some measure of it.

By the usual standards of judging a consulting engagement, mine was successful. A new program for that school of administration did emerge, and it has been sustained. Also, in this period, I believe I learned something about the steps that needed to be taken in India to develop a new leadership to recover that great nation from the deprivation of three hundred years of colonial rule during which the Indians had been educated for, and participated extensively in, routine administration, but they had not been allowed to learn such essential skills as goal setting, negotiation, or institutional design. These had all been done for them by their colonial masters,

In 1970, I made my last visit to India. This time I went only to New Delhi to confer with the foundation staff that was based there about the new conditions they faced in India and how the foundation might best serve while it still had the opportunity. It was then clear that the future of that country was not likely to accord either with Gandhi's dream of a village-based nation or Nehru's classical socialist aim of an industrialized one. Rather, it seemed that they were embarked on their own evolutionary path on which they would move forward, much as the rest of the world does, not according to an idealistic plan but by responding creatively to world conditions and the current state of their own society. And I felt that there needed to be a new concept of how things get done in India under these new conditions, both for the benefit of the Indians in building their new institutions and for the guidance of those whom they might choose to advise them. Otherwise, these advisors would have to learn for themselves, the hard way as I did, how things get done there—if, indeed, they ever learned. But, alas, it was a tardy suggestion. The opportunity for the foundation to give that kind of service in India was very soon to be gone. The advice was twenty years late.

In 1971, when I signed off on this foundation relationship, I had some things to say in my report that have a bearing on the question of how those in a position to lead can best lead, and why Americans who try so hard at it are seen as arrogant by so much of the world. But, first, I want to comment on the Indian view of aid when I first went there, while Jawaharlal Nehru was still prime minister, a post that he held for the first seventeen years after independence.

Nehru was Oxford educated and Western in outlook. Furthermore, he denigrated both Indian religion and culture, and he welcomed technical assistance the way I, and many others like me, were prepared to give it as one of the means for helping India to take a fast course into the family of advanced (Westernized) nations. This was 180 degrees off the course that Gandhi had charted for them and prompted Nehru in his autobiography to make such comments as: "How very different was his [Gandhi's] outlook from mine…and I wondered how far I could cooperate with him in the future." "He has a peasant's outlook on affairs, and with a peasant's blindness to some aspects of life." "In spite of the closest association with him for many years, I am not clear in my own mind about his objective. I doubt if he is clear himself." Part of the confusion about goals that I sensed there stems, I believe, from this very basic conflict in outlook between Gandhi, who gave the masses of common people a great dream of their own good society, and Nehru, who headed the first government and led them in quite another direction.

With the perspective of my own experience in India and much reading of its history and biographies of its leaders, I made the following comment in my final report to the foundation that employed me:

> Anyone who has spent even as little time as I have in India cannot help having views about the whole aid-giving, aid-receiving relationship…It does not seem to

me to be a sound basis for a relationship for one nation to be aid giver and another aid receiver for a long period of time. A one-way flow of aid is all right for an emergency or a short period of readjustment, but not as a term thing—and twenty years [the time this foundation had been working in India] is a long period. I believe, further, that, on balance, the Indians have as much to give us as we have to give them (different things, perhaps, but just as much). And it seems presumptuous, over a long period of time, for us to assume that, because we happen to have a surplus of money, the giving should be one way. Therefore, I believe that if we want to continue to be useful to the Indians, we should use our resources as much to learn from them as to facilitate their learning from us.

By a quirk of fate, in the years that I have been available to do it, I have served as a consultant to several foundations, both large and small. In addition, I was a trustee for some years of a middle-sized one, so I have had a rather concentrated immersion in the field of giving, and I have had a good deal of occasion to reflect on the role of giving. Recently I have summarized this experience in two articles in *Foundation News*, the journal of philanthropy (see chapter 6 herein). In one of them I made this observation:

Those who have been deeply involved in foundation staff work, particularly in a large foundation, are aware of the incessant pressure of grant requests. They know how difficult it is to judge the merit of a request. And they know that many meritorious ones must be turned down. Sensitive people have referred to this as "corrupting work" because grant applicants, no matter how prestigious and powerful they may be, approach the foundation as supplicants. Communication is warped to the extent that a feeling of omniscience is a serious occupational disease of foundation staff work. Not all who are exposed contract the disease, but the incidence is high. An early foundation officer recommended a ten-year limit of tenure to reduce the liability.

In his book *Private Money and Public Service*, Dr. Merrimon Cuninggim, former president of the Danforth Foundation, takes a more theological view when he suggests that "giving is a potentially immoral act." He continues:

> Its danger lies in its assumption of virtue by the agent, of the virtue of agentry, with an accompanying train of unvirtuous assumptions. The relatively innocent desire to help is so thinly distinguished from wanting to be the helper. But the latter is capable of all sorts of distortions: wanting to be well known as the helper, wanting to dictate, to paternalize, to manipulate. It is not likely that a foundation, any more than a person, will escape these faults by thoughtlessness or accident. Only by being conscious of the danger is there a chance to escape. In other words, a foundation must believe in the potential immorality of giving.

Out of reflection on my own experience, and particularly in the context of this conference where the arrogance of power has been so sharply highlighted, Dr. Cuninggim's admonition to the giver to be conscious of the danger and believe in the potential immorality of giving seems not enough. We in the United States who are placed in a position of power by our massive surplus (relatively) for giving, from both public and private resources, will not escape the opprobrious label of "arrogant," nor will we have a chance to achieve that possible wholeness of existence, as individuals and as a nation, simply by being aware—unless that awareness opens the way to a new basis of relationship between aid giver and aid receiver, both among individuals and institutions in our country and between our nation and others, particularly the developing nations.

In this regard I see no middle ground between arrogance and humility. One may not safely give unless one is open and ready to receive the gifts of others, whatever they may be. Scripture holds that it is more blessed to give than to receive. But if one has the great power of affluence in modern terms, a condition which the writers of scripture may not have foreseen, this may be a questionable generalization, because *receiving* requires a genuine humility that may be uncomfortable and difficult to achieve, whereas *giving* poses the risk of arrogance, which, unfortunately, is easy to come by—and some seem to enjoy it.

An important dimension of leadership within a nation that has the substantial power of affluence, such as we in the United States have, will be the ability to persuade those who are in a position to give, whether an individual, an institution, or the nation, that they should reach out for, gratefully receive, and help pay the cost of the giving to themselves by the less favored.

In the contemporary world it is at least as blessed, especially for the powerful, to receive as to give—and much harder to do.

XI

An Inward Journey

It was my privilege to see a bit of Robert Frost in his last years and, having a feeling for the man as a person, his poetry has a special meaning for me.

Philip Booth, in a review, said: "Poems like 'The Demiurge's Laugh,' 'The Road Not Taken,' 'Stopping by Woods on a Snowy Evening,' 'On a Tree Fallen Across the Road,' 'Desert Places,' 'Come In,' and 'Directive' map, in sequence, the road Robert Frost took into the dark woods, and record the serial ordeal he survived by surrendering himself to the conflicts such poems dramatize." Earlier, in chapter 9, "Servant Responsibility in a Bureaucratic Society," I quoted from "New Hampshire" and "The Night Light" passages that suggest the contrast between the gay and light-hearted conversationalist I knew in face-to-face meetings and the vast inner world of both terror and laughter that he confronted in his poetry.

In a group conversation with him one evening, he digressed on the subject of loyalty. At one point I interjected with: "Robert, that is not the way you have defined loyalty before." He turned to me with a broad friendly grin and asked softly, "How did I define it?" I replied, "In your talk on Emerson a few years ago, you said, 'Loyalty is that for the lack of which your gang will shoot you without benefit of trial by jury.'" To this man who had struggled without recognition until he was forty, and then had to move to England to get it, nothing could have pleased him more in his old age than to have an obscure passage like this quoted to him in a shared give-and-take with nonliterary people.

After Robert Frost died in 1963, I wrote the following engagement with his poem "Directive," partly as an acknowledgment of his influence on me and partly as a sharing with those who are on the search for what I have now come to see as *servant leadership*, and who, sooner or later—and in their own way—come to grips with who they are and where they are on the journey.

Directive

Back out of all this now too much for us,
Back in a time made simple by the loss
Of detail, burned, dissolved, and broken off
Like graveyard marble sculpture in the weather,
There is a house that is no more a house
Upon a farm that is no more a farm
And in a town that is no more a town.
The road there, if you'll let a guide direct you
Who only has at heart your getting lost,
May seem as if it should have been a quarry—
Great monolithic knees the former town
Long since gave up pretence of keeping covered.
And there's a story in a book about it:
Besides the wear of iron wagon wheels
The ledges show lines ruled southeast northwest,
The chisel work of an enormous Glacier
That braced his feet against the Arctic Pole.
You must not mind a certain coolness from him
Still said to haunt this side of Panther Mountain.
Nor need you mind the serial ordeal
Of being watched from forty cellar holes
As if by eye pairs out of forty firkins.
As for the woods' excitement over you
That sends light rustle rushes to their leaves,
Charge that to upstart inexperience.
Where were they all not twenty years ago?
They think too much of having shaded out
A few old pecker-fretted apple trees.
Make yourself up a cheering song of how
Someone's road home from work this once was,

Who may be just ahead of you on foot
Or creaking with a buggy load of grain.
The height of the adventure is the height
Of country where two village cultures faded
Into each other. Both of them are lost.
And if you're lost enough to find yourself
By now, pull in your ladder road behind you
And put a sign up CLOSED to all but me.
Then make yourself at home. The only field
Now left's no bigger than a harness gall.
First there's the children's house of make believe,
Some shattered dishes underneath a pine,
The playthings in the playhouse of the children.
Weep for what little things could make them glad.
Then for the house that is no more a house,
But only a belilaced cellar hole,
Now slowly closing like a dent in dough.
This was no playhouse but a house in earnest.
Your destination and your destiny's
A brook that was the water of the house,
Cold as a spring as yet so near its source,
Too lofty and original to rage.
(We know the valley streams that when aroused
Will leave their tatters hung on barb and thorn.)
I have kept hidden in the instep arch
Of an old cedar at the waterside
A broken drinking goblet like the Grail
Under a spell so the wrong ones can't find it,
So can't get saved, as Saint Mark says they mustn't.
(I stole the goblet from the children's playhouse.)
Here are your waters and your watering place.
Drink and be whole again beyond confusion.

—ROBERT FROST

If Robert Frost had a deliberate strategy of influence in mind when he wrote "Directive," he kept it to himself the one time I heard him asked about its meaning. His answer was, "Read it and read it and read it, and it means what it says to you." He read this poem in a way that carried the impact of its obviously great importance and meaning to him.

What one gets by reading and reading and reading this poem cannot be predicted. One gets what one is ready for, what one is open to receive. Of course, this is what the poem is about. Our problem is circular: we must understand in order to be able to understand. It has something to do with awareness and symbols.

Awareness, letting something significant and disturbing develop between oneself and a symbol, comes more by being waited upon rather than by being asked. One of the most baffling of life's experiences is to stand beside one who is aware, one who is looking at a symbol and is deeply moved by it, and, confronting the same symbol, to be unmoved. Oh, that we could just be open in the presence of symbols that cry out to speak to us, let our guards down, and take the risks of being moved!

The power of a symbol is measured by its capacity to sustain a flow of significant new meaning. The substance of the symbol may be a painting, a poem or story, allegory, myth, scripture, a piece of music, a person, a crack in the sidewalk, or a blade of grass. Whatever or whoever, it produces a confrontation in which much that makes the symbol meaningful comes from the beholder.

The potentiality is both in the symbol and in the beholder. But one does not read old crystallized meaning into a new symbol. One does not even look to an old symbol as the justification for old meaning. All symbols are potential sources of new meaning. Nor is meaning a product of the conscious intent of the creator of the symbol. The poet is sometimes as surprised by new meaning in his own poem as is anyone else. Meaning from an interaction with a symbol is a new creation. It can be new with each opportunity. Taking the opportunity may be the measure of one's growth.

If one views inward growth as a unique and personal journey, then what one makes of a symbol is to some extent unique and personal. A symbol may say something in common to all beholders, but the real lift and insight is beyond the range of verbal communication. Yet it is important that we try to share our symbolic experiences because, as responsible people, we need the check and guidance of other responsible people. All of us encounter obstacles to growth. We may find new paths in the accounts of fellow seekers. It is in this spirit of sharing that I offer my experience with "Directive."

Back out of all this now too much for us,

Those of us who undertake the journey must accept that, simply by living in the contemporary world and making our peace with it as it is, we may be involved in a way that blocks our growth. Primitive people may have suffered much from their environment, but they were not alienated; the Lascaux cave paintings attest to this. They probably did not articulate a theology, but they may have been religious in the basic sense of "bound to the cosmos." With us, sophistication, rationality, greater mastery of the immediate environment have taken their toll in terms of a tragic separation from the opportunity for religious experience, that is, growth in the feeling of being bound to the cosmos.

So we must go:

Back out of all this now too much for us,
Back in a time made simple by the loss
Of detail, burned, dissolved, and broken off
Like graveyard marble sculpture in the weather,

To go back, something must be lost. This is the key to the journey: something must be lost in order that something may be found. (*May be*, but not necessarily found.) And it is not an easy loss! *Burned, dissolved, broken off.* These are radical, searing losses. But they are the losses we must contemplate if the *time made simple*, spontaneity, the indispensable condition for progress on the inward journey, is our goal.

What follows in the poem after the *time made simple* has been achieved—an enigmatic symbolism, something to puzzle over, something that both is and is no more. A transmutation?

There is a house that is no more a house
Upon a farm that is no more a farm
And in a town that is no more a town.

Then we turn to the poem for direction.

The road there, if you'll let a guide direct you
Who only has at heart your getting lost,

If you'll let a guide direct you who only has at heart your getting lost! This is a big *if;* who wants that kind of guide? Don't we ask for a guide who is certain of the destination, and then only after we are certain that it is a destination we want to go to? No, this is not the kind of guide many of us are looking for. We already feel lost. Why then would we want a guide who only has at heart our getting lost?

This is the ground on which the great religious traditions of the world have always stood. The tradition built around the ministry of Jesus of Nazareth, the one in which I grew up and which has the greatest symbolic meaning to me now, seems especially emphatic on this point. Jesus seemed only to have at heart our getting lost; he was mostly concerned with what must be taken away rather than with what would be gained. We find clues to what must be lost in such sayings as "Unless you turn and become like children you will never enter the kingdom of heaven," "It is easier for a camel to go through the eye of a needle than for a rich man to enter the kingdom," "Cleanse the inside of the cup, that the outside also may be clean," and "Unless one is born anew, he cannot see the kingdom of God."

A few general terms describe what will be received: heaven, eternal life, salvation, the kingdom of God. The believers of the literal word know what these terms mean; they have to. But seekers who are responding to symbols don't know, don't have to know, wouldn't be helped by knowing. They are not too interested in meaning as bounded by the vagaries of language. Rather they seek a guide who only has at heart their getting lost.

The road there, if you'll let a guide direct you
Who only has at heart your getting lost,
May seem as if it should have been a quarry—
Great monolithic knees the former town
Long since gave up pretense of keeping covered.

Grotesque dream imagery perhaps?

And there's a story in a book about it:

Could it be the story of the search for the Holy Grail, that
great legend from many ages and cultures in which the object of
the search is that symbolic cup which holds the source of spiritual
life? In the version that comes to us from Malory, the knights
who search for the Grail largely pursue their missions alone,
although they are gathered for the consummation of the search.

Besides the wear of iron wagon wheels
The ledges show lines ruled southeast northwest,
The chisel work of an enormous Glacier
That braced his feet against the Arctic Pole.
You must not mind a certain coolness from him
Still said to haunt this side of Panther Mountain. *

Along the way, as your guide directs you who only has at
heart your getting lost, perhaps you will be chilled to discomfort,
but you must not mind.

Nor need you mind the serial ordeal
Of being watched from forty cellar holes
As if by eye pairs out of forty firkins.

---

*"Connecticut where I live is full of very real and concrete towns that are no more
towns, places in the deep woods which are exactly as described in this poem, from the
wagon wheel marks on the ledges uncovered on the old wood roads to the springs and the
children's playhouses and the cellar holes and the trees which have shaded out old apple
orchards. I can show you three or four on my own property here. And there is a ghost
town a few miles away, lost in deep woods, with at least a hundred and forty cellar holes
which watch as you walk through it." (From a letter from a friend commenting on an
early draft of this chapter.)

These may be the curious eyes from curious places that could add to your discomfort. In "Ali Baba and the Forty Thieves" the maid had gone to the shed at night to get oil for her lamp, but all but one of the firkins that presumably contained oil held, in fact, a thief.

As for the woods' excitement over you
That sends light rustle rushes to their leaves,
Charge that to upstart inexperience.
Where were they all not twenty years ago?
They think too much of having shaded out
A few old pecker-fretted apple trees.

The immature and the superficial may flap their wings in a way that diverts and distorts with a seeming excitement. Pass them by.

Make yourself up a cheering song of how
Someone's road home from work this once was,
Who may be just ahead of you on foot
Or creaking with a buggy load of grain.

Why would you need to make up a cheering song? Would you by chance be feeling lonely as you get more and more lost? Then you supply your own cheer. You imagine that you are following someone just ahead—a simple person, a workman on foot, or a tender of a small farm—symbolically, people who never had much veneer or from whom much of the veneer has been stripped as it is now being stripped from you. Believing this, the song you make up can really cheer!

The height of the adventure is the height
Of country where two village cultures faded
Into each other. Both of them are lost.

You are now at the height where the artificiality of culture has faded away. You are not constrained. There is no certainty. You are on your own. This is the real adventure.

And if you're lost enough to find yourself
By now, pull in your ladder road behind you
And put a sign up CLOSED to all but me.
Then make yourself at home.

You must be *lost enough* before you can find yourself. The test, maybe, is: *If you can't find yourself, you're not lost enough.*

Pull in your ladder road behind you—this is interesting symbolism. Could this be echoing Herman Melville in *Moby Dick* when Father Mapple climbed to the pulpit to preach that great allegorical sermon? Ishmael, telling the story, describes how this venerable seafaring-man-turned-chaplain mounted to the pulpit on a rope ladder and then turned around and slowly pulled the ladder up into the pulpit. Said Ishmael, "Thought I, there must be some sober reason for this thing; furthermore, it must symbolize something unseen. Can it be, then, that by the act of physical isolation, he signifies his spiritual withdrawal for the time, from all outward worldly ties and connection? Yes, for replenished with meat and wine of the word, to the faithful man of God, this pulpit, I see, is a self-contained stronghold—with a perennial well of water within the walls."

"Put a sign up *Closed* to all but me. Then make yourself at home." You have lost some affiliations you once valued. But you welcome the separation. You are alone, and yet you are not alone because you are beginning to feel at home. But there is more, much more.

The only field
Now left's no bigger than a harness gall.

Is this the farm that is no more a farm?

First there's the children's house of make believe,
Some shattered dishes underneath a pine,
The playthings in the playhouse of the children.
Weep for what little things could make them glad.

Weep? Why weep? Perhaps because as adults little things no longer make us glad? Or have we lost the capacity to be glad?

Then for the house that is no more a house,
But only a belilaced cellar hole,
Now slowly closing like a dent in dough.
This was no playhouse but a house in earnest.

The thing that we built as our abode is but a hole closing like a dent in dough. How ephemeral are human works.

Your destination and your destiny's
A brook that was the water of the house,

Destination and *destiny*—two interesting words. They could be synonymous. But if one may choose among many meanings, *destination* could be the end of the journey and *destiny* could be the ultimate (therefore unachievable) goal. Paradoxically, at one time one might be at the end and the beginning of one's journey.

Then *water,* the great symbol of wholeness. The house, the ephemeral, is gone but the water is here. And it is near its source.

Cold as a spring as yet so near its source,
Too lofty and original to rage.
(We know the valley streams that when aroused
Will leave their tatters hung on barb and thorn.)

Cold, near its source, lofty, and original. Nothing old and shopworn here. This is new and fresh. It is not in doctrines and dogmas. It is not substantive and codified. To make the point clear we parenthetically note that we know all about the turbulent contention of historical ideas. But what is before us now is too lofty and original to rage. It is not the confused and raging torrent of the valley stream after the waters (no longer cold, fresh, and original) have merged from many sources.

This is a painful confrontation for those who cling to the comfort and security of old ways, or who would like to remake the new world into an old image. Look at the past, yes; but don't expect historical ideas to have cool freshness, to be lofty and original.

This is powerful symbolism. Cold water, near its source, lofty and original. This is the kind of water one would like to drink—a long hearty drink. But who shall drink this water?

> *I have kept hidden in the instep arch*
> *Of an old cedar at the waterside*
> *A broken drinking goblet like the Grail*
> *Under a spell so the wrong ones can't find it,*
> *So can't get saved, as Saint Mark says they mustn't.*
> *(I stole the goblet from the children's playhouse.)*

The cup, the Grail, that ancient symbol of the quest for wholeness, is a broken goblet from the children's playhouse. It has the imperfection of the rejected and the discarded. It was once one of those little things that make children glad, the kind of thing for which many adults, immersed in cumber and Martha-like involvements, no longer can be glad.

And it is under a spell so the wrong ones can't find it, so can't get saved, as Saint Mark says they mustn't. What an awful injunction! What did Saint Mark say?

Is it the fourth chapter of Mark? Jesus had just spoken the parable of the sower as he sat in a boat at the edge of the sea. Having concluded the parable, he said, "He who has ears to hear, let him hear." *And when he was alone, those who were about him with the twelve asked him concerning the parables. And he said to them, "To you has been given the secret of the kingdom of God, but for those outside everything is in parables; so that they may indeed see but not perceive, and may indeed hear but not understand; lest they should turn again and be forgiven."*

Here we have the inner and the outer circles. To the inner circle, to those who have the secret of the kingdom, he explains everything. To the outer circle, those who know not the secret, he speaks only through parables so *the wrong ones can't understand it,* so that they may indeed see but not perceive, and may indeed hear but not understand, lest they should turn again and be forgiven!

Poetry, my friend has said, is a way of writing in parables so the wrong ones won't understand.

There are several "tests" suggested in other of the gospel accounts. The one given in this passage in Mark is the most demanding, the most baffling. In the twenty-fifth chapter of Matthew the test is one of *humanity:* "I was hungry and you gave me food, I was thirsty and you gave me drink, I was a stranger and you welcomed me, I was naked and you clothed me, I was sick and you visited me, I was in prison and you came to me— truly, I say to you, as you did it to one of the least of these my brethren, you did it to me." And the reward to the righteous who meet this test is "eternal life." But here, too, the righteous and the unrighteous are separated by the vivid imagery of the sheep and the goats.

In the third chapter of John, in the conversation with Nicodemus, the test is *faith:* "Whoever believes in him (the Son) will have eternal life."

The requirement laid down in the fourth chapter of Mark is clearly one of spiritual growth; it is the route of initiation, of ordeal, a journey for which "Directive" is a guide. Could it be that such is requisite to being fully human, to the capacity for faith? Unless one perceives and understands, unless one is *aware*, can one, in fact, be human and believe?

All of this forces me to view this passage from Mark as symbolism in a particular way. Privately, to the inner circle, he explains everything. To those without he speaks in parables, symbols, symbols with which there must be a searching confrontation and a mutual response.

How, then, may we view Jesus symbolically at this point? I can see two quite different possibilities, and I find them both important. The first is Jesus as the greatest of the avatars, the symbolic consummation in one human being of the total Judeo-Christian tradition—and what a tough and demanding tradition it is. Here is the one who could, with all gentleness, say to the woman taken in adultery, "Neither do I condemn you; go and sin no more." And who could answer the question "And who is my neighbor?" with the Good Samaritan story. Yet he did not say to the woman that because she was not condemned she was within the circle of those who have the secret of the kingdom and to whom everything is explained. Nor did he imply that the Samaritan was such a person. He was, of course, the great teacher, and when he was speaking in parables he was holding out the opportunity for his hearers to proceed on with the journey. But there is the suggestion that only the complete dedication of the disciple will make it to the inner circle.

The second view is to see Jesus in this passage in Mark as symbolic of an aspect of people's understanding rather than as people in their entirety. I find this view also necessary because there is something in me that hesitates to accept him as a man who is wilfully condemning the ignorant and the befuddled to eternal darkness.

With this reservation, *what* then is Jesus at this point in the story? Can he be *meaning?* Could meaning be what is speaking in this passage? If so, on what terms is meaning available?

To those who are without, who have *not* lost what must be lost, it will be enigma, confusion—meaning does not come through. To those who are within, who have accepted the guide who only has at heart their getting lost, who have traveled the road of grotesque imagery, the coolness of the glacier, the curious spying eyes, the flutter of frivolity, the aloneness and self-cheer, and who have reached the height of the adventure where they are lost enough to find themselves—they have joined that group to which all may aspire to whom meaning comes through and is clear beyond confusion. But meaning is a stern taskmaster: one must *aspire,* one must *persevere,* one must accept the *discipline* of dealing thoughtfully with symbols.

"Directive" offers a promise to those who do aspire: When we have gone back out of all this now too much for us, when we are lost enough to find ourselves and have pulled in our ladder road behind us, then we shall have the opportunity to drink of the waters of wholeness.

Here are your waters and your watering place.
Drink and be whole again beyond confusion.

Yes, here is the water to drink and be whole *again*. Were you once whole? In your childish naiveté perhaps? Possibly in your own uniqueness, which you have denied—the opportunity to live in the light of your own inward experience? And what is beyond confusion?

A measure of people's wholeness will not bring them certainty or tranquility (although brief moments of these delights may be theirs). *Beyond confusion* is the promise. Their state may be moving, developing, uncertain, even dangerous. But they will not be confused because they will be at one with the circumstance, both far and near. In fact, they will *be* the circumstance; they will no longer be alienated. Rightness, responsibility, courage will define their character. They will be bound to the cosmos. They will be at home in this world as it is, as it always is.

For modern people this is probably not achievable, not wholly, but one can move toward it. Depending upon age, interest and drive, the deepness of the set of attitudes and habit patterns, and other factors (some unknown)—depending on such as these one person will move farther and with greater facility than another.

No one can judge, from where one now stands, how difficult the next step along the road of spiritual growth will be. Those of good works, the upright moral citizens, the pillars in the church may find the next step of staggering proportions. Their seeming opposites—the unsuccessful, the misfit, the unlovely, the rejected—may take the next step with ease. We cannot assume with assurance that we are relatively advantaged or disadvantaged for any stage of the inward journey.

To be on with the journey one must have an attitude toward loss and being lost, a view of oneself in which powerful symbols like *burned, dissolved, broken off*—however painful their impact is seen to be—do not appear as senseless or destructive. Rather, the losses they suggest are seen as opening the way for new creative acts, for the receiving of priceless gifts. Loss, *every loss one's mind can conceive of,* creates a vacuum into which will come (if allowed) something new and fresh and beautiful, something unforeseen—and the greatest of these is *love.* The source of this attitude toward loss and being lost is *faith:* faith in the validity of one's own inward experience; faith in the wisdom of the great events of one's history, events in which one's potential for nobility has been tested and refined; faith in doubt, in inquiry, and in the rebirth of wisdom; faith in the possibility of achieving a measure of sainthood on this earth from which flow concerns and responsibility and a sense of rightness in all things. By these means mortals are raised above the possibility of hurt. They will suffer, but they will not be hurt because each loss grants them the opportunity to be greater than before. Loss, by itself, is not tragic. What *is* tragic is the failure to grasp the opportunity which loss presents. I find these assumptions necessary for the acceptance of "Directive" as a guide

For those who, having followed thus far, would be on with the journey, I submit "Directive" as a dependable guide *providing* they will let something develop between themselves and the poem, a new level of meaning about the inward journey, something unique and personal for each reader, a continually evolving awareness.

Awareness, below the level of the conscious intellect, I see as infinite and therefore equal in every human being, perhaps in every creature. The blinders that block our conscious access to our own vast awareness are the uncompensated losses we have sustained; and the errors we have acquired from our cultural inheritance, from the undigested residues of our own experience, and from our conscious learning. "Directive" would seem to say: Remove the blinders from your awareness by losing what must be lost, the key to which no one can give you, but which your own inward resources rightly cultivated will supply. Then set forth upon your journey and, if you travel far enough, filling the voids of loss with the noblest choices, you *may* be given the secret of the kingdom: awe and wonder before the majesty and the mystery of all creation. Then, and only then, will the parables be explained (the drinking of the cold, lofty, original water). I submit this as a hopeful hypothesis at a time when hope is dim. I will bet my life upon it.

XII

Postscript

Who is the servant-leader?

Is not every servant a leader because of influence by example? Walt Whitman may have answered this when he wrote, "We convince by our presence."

Servant-leaders differ from other persons of goodwill because they act on what they believe. Consequently, they "know experimentally" and there is a sustaining spirit when they venture and risk. To the worldly, servant-leaders may seem naive; and they may not adapt readily to prevailing institutional structures.

The hierarchy of contemporary institutions that exist to serve humankind may be seen to be on three levels. In the base group are families, communities, businesses, governments, schools, and health and social agencies. Standing next above, in a position to serve both individuals and institutions, and with power to exert a value-clarifying influence, are churches and universities. At the third level, because of the great opportunity to harbor and nurture prophetic voices that give vision and hope, I see theological seminaries and foundations. In a sustained good society, the gap between opportunity and performance narrows progressively at levels two and three. When there is faltering, as there seems to be now, the gaps between opportunity and performance may have widened, perhaps most at the third level.

The transforming movement, should there be one, may come from anywhere and may spread in unaccountable ways. But that movement will be favored if seminaries and foundations give shelter and encouragement to the originators, and if churches and universities are effective mediators to base-line institutions. All have the opportunity to convince by their presence, by acting on what they believe *in their internal affairs*, and by being more hospitable to servant-leaders.

In the absence of solid evidence of such initiatives, servant-leaders may stand alone, largely without the support of their culture, as a saving remnant of those who care for both persons and institutions, and who are determined to make their caring count—*wherever they are involved*. This brings them, as individuals, constantly to examine the assumptions they live by. Thus, their leadership by example sustains trust.

They also serve who only stand and wait.

—JOHN MILTON

Peter M. Senge

Afterword

I don't think there are many great books, books that cause
something to happen. There are many good books, many
interesting books. There are books that you read and you say,
"Well, that's got some good ideas." "Maybe I'll recommend it to
a friend." But ten years later, you couldn't say something has
really changed as a result of that book, changed on a scale that
matters in the world. But that is exactly what I think *Servant
Leadership* has done. Moreover, I expect the impact of *Servant
Leadership* to be greater in the next twenty-five years than the
past twenty-five years.

Why do I think it's a book that has had and will have such an
impact? I first read the book around 1982. If I remember correctly, Joe Jaworski gave it to me, and I think John Gardner told
Joe to read it. That says something right there. Clearly, the ideas
in the book struck some important chords for some important
thinkers about leadership. To appreciate the greatness of *Servant
Leadership*, we have to look at the *context* as well as the *content*.

An Era of Institutional Failure

I have a very simple hypothesis about why this is an
important book. As Dee Hock, founding CEO of VISA and one
of the great institutional innovators of our time says, "We live
in an era of massive institutional failure." The need for fundamental institutional change is enormous, and it is not likely to
decrease. It's very hard to point to any institutions that we can
say are thriving and truly serving the larger public interest.
Arguably, you might say business is the most healthy institution. In most countries you'd be hard pressed to say that public

education, or government, or nonprofits in general are in better shape. But having spent much of my last twenty years in business, I would be hard pressed to call business a healthy institution either, if only from the standpoint of its impact on its members.

How many of us work longer hours today than we worked ten years ago—total work at our work site, at home, on our email, voicemail, and our other "personal work technologies"? How many of us think we can continue to increase our hours worked by a similar amount over the next ten years? This is but one of many unsustainable trends in the way our institutions function, and especially the way they affect the larger social and living systems upon which they depend. Many of these trends will simply not continue. It's very hard to know what will happen, or how change will come about, but we can be pretty sure we can't sustain more of the same. In the United States we've already sent our families' second potential wage earners to work in order to sustain family incomes. Unless we revert to child labor, we don't have a third potential wage earner to send to work. So that trend's over. Can we continue to heat up the globe and destroy species? I doubt it. As the ecologists have always said, nature bats last, and she hasn't had her last time at bat yet. Can we continue to ignore the effects of the spread of global institutions on the social divide?

But we don't even have to look at global breakdowns to see that something is very much amiss. It seems to me very few people are truly happy with their work lives. I don't mean it's not exciting, or that we don't have a lot of fun things to do. But I haven't heard people raving lately about going home at ten o'clock in the evening and starting to work on their email, about breakfast meetings or Saturday meetings, or meetings in general. And I haven't heard many teachers lately raving about how wonderful standardized testing is, and then there is also the growing stress and workload pressure for students, teachers, schools, and even school districts who fear that their test scores will be at the bottom of the state rankings in next Sunday's paper.

So, it is not hard to find evidence to corroborate Dee Hock's assessment of institutional health. In an era of massive institutional failure, the ideas in *Servant Leadership* point toward a possible path forward, and will continue to do so.

The second reason I think this book will grow in importance is that the changes ahead will be difficult. A mentor of mine, William J. O'Brien, retired a few years ago as the CEO of a property and liability insurance company. O'Brien was instrumental in leading a firm, over twenty years, which went from being bankrupt to being one of the top performers in US industry. Bill used to say, "I go every place in my organization and talk to people about our vision; about our commitment to distribute power and authority so that people can genuinely feel they have real impact on the business from wherever they are; about trust; about openness; about eliminating political game-playing and confronting difficult issues publicly rather than in back rooms. The amazing thing is," he continued, "you almost never find anybody who says, 'No, I'm not interested in that.' On the contrary, almost everyone is genuinely drawn to the idea of creating work environments like this."

So, O'Brien suggests, that leads to one obvious question: "If most of us would like to work in that sort of work environment, then why don't such work environments pervade all institutions? Why aren't they the norm rather than the exception?" Then he said, "I've come to one conclusion: We have no idea the depth of commitment required to build such an enterprise."

I expect *Servant Leadership* to become more important in the future because it is one of the very few books that illuminates the depth of commitment required to build truly innovative organizations. We are just starting to get an inkling of the depth of commitment required to build truly healthy enterprises for the future. It is a profound journey, and Bob Greenleaf understood that right from the start—and he described it more cogently and evocatively than almost anybody else.

Still, the work sits on the periphery of management think-ing, as indeed does our work on knowledge creation, learning, and fundamental institutional change. What will it take to pene-trate the mainstream of management practice?

Learning, Knowledge, and Change

Dr. W. Edwards Deming was another mentor to me. Dr. Deming was world famous for his pioneering work in quality management. Yet, he was deeply disappointed at the failure, especially of American firms, to grasp his thinking about what he called "the transformation of management." Despite all the qual-ity-management programs, you could count on one hand the companies who had internalized his message to the point of shifting the fundamentals of how they are managed. One was Toyota, which has dominated the world auto industry for twenty years. Despite a weak domestic economy and depressed value of the yen over the past decade, Toyota's market capitalization has exceeded the *sum* of the market values of General Motors, Ford, and Daimler-Chrysler for most of the past twenty years. Dem-ing's attitude toward this was, "Well that's all pretty good, but it hasn't transformed management. What has kept the others from getting it? One percent or 2 percent penetration of management thinking is not 30 percent." To paraphrase Bill O'Brien, "If this stuff is so good, why isn't it *everywhere?*"

Were we to take another industry context—say public pri-mary and secondary education—I do not think our assessment of the success of fundamental innovation would be much more favorable. There are countless examples of ideas and methods of comparable significance to quality management—for example, the theory of multiple intelligences, learner-centered learning, action learning—that have failed to penetrate public education.

Failures in fundamental change efforts are the norm rather than the exception. Why?

Speaking from the vantage point of the work we've done on organizational learning, I would say the problems start with our basic change strategies, problems Greenleaf understood very well. There is a basic difference between *change* and *learning*. Learning requires change. You would not say you had really learned anything, like walking or skiing, if no change was produced. But change does not require learning. The heart of learning lies in the development of new capacities, a new level of ability to reliably produce a quality of result. This is the difference between walking one time and *learning to walk*. The same principle applies to collective or organizational learning, which concerns developing new collective capacities.

Efforts to produce such learning invariably fail for two reasons. First, the approaches taken usually do not allow a realistic amount of time for capacity-building. Typically, today, somebody in top management meets with a consultant, reads a book, gets excited about a new idea, and begins to talk about it. Next there is a three-day training program, the program "is rolled out" across the organization, and everyone is expected to participate. Can you think of anything in your life that was a significant development for you, a significant learning, that could have been done like this? Does anybody learn to play the violin in a three-day intense training program? Or become a nuclear engineer? Nor does being able to talk about being a pianist make you one. Significant capacity-building takes months and years, not hours. It takes deep commitment; it takes a willingness and a possibility to practice, to try out new approaches repeatedly, and to learn from experience. That's the way we learn anything that's significant. So by definition, three-day training programs, by themselves, are only for learning what is not significant. Or, to be a bit cynical, our organizations excel at learning what is trivial.

The second problem concerns *whom* most change programs are designed for. In one of the early sections of "The Servant as Leader" (chapter 1), Greenleaf tells a story. "A king once asked Confucius for advice on what to do about a large number of thieves. Confucius responded to the king and said, 'If you, sire, were not covetous, although you should reward them to do it, they would not steal.'" This is in a little subsection of the essay titled, "In Here, Not Out There." The real territory of change is always "in here." Now, the consequences must be "out there" if we're really interested in institutional change. But we can't get there from just focusing on "out there." That is the paradox. That's what it means to take a capacity-building approach. We want something new to be created in our organizations. We ask, what capacities do we need that we do not now have? It's very simple—and extraordinarily unusual, as Greenleaf knew.

Among the particular areas of capacity-building at the heart of our work, the first has to do with aspiration. All learning—all real, deep learning—is driven by the aspirations of learners. There's an old saw, that there are only two fundamental sources of change in human affairs: aspiration and desperation. We are familiar with the phrase, "Nothing will ever change unless there is a crisis." That's *desperation*. As far as I can see, the number one leadership strategy in America is quite simple to describe: Create a crisis. Or if you're really clever, create the *fear* that a crisis is about to hit. That shows the extent to which we have allowed the diminishment of our capacity for aspiration.

Aspiration drives virtually all fundamental learning. Why did we learn to walk? Why did we learn to talk? Why did we learn *anything* that we consider really significant in our lives? Did we suddenly wake up one morning at the age of eight months and say, "Oh my gosh, my life is never going to turn out. I'm going to be a total loser if I don't learn to walk!" Or, did we learn to walk because we wanted to? That's *aspiration*. Just imagine: What if nine out of ten change initiatives, in our organizations or in our societies, were driven by excitement, by the idea that this would serve somebody in a different way, that this would give us a better way of living? This would be very different from crisis and fear, our current primary motivators for change.

In another early section in "The Servant as Leader," Greenleaf asks, "What are you trying to do?" He continues: "Every achievement starts with a goal, but not just any goal." Here, Greenleaf hints at a key to why aspiration is not more prevalent as a motivator of change. Why are some goals more important than others? Because they're more meaningful to us. They represent "a greater cause," something beyond ourselves, a dream, a symbol of what we deeply care about. That's the force of aspiration. Some goals are more meaningful than others. The goals that are most meaningful are those that we somehow sense—intuit, feel, hear—are what I'm here to do. We all know the difference in ourselves between *doing what we're here to do* versus *doing what someone said we ought to do.* That's the difference between aspiration and compliance. When we fail to tap the power of aspiration, deep learning and change are virtually impossible.

A second area of capacity-building vital to our work is our understanding of complexity. One of the sections in "The Servant as Leader" that few people pay enough attention to is the section on conceptual leadership. Greenleaf calls conceptualizing "the prime leadership talent." Conceptualizing means, for example, how we make sense of a complex situation. Most of the time, people in positions of authority trivialize complex issues. "The problem is we're not competitive because we've got old technology. So we're going to buy this new company to bring us new technology." This sort of statement says nothing about *why* our technology has become old or *what* will keep us from neglecting innovation in the future. If anything, trivializing complexity is even more of a problem for our public-sector leaders, who find themselves continually offering pat solutions to highly complex issues. As Oscar Wilde once said, "For every great problem, there is a simple solution—and it's wrong."

Why do people in leadership positions trivialize the complex? I think there are two reasons. One is that those in positions of authority want to appear to have the answers. To stand up in front of people and say, "You know, this is really a complex issue, and I don't think I understand it very well," does not sound like leadership to most people in most institutions. A second reason, I believe, is that we think people can't handle anything but a trivial solution. In other words, our assumption is that people don't have the capacity to think for themselves, to deal with dilemmas, to consider the possibility that complex issues are actually complex.

These are reasons that Greenleaf considered the ability to conceptualize so vital to leadership—to see a complex situation as complex but somehow still make some sense of it. I remember once hearing a famous radio broadcast by Franklin Delano Roosevelt, from 1933, when he had declared the "bank holiday" that closed US banks in order to stop a run on their assets during the Great Depression. There was great fear in the country, and a particular fear that the whole banking system would collapse. This fear was driving more people to withdraw their savings, which was in fact precipitating the collapse. A disastrous self-fulfilling prophecy was unfolding. When I heard this recording, I was stunned. Roosevelt was not just telling people that he had made this decision because it was "the right thing to do and everyone would be better off." In a radio broadcast that lasted about a half hour, he explained to every citizen who was interested in listening how the modern banking system worked. That was not a trivial task. He explained it so that people could understand why we were closing all the banks, and why they would not be able to withdraw their funds. He explained how this would allow the banks to reestablish their liquidity, assess how vulnerable each was, and agree what particular needs each bank had for federal assistance. But he also explained the role of public perceptions in the banking system—that in some ways we all make the banking system work or fail. By the time he had finished, not only did people know the basics of modern banking, but they also felt personally responsible for a sound banking system. *That is conceptual leadership.*

Can we imagine a president today doing something similar to help citizens understand a contemporary crisis? Perhaps one reason it is difficult to imagine this is because, when you do this, it's quite clear that you are laying out a *theory*, not an *answer*—a way of looking at a problem, a way of thinking about it, not a fixed solution. When you do this, you are vulnerable; you are no longer pretending to be infallible. This is not easy to do. And, you must presume that you're talking to an intelligent listener, someone who is genuinely interested in understanding what is going on, not just looking for a quick fix. These are examples of capacity-building that Greenleaf knew to be vital to leading. But he also knew that there would be no progress in this area without a genuine spirit of learning. Recall Gandhi's words, "We must be the change we seek." That's the principle of capacity-building, the principle that embodies "in here, not out there." There is no reason to expect change in our organizations or societies if that change doesn't happen *in here*, in us.

If only more leaders understood this principle, many of the problems with "resistance to change" would disappear. Think about how often people in organizations, in the midst of any change process, think that "someone up there is trying to change us." Is that not the way most change efforts are perceived? "They're trying to change us." What do virtually all human beings do if they perceive someone is trying to change them? They resist change! So, we've got all these CEOs wondering "Why do people resist change?" or "How can we overcome people's resistance to change?" Yet a primary reason for this resistance lies in the leader's very strategies. When people perceive that someone is trying to change them, they are very likely to resist that change at some level, even if on the surface they proclaim support.

Rather than understanding the source of the resistance, most self-proclaimed "change leaders" are busy seeking "buy in." You hear this a great deal from people seeking to produce change. "How do I get people to buy in?" It has become an almost universal refrain among CEOs. But "buy in" is often a superficial type of commitment. People will "buy in" to one idea today and another tomorrow. This is not what Bill O'Brien meant when he suggested that we probe "the nature of the commitment" required in order to build a great enterprise. It must start with a commitment to be willing to change myself. There is an old saying in Buddhism, "There is nothing so difficult as changing oneself." So, I always have to ask the question, "What capacities do *I* lack and what am *I* doing to build those capacities?"

Learning to Serve

But here Greenleaf "upped the ante." In what I have always regarded as one of his seminal thoughts, he offered this little line, which always keeps coming back to me, to express the spirit of servant leadership. "The servant-leader is servant first, it begins with a natural feeling that one wants to serve, to serve first, as opposed to, wanting power, influence, fame, or wealth." Greenleaf doesn't discount these motivations. After all, we are human beings, and naturally we have interests and aspirations in these areas. The real question is, what is primary and what is secondary? It's so easy to say—and probably most of us would like to think—that our first orientation is to serve. "That's really why I'm here—to serve." But turn this around and ask, "How many people perceive me as *first* and *foremost* a servant?" How many people perceive those in positions of authority to be first and foremost servants? Obviously, these are demanding questions. What kind of success rate do you think you would get on these questions in your organization? Would you get 50 percent? 20 percent? 10 percent? When I ask this question of groups, typically I get a smattering of hands raised, perhaps 5 percent or 10 percent. That seems realistic to me. Certainly, I question the extent to which I measure up to this question. Clearly, it's easy to espouse servant leadership but it's not so easy to do. In many ways, this is the first point in the book. It is foundational to Greenleaf's contribution.

What does it take to cultivate a genuine desire to serve? I can't think of any more important question. What keeps us from accessing, realizing, and acting from an innate desire to serve? I do not think these questions have simple answers. But I do think they are the right questions. The answers have to be personal. They also have to be situational. But this is where the journey starts.

True Commitment

I believe that there is a special character to the type of commitment that lies at the heart of servant leadership, a type of commitment that is not well understood.

To get at this, we can start with a simple question: "What is the difference between someone who is committed and someone who is fanatical?" That's not a trivial point. History is full of people who are absolutely committed and very dangerous. But the world is full of people who are neither fanatical nor committed to much beyond themselves. It is easy to avoid fanaticism by avoiding commitment. But if we seek commitment, in ourselves and others, we had better understand its shadow, fanaticism. If we don't, I would forget about servant leadership. Because I will guarantee you that many fanatics see themselves as genuinely committed to serving a larger cause.

Some think the difference lies in selflessness. But many who are fanatical are willing to give up their lives. Some think the difference lies in empathy. But many who are fanatical have deep empathy for others whose plight they have taken up. Others say the difference lies in values. Believe me, I don't know of any fanatics who don't have values. We may not like their values, but they have values. There are ideas that they are absolutely committed to that they consider of transcendent importance.

Eric Hoffer's classic *The True Believer* includes the best examination of fanaticism I have ever encountered. Eric Hoffer was a San Francisco longshoreman with little formal education. By the time he died he was considered one of the great mid-twentieth-century American philosophers. Hoffer argued that the fundamental distinction between commitment and fanaticism was *uncertainty*. A fanatic is *certain*. A fanatic has *the* answer. A fanatic knows what *really* is happening. A fanatic has *the* plan. When you understand this, you realize that fanaticism is not limited to just the extreme fringes of civilized society. Fanaticism is alive and well in mainstream society. It arises in all kinds of positions of authority. In fact, I would argue it is the first and most fundamental abuse of all positions of authority.

Greenleaf understood this as well. In his discussion about commitment, he says, "Finally, one must make choices. Perhaps one chooses the same aim or hypothesis again and again. But, it is always a fresh and open choice, and it is always under a shadow of doubt." *It is always under a shadow of doubt.* From my standpoint, all true commitment lives in the domain of doubt. Anything less than that is calculation based on a belief that is held as absolute: "If this is the way it is, then this is what we must do." Without uncertainty or doubt, there is no foundation for tolerance. If there is one "right view," which we will generally see as our own, we have no space for the possibility that a different point of view may be valid. Because of that, we have no empathy for those with different views. Because of that, of course, we have no humility. How can we have humility if we've got the answer?

The great Chilean biologist and philosopher Humberto Maturana expresses this idea very poignantly. He says, "When one person tells another person what is *really* going on, they are making a demand for obedience." They are making this demand because "they are asserting that they have a privileged view of reality." And that is something that, from a biological standpoint, no person can claim. Maturana's famous Santiago Theory of Cognition shows that there is no such thing as a privileged view of reality. We are all blind, biologically blind. We do not see the world around us. We see the world we are prepared to see.

How can we be genuinely committed and in that shadow of doubt? Many think the two are mutually exclusive. I think the two are inseparable. Only if we are in that shadow of doubt will we have a chance of actually hearing what *another* says that doesn't match what *we* say. Only if we are in the shadow of doubt do we have a chance to learn. Many people think that we must be 100 percent committed, and that this means we must suppress all doubts. Yes, we must be 100 percent committed—and we must be prepared to be wrong.

Gandhi once stopped a huge protest march about halfway through. It had taken a long time to organize the march, so his attendants came running over to him, saying, "Mahatmaji, how can you do this? There are thousands of people here. They've come from all over India to participate in this march. How can you disband it and send them home?" Gandhi responded, "My commitment is to the truth as I see it each moment, not to consistency. This is not the right thing to do right now." This is a very tricky story, because it could be heard as Gandhi expressing an absolute authority over his followers. But I would suggest that he had earned the right to serve them through his lifetime of genuine commitment and questioning. He had earned their trust and thus was able to say, "Maybe we're wrong." This is the nature of commitment—that it requires us to serve through embracing uncertainty.

Stepping Ahead

Embracing uncertainty might lead to equating servant leadership with timidity, and waiting until everyone has had a vote, until everyone is in agreement, and then we move ahead with less doubt. But this would not be leadership at all. If leadership means anything, it means the courage to step ahead.

This is why the type of relationship between leader and follower articulated by Greenleaf is so important. He says, "When all is said and done, the leader needs one more thing. The leader ventures to say, 'I will go, I will go. Come with me if you will.'"

I once spoke with a woman who was doing research on the theory of leadership at Hewlett-Packard. She had arranged an interview with David Packard, one of the company's founders. He was quite old, a revered figure in the company. She said to him, "I am doing a study on leadership, and we all want to know what your theory of leadership is." She said he looked at her and didn't say anything. She thought, "Well, you know, maybe his hearing aid isn't quite working...I'll try again." She tried a little differently. "We all know you have deep convictions about leadership that have inspired thousands and thousands of people. What is your theory about the essence of leadership?" And she said he cocked his head and looked at her—it was clear that he had heard her. Finally, he said, "Well, I don't know. I don't think I have any theory of leadership. Bill Hewlett (his good friend and co-founder) and I just always did the things we loved to do, and we were so happy that people wanted to join us." Notice the difference in the spirit of that comment from the one that says, "We've got the vision, now we've got to go enroll people in the vision."

This story illustrates the way that true commitment opens the door for other people to make choices. It's not only about the choices of the person making the commitment. *True commitment actually creates choice for others.*

Vulnerability

The last aspect of commitment is vulnerability. This follows in a sense from uncertainty, but it's a little more personal. My comments about fanaticism and uncertainty are a bit conceptual. What they mean *personally* is that occupying a leadership position becomes an exercise in *vulnerability*.

Vulnerability starts with our embracing complex issues and not trivializing them. We lead from theories—assumptions, really—and sharing our assumptions openly is rarely comfortable, especially when people expect certainty. When we make our assumptions visible, we are in effect inviting others to help us in discovering how we are wrong. They will often be only too happy to oblige.

Shortly before he retired as CEO of Shell Oil, Phil Carroll reflected on his personal journey as CEO by saying, "Every process of transformation begins with yourself. It has to start with personal change. The abstraction of corporate transformation—that's a result, that's not a method." He then talked about how difficult the journey had been. "I had to do a lot of soul-searching about how I behaved, what I thought was important. Were my personal objectives and aspirations consistent with what I would try to hope for in the company?"

One of his great discoveries was that "vulnerability is a very important element in leadership. If you're not willing to make yourself vulnerable, then you can't provide good leadership." Phil, and other CEOs I have known, have discovered a paradoxical quality of leadership: Vulnerability can actually *increase* your effective power. When he became CEO, Shell Oil was coming out of one of its worst financial crises in history, including record layoffs. "Everyone expected me to tell them what we were going to do," said Carroll. "But I knew that I didn't have the answer." By being honest about it, he communicated a signal that many others would have to step up to their own responsibility to help shape the future. One result was an outpouring of creative initiatives in the ensuing years that eventually contributed to record profitability. Another outcome was a strong internal network of leaders, especially younger leaders—many of whom are in important positions today in Shell worldwide. Carroll concluded that there are "two qualities of leadership that ought to be present, whatever the situation or the style of the individual." The first is "humility—if you're not aware of your own flaws and shortcomings and lack of judgment, you will lead people in wrong ways. If you don't have a fundamental commitment to the truth and telling the truth, you can't lead. And telling the truth is so much more difficult than just not lying."

As I reflect on Phil's comments and similar ones I have heard by others who have had to come to terms with the ambiguities and challenges of executive leadership, I am reminded of Greenleaf's acid test of servant leadership. How do you tell a servant-leader is at work? —"Do the people around the person grow?"

Is All the Talk About Leaders Becoming Counterproductive?

Lastly, I want to share two concerns I have with the way we talk about leadership. Both relate to the way we use the word *leader*.

First, many people in the private and public sectors confuse authority and leadership. People commonly make statements like, "The problem around here is we don't have good leaders." Or, "What we need here is a leader who can really drive change."

Or, in considering a new initiative, "Nothing will happen if the leaders aren't on board." Who are people referring to in each of those statements? Who are these "leaders"? In most cases it is pretty clear they mean the CEO, or perhaps a management team, or the senior management. Why not just say, "Nothing will happen unless the CEO is on board"? I'm not disputing the *validity* of these statements, only their *clarity*. Do we need two words to describe the same thing? If formal management hierarchies exist, then there are positions of authority. Moreover, when people say, "Nothing will ever happen unless the leaders are on board," the obvious implication is that power is concentrated at the top. It is not just a problem of confusing authority with leadership, *it is an assertion that only those at the top of the hierarchy can create change.* This is not just disempowering, it is wrong. Experience has proven, again and again, that many of the most important change processes arise from line managers, internal networkers, and others with far less positional authority. So one reason I wonder if all the talk about leaders is counterproductive is that, in everyday use, leader has become a synonym for *boss*.

My second concern can be illuminated by considering an alternative definition of leadership, one which is independent of hierarchy. The criteria for assessing a definition should not be about right or wrong but whether it reflects important aspects of our experience and is useful. A definition we have found helpful in the Society for Organizational Learning is that leadership is "the capacity of a human community to shape its future."

I think this definition gets to the heart of *why we care* about leadership, and servant leadership in particular. We really do care about whether we feel we are victims, powerless and ineffective, or whether we feel we can do something about our future. I think that matters to every human being in every setting. It is one of the reasons leadership is an important idea: it matters to all of us whether we operate in a fatalistic, reactive, disempowered mode versus believing that we have agency, that we can actually have some influence over our future.

There is another key word in this definition: *community*. When we talk about leadership today, we tend to think of it as an individual phenomenon. Over time, I find this more and more limiting. In every case I know where significant change processes have been sustained, it has been due to the workings of large numbers of people, not just isolated individuals. For example, Phil Carroll's comments about vulnerability point in this direction. When a person in a position of authority allows himself or herself to be honest and therefore vulnerable, that person enhances collective leadership. "If the boss doesn't have all the answers, we'd better get our act in gear. Who are we waiting for?" Or, as someone observed recently, "*We* are the leaders we have been waiting for."

When we aspire to increase servant leadership, I would suggest that does not refer only to servant-leaders at the top. We must recognize that the capacity for servant leadership must be distributed *throughout* an organization; we need to increase the number of servant-leaders *everywhere*. Anything less will fail to accomplish the radical benefits for human institutions that Greenleaf's work promises. Anything less would deny the profound paradox that sits at the heart of servant leadership: that genuine leadership is deeply personal and inherently collective.

Peter Senge is a senior lecturer at the Massachusetts Institute of Technology and the founding chair of SoL (Society for Organizational Learning). He is also the author of The Fifth Discipline, *which hit a nerve deep within the business and educational communities by introducing the theory of learning organizations. Since its publication in 1990, more than 750,000 copies have been sold. In 1997,* Harvard Business Review *identified it as one of the seminal management books of the past seventy-five years. In 1999 the* Journal of Business Strategy *named Dr. Senge one of the twenty-four people who had the greatest influence on business strategy over the last one hundred years.*

Index

Acceptance, 33–34
Acton, Lord John, 116, 182
Administrators, 70, 101, 105, 109, 118, 163
Alcohol, prohibition of, 148
Alcoholics Anonymous, 50, 102, 233
Almoner's disease, 221
Ambiguity in the institution, 117–20, 204
American Telephone and Telegraph Company, 16–17, 110, 152
Andersen, Hans Christian, 176
Anti-innovative, 241
Anti-leader, age of, 8, 240–41
Association of American Colleges, 287
Assumption that one knows what another ought to learn, 180–82
Authority, 23–24, 55–56, 95, 115, 178
Awareness, 40–41, 329, 340

Basho, 235
Bea, Cardinal Augustin, 266
Beauty, 312
Beethoven, Ludwig von, 312

Belief, tension with criticism, 119–20
Berrigan, Philip, 268
Bigness, the implications of size, 120–23, 162–70
Blake, William, 41
Boards of Directors, see trustees
Body-field theory, 35
Boe, Lars, 297
Booth, Philip, 326
Bridges, Robert, 312
Bridgman, Percy, 32
Buber, Martin, 265
Buddhist ethic, 155
Build a life like a work of art, 262
Builders, affirmative, 24
Bureaucracy, defined, 307
Burnham, Daniel, 268
Business, 341; business practice, 66, 152; business as servant, 85–87; growing larger, 162–70; servant leadership in, 147–75
Business directors initiate social policy, 110–75
Business ethic, 155–56

Campus turmoil, 17, 246

Campus use of resource people, 207–14

Camus, Albert, 25, 61, 235

Caring, 62, 142, 255–56

Carleton College, 262–63, 268–303

Carlyle, Thomas, 315

Catholic Church, an assessment, 248

Certified financial audit, 110

Chair persons, trustee, 69, 84, 101, 128–30, 132

Change, 118, 185

Chesterton, G. K., 198–99, 201

Chief, of business, 74–78, 84, 124

Church, 62, 67, 341; the growing edge, 92–95, 258; as painter of a dream, 101

Churches, servant leadership in, 231–61

Coach, for trustees, 137

Coleman Report, 179

Competence and disability, 118–19

Communication, 31

Community, 50–53, 169–70, 204, 341

Conceptual flaw (in organization), 105–6

Conceptual leadership, 79–82

Conceptualizing, 45–47

Confucius, 57, 186

Confusion, 245, 339

Conn, Howard, 296

Connelly, Marc, 315

Consciousness, levels of, 40

Constitution, U.S., 44, 65, 148, 292

Consumerism, 85

Controlling, 108

Corporations, 65, 105

Cowling, Donald John, 262–63; an appreciation, 268–303

Cox, Harvey, 318

Create dangerously, 25–26

Creative process, 39

Creativity, 225; and prudence, 223–30

Criticism, 25, 217; tension with belief, 119–20

Critics, social, 309

Cuninggim, Merrimon, 181–82, 218, 324

Dartmouth College, 264, 272

Declaration of Independence, 44–45, 292

Deschooling Society, 176

Detachment, 41, 134

Dewey, John, 290

Dickinson College, 196

Dogma, need for, 117

Dreams, necessity of, 14, 100

Education, 25, 51; based on coercion, 183–84;

servant leadership in, 176–214
Educational enterprise, three major faults, 176–77
Eisenhower, Dwight D., 130, 284
Elderly, care of, 51–52
Emerson, Ralph Waldo, 25, 160, 326
Empathy, 33–34
Enemy, discernment of, 58
Environment, protection of, 85
Ethics and manipulation, 149–62; *also see* business ethic
Ethical failure, 39–40
Executive growth and selection, 127
Expectation, revolution in, 85, 223
Experimental knowledge, 237, 242

Faculty members as entrepreneurs, 222
Faith, 23, 39, 232, 340
Family, 341
Fitch, Albert Parker, 277
Folk High School, Danish, 45, 184
Followership, 256
Ford, Henry, 157
Foreman Conferences, 16
Foresight, 35–40
Fosdick, Harry Emerson, 278

Foundations, 121–22, 215–30; distinguished from other institutions, 223–24; servant leadership in, 215–30
Foundation News, 215
Foundation personnel, hazard to, 227
Foundation trustees, 216–23
Fox, George, 94–95, 156, 233–44
Francis of Assisi, 31, 313–14, 318
Friends Journal, 231, 236, 262
Friends schools, 178–88
Friere, Paulo, 49
Frost, Robert, 34, 242–43, 315–16, 326–41

Gandhi, Mohandas, 321–22
Gardner, John W., 317
General Electric Company, 110, 152
General Motors, 153
Goals, 29–30, 99, 107, 126, 252
Goldberg, Arthur, 143
Goodman, Paul, 29
Gould, Laurence M., 290–91
Government, 66, 86, 341
Green Revolution, 225
Growing edge church, 258–61
Gregg, Richard B., 234
Grundtvig, Nikolai, 45–48, 185

Harvard Business School, 167
Healing, 49–50
Health services, 51, 67, 341
Hebrew Union College, 265
Helming, Oscar, 19
Heschel, Abraham Joshua, 56,
    146, 243, 262–68
Hesse, Hermann, 21–22, 57,
    60–61
Hierarchical principle, 74
Holy Grail, 332, 336
Hope, 23, 184
Hopkins, Mark, 134
Hospitals, 51, 133
Humanity, 337
Humor, 315
Huxley, Aldous, 236
Hypothesis, 28

I Ching, 186
Idealistic pretensions, 182
Illich, Ivan, 176, 183
Imagination, 31–32
India, 320–23
Information gap, 36
Information, key to trustee
    role, 131–33
Inge, Dean, 23, 232
Initiative, individual, 28–29
Institutions, 53–54, 62, 152,
    182, 239, 249–50;
    building, strategy for,
    252–54; crisis in, 65–68;
    three levels of, 341
Integrity, 220, 222

Intuition, 27–29, 36, 239
Inward radiance, 308

Jaures, Jean, 236
Jefferson, Thomas, 44–45, 178
Jesus of Nazareth, 42, 181,
    199, 236, 331, 336–37
Jethro, father-in-law of
    Moses, 96–97
Jewish Theological Seminary,
    263
Johnson, Ben, 247
Jones, Rufus, 185, 258
Journey to the East, 21, 60
Joy, 57, 155, 260

Kabbalah, 265
Kazantzakis, Nikos, 289, 307,
    311, 318
Kesey, Ken, 57
Kibbutzim, Israeli, 52
King, Martin Luther, Jr., 266
Know the unknowable, 35
Knowing, the art of, 236–44

Language, 31–32
Lascaux cave paintings, 330
Law, 148–49
Leader, is servant first, 21;
    trustee as, 83–85; also see
    servant leaders
Leadership, 109, 150, 256;
    conceptual and
    operational, 79–82; by
    persuasion, 42;

preparation for, 60; *also see* servant leadership
Lebanon Valley College, 274
Lewin, Kurt, 199
Liberal arts education, 196
Lifestyle, 294, 308, 311; of greatness, 268
Listening, 30–31, 268, 313–14
Loss, 339–40
Love, 52, 149
Luther, Martin, 94–95

Machiavelli, Niccolò, 38–39
Management, 106–8, 149–50, 165
Manipulation, 55, 149–50, 160, 162
Marijuana, control of, 148, 199
Masefield, John, 238
Meaning, 31, 338
Mediocrity, 96, 259, 309–10, 162
Melville, Herman, 334
Minninger Foundation, 295, 300–301
Menninger, William, 295
Mental retardation, 51
Milton, John, 342
Miro, Juan, 239
Moby Dick, 334
Momentaneity, 313
Moral law, flaw in the traditional, 260
Morgan, J. P., 110–11, 140–42

Moses, 74, 96–97, 259
Motivation, 152

Nason, John W., 273, 290
Nehru, Jawaharal, 321–22
Neibuhr, Reinhold, 65

Openness, 313–14
Operational leadership, 79–82
Optimum, finding one's, 32–33
Order, 59
Organization, of business, 71–79, 108; student of, 16; of the top executive office, 127; two traditions of, 74–76
Organizing to serve, 244–58
Orphans, 51

Parables, 336–37
Passion for Truth, A, 268
Patton, George, 130
Pedagogy of the Oppressed, 49
Penal institutions, 51, 199
Perception, 40
Performance, review of, 108, 127; performance gap, 341
Persuasion, 42–44, 115
Planning, 108
Pope John XXIII, 247–48, 307–08
Pope Paul VI, 266
Porgy and Bess, 202

Power, and authority, 23, 55–56, 115, 140, 178, 180; coercive, 55, 98, 121; countervailing, 98; legitimize, 19; of persuasion, 42–43; the problem of, 95–98; in schools, 42–43; tends to corrupt, 116

Powerlessness, 98

Primus inter pares, 74, 80, 83, 126, 163

Profit and not-for-profit organizations, 63

Prophecy, 22

Prophet, The, 265

Prophets, speaking all the time, 232; Old Testament, 56

Prudence and creativity, 223–30

Purpose, 98

Quakers, 42–44, 94, 156, 185, 233, 236–38, 240, 242, 268

Rationality, beyond consciousness, 35

Real world, 205, 212

Reason, 27

Redlands, University of, 304

Rejection, 33–34

Religion, 93, 231; *also see* church

Remnant, saving, 341

Rosenwald, Julius, 152

Resource people, campus use of, 207–14

Responsibility in a bureaucratic society, 305–18

Roethlisberger, Fritz, 167–68

School Sisters of St. Francis, 231, 244

Schools, 51, 246; *also see* education; university

Schmidt, Karl, 277

Schweitzer, Albert, 318

Scopes trial, 278

Sears, Roebuck Co., 152–53

Seekers, 22, 232–35, 259

Seminaries, conceptual resource for churches, 95

Serrano, Miguel, 44

Servant leaders, 262–90; concept emerges, 17; discernment of, 56; program for training, 204–05; tests for trainers of, 204; who they are, 341

Servant leadership in churches, 231–261; in foundations, 202–17

Servant, natural, learning to be, 31

Serve and be served by, 189–94, 203, 250

Servant first, 27, 48

Shakespeare, William, 56, 312

Silence, 31
Single chief, flaws in the
    concept of, 76–79, 105
Slaveholders, 43
Sloan, Albert, 152
Sloan School of Management,
    239
Smith, Margaret Chase, 209
Social performance, criteria
    for judging, 172–74
Society of Friends, *see*
    Quakers
Spender, Stephen, 302
Staff, 109, 166; for trustees,
    221, 227–28
Stern, Carl, 263
Strategy, 71
Structure, formal and
    informal, 72–73
Structural dynamic, 39
Symbol, power of, 329
System, the, 24, 58

Tax Reform Act of 1969, 219
Teams, building teams, 85,
    169; design of work
    groups, 224
This is the day, 313
Thurber, James, 304, 315
Tolerance, 315
Tonna, Benjamin, 320
Trans World Airlines, 143
Trust, 24, 52, 63, 100–103,
    113–15, 127–28, 134,
    139, 156, 222, 341
Trustees, 63, 68–71; failure to
build trust, 113–14;
    foundation trustees,
    216–23; function of,
    126–27; initiative, 107,
    110; judgment, 133–36;
    motivation, 143;
    opportunities in large
    institutions, 122–23;
    power, 115, 140; role,
    conditions that need to
    be met, 116; role,
    initiating rather than
    reacting, 110–11, 125;
    role, limitations in
    conventional, 111–13; as
    servants, 54–55, 62–63,
    68–71, 104, 179; *also see*
    trusteeship
Trusteed society, 138–40
Trusteeship, defined, 107;
    failure of, 65; pedagogy
    of, 136–38

Understanding, 30–31, 100
Unicorn, 304, 319
Union Theological Seminary,
    266
Unions, 168–69
United Nations, 291
United States Steel
    Corporation, 110
University, 62, 67, 221–22,
    341; as an institution,
    87–92; operating versus
    thinking about, 92;

trustee role, 62, 88–90, 188–96

Vail, Theodore N., 152
Values, teaching of, 177–78
van der Post, Laurens, 258
Vatican Council II, 266, 307
Vining, Elizabeth Gray, 185
Virginia Legislature, 45
Voluntary striving for excellence, 148

Washington, George, 104
Whitehead, Alfred North, 31, 269
Whitman, Walt, 103, 244–45, 341

Wilhelm, Hellmut, 186
Wisdom, 16
Withdrawal, 32–33
Woodrow Wilson Fellow, 196
Woolman, John, 42–44
Word, the, 23
Work, world of, 154–55, 159, 168, 196–206
World leadership, 320–25
Wright, Frank Lloyd, 176
Wythe, George, 44

Yale University, 274–75, 288

Zechariah, 180

About Robert K. Greenleaf
and the Greenleaf Center
for Servant-Leadership

Robert K. Greenleaf (1904–90)

Robert K. Greenleaf spent most of his organizational life in the field of management, research, development, and education at AT&T. Just before his retirement as director of management research there, he held a joint appointment as visiting lecturer at M.I.T.'s Sloan School of Management and at the Harvard Business School. In addition, he held teaching positions at both Dartmouth College and the University of Virginia.

His consultancies included Ohio University, M.I.T., Ford Foundation, R. K. Mellon Foundation, Lilly Endowment, and the American Foundation for Management Research.

As consultant to universities, businesses, foundations, and churches during the tumultuous 1960s and 1970s, his eclectic and wide-ranging curiosity, reading, and contemplation provided an unusual background for observing these institutions.

As a lifelong student of organization (that is, how things get done) he distilled these observations in a series of essays, books, and videotapes on the theme of the servant as leader, the objective of which is to stimulate thought and action for building a better, more caring society.

The Robert K. Greenleaf Center
for Servant-Leadership

The Robert K. Greenleaf Center for Servant-Leadership, headquartered in Indianapolis, Indiana, is an international not-for-profit educational organization that seeks to encourage the understanding and practice of servant leadership. It was originally founded in 1964 as the Center for Applied Ethics and was renamed the Robert K. Greenleaf Center in 1985. Larry C. Spears, editor of *Servant Leadership* and six other books, was named the first full-time executive director of the Greenleaf Center in 1990, shortly before Robert Greenleaf's death.

The Greenleaf Center for Servant-Leadership exists to support those who, through the practice of servant leadership, seek to create organizations in which individual stakeholders become healthier, wiser, freer, and more autonomous, and, in so doing, build a better, more humane society that welcomes the full diversity of the human family.

The Greenleaf Center currently has offices in Australia/New Zealand, Canada, Europe, Korea, the Philippines, Singapore, South Africa, and the United Kingdom. The Center's mission is to improve the caring and quality of all institutions through servant leadership.

The Greenleaf Center's programs and resources include the worldwide sale of books, essays, and videotapes on servant leadership; an annual international conference on servant leadership held each June in Indianapolis; a variety of workshops, institutes, retreats, and speakers; a membership program; and other activities around servant leadership.

Servant leadership is being practiced today by many individuals and organizations. For more information about servant leadership and the Greenleaf Center, contact:

The Greenleaf Center for Servant-Leadership
921 East 86th Street, Suite 200
Indianapolis, IN 46240
Phone: (317) 259–1241; Fax: (317) 259–0560
Email: greenleaf@iquest.net
Website: www.greenleaf.org

Paulist Press is committed to preserving ancient forests and natural resources. We elected to print this title on 30% post consumer recycled paper, processed chlorine free. As a result, for this printing, we have saved:

45 Trees (40' tall and 6-8" diameter)
19 Million BTUs of Total Energy
4,527 Pounds of Greenhouse Gases
20,413 Gallons of Wastewater
1,294 Pounds of Solid Waste

Paulist Press made this paper choice because our printer, Thomson-Shore, Inc., is a member of Green Press Initiative, a nonprofit program dedicated to supporting authors, publishers, and suppliers in their efforts to reduce their use of fiber obtained from endangered forests.

For more information, visit www.greenpressinitiative.org

Environmental impact estimates were made using the Environmental Defense Paper Calculator. For more information visit: www.papercalculator.org.